Praise for the Book

"In this thought-provoking book on employee engagement, the author emerges as a true believer in its transformative power. Van Belle compellingly argues that engagement isn't just a vital pillar for organisational success; it transcends the workplace, extending into families, teams, communities, societies, and even nations.

The book deftly illustrates how engagement cuts across cultures, highlighting its universal importance and applicability. Through insightful concepts, the author invites readers to reflect on and explore what strategies resonate most with them, rather than following a prescriptive 'how-to' guide. This approach makes the book refreshing and applicable to various aspects of life, encouraging leaders and individuals alike to think critically about their unique contexts and what fosters genuine engagement within them. The author's fervour and multifaceted perspective ensure that readers come away with a broadened understanding and appreciation of engagement's profound impact."

—George Karam,
Managing Director
Korn Ferry Advisory MENA

"'Engagement is the story we tell ourselves about our work experience.' This is one of the powerful ideas explored in Inge's book, which highlights a fundamental truth: the way employees perceive their work shapes their motivation, performance, and long-term commitment. In the dynamic and multicultural environment of the United Arab Emirates, where professionals from all corners of the world collaborate, engagement is not just an HR metric; it is the foundation of a thriving workplace.

Belgium—where Inge proudly comes from—much like the UAE, has built its success on diversity, innovation, and global connectivity. Belgian companies and professionals contribute significantly to the UAE's vibrant business ecosystem, bringing a deep-rooted culture of adaptability and excellence. As the book rightly points out, engaged employees transcend the average with their dedication, and the same applies to nations, businesses, and leaders who foster environments where individuals feel valued and empowered.

In an era of rapid change, engagement is the key to turning workplaces into communities of purpose. *Employee Engagement, What Else?* provides essential insights for leaders who aspire to create or support organisations where employees don't just work, but where they belong, contribute, and excel. This book was an eye-opener and allowed me to put into words and better understand situations that I witness every single day. Whether in Dubai, Brussels, or anywhere else, the most successful teams are built on shared commitment, passion, and a compelling story of engagement."

—Antoine Delcourt,
Ambassador of Belgium
to the United Arab Emirates

continued at the end...

Employee Engagement What Else?

The Leader's Guide to Customer Happiness and Organisational Success

"I'm excited about this book. It's about people, about the customer, about emotion and passion. And that's exactly what the world needs right now."

**—Ignace Van Doorselaere,
Former CEO Neuhaus**

Inge van Belle

Global Book
Publishing

Employee Engagement. What Else?
Inge van Belle
©2025 Inge van Belle. All rights reserved.

ISBN: 978-1-964644-27-1
Book Design & Publishing done by:
Global Book Publishing
www.globalbookpublishing.com

This book is dedicated to the people of the UAE.

To your kindness, resilience, and patience. And to your hopes and dreams.

Every morning, when I wake up early with the warm touch of the sun on my face, I look out at the bustling city of Dubai from the 48th floor. The vast view stretches from the sea to the desert, framed by the Burj Khalifa, the Burj Al Arab, and the many roads busy with hundreds of cars, delivery bikes, taxis, and buses, each carrying people working hard toward a better future for their families, for themselves, and for this country.

It reminds me that, despite our differences and challenges, we have so much more in common than we think. I think that we truly are becoming a nation. And I feel humbled, proud, and immensely grateful to be part of this journey.

Table of Contents

Letter to the Reader

This is not an HR book. Neither is it a book written purely for HR professionals—though they'll probably get the most mileage out of it, and they're one of the main characters. My book tackles employee engagement, a subject far too vital to drop at the doors of one department. Employee engagement touches EVERYONE in the organisation, especially the leaders and it is deeply intertwined with performance.

This book is for business leaders who are serious about raising their game. Not just with their people. But also with their clients, stakeholders, board members, and suppliers. And ultimately in life.

Now, let's be clear: Employee engagement isn't just a buzzword. It's an art. And a craft. A cornerstone of successful business practice. Globally, leaders mark employee engagement as a top 3 priority, knowing full well its correlation with success. Yet here's the kicker: fewer than 20% of employees are actually engaged, meaning that they feel intrinsically motivated and emotionally connected to their organisations. Alarmingly, around 17% are actively disengaged, leading to apathy or even workplace sabotage. For these individuals, work is an exhausting drain on their energy, overshadowing their lives. Gallup's research underscores the impact of this phenomenon, with billions of dollars lost annually due to disengagement.

Why is there such a disconnect between the talk and the reality? Business leaders are looking for the secret formula to enhance engagement as an accelerator for growth and, ultimately, profitability. I won't promise you a magical recipe book. But what I do offer you, is a way to elevate your engagement strategies, by sharing some fundamental principles drawn from the worlds of marketing and technology, where I've spent my career. Apply these, and you'll very likely see a positive impact on your bottom line. Employee engagement, after all, is the engine that drives profit. You will also find that the factors influencing engagement are more complex than they might initially appear. I will share real-life stories, along with some surprising insights from organisations and leaders who've mastered the art of engagement.

The first version of this book was published during the pandemic. I wrote it in Dutch, together with Klaus Lommatzsch, Managing Partner at Duval Union. At that time, the work environment was undergoing unprecedented changes, and navigating this new reality was no small feat. Now that I'm finalising the second edition, I have come to realise how much the world has changed since its first release. Just as organisations were settling into a *new normal,* with a focus on hybrid work, well-being and digitalisation, Generative AI burst onto the scene. GenAI has been met with both excitement and unease, and it's changing our entire world. The impact on our work is so huge, that I will give it the attention it deserves.

My personal life has also changed dramatically since our first book was released. In 2020, in the midst of the pandemic, my family and I made the bold move to the United Arab Emirates. After over a decade of commuting between the Middle East and Europe and contemplating the move, my husband and I finally decided to make it happen—with the reluctant blessing of our teenage children, who faced leaving behind a warm circle of family and lifetime friends.

When we arrived in our new home country, we found our beloved UAE in a different state than how we remembered it. The streets were empty, real estate prices were at an all-time low, and strict COVID-19 safety measures were in place. It was hard to reimagine the liveliness and buzzing life that characterised this young nation. The atmosphere felt all too familiar—like home or any other place shaped by the relentless grip of the pandemic. Yet we felt estranged. However, despite the seeming silence, we could feel that something was happening underneath the surface. There was an almost imperceptible buzz, a signal of something imminent. The country was holding its breath, as if on the brink of an unseen revelation. Dubai was ramping up and more determined than ever to host the World Expo 2020, albeit with a year of delay. The small Emirate wanted to show the world that it was able to safely open its doors to millions of visitors as the first nation after the global pandemic. It felt almost surreal in an era dominated by the horrible facemask and sanitiser and when most of the population was wary of getting too close to strangers.

And for those who wonder: yes, absolutely. Moving to the UAE as entrepreneurs was definitely a bold decision. It wasn't one that came with the cushy benefits package of a Western expat. For many years, we have been closely observing this country while it emerged like a mushroom after the rain. We saw the UAE navigate the financial crisis of 2008 and its aftermath. We strolled in awe through Dubai Mall (the biggest mall in the world) when it was still more empty space than a shopping destination, uncertain whether this was megalomania or a calculated stride towards an extraordinary future. Every time, the UAE bounced back stronger, with even more determination and resilience.

What captivated us, was more than the rapid growth. It was the vision behind it, the charismatic leadership, and the incredible multicultural environment that thrives here. Although the pioneering days are long behind it, we felt like modern immigrants. Not driven by famine, war, or disaster, but by the hunger for something more. Our journey didn't involve perilous seas or relentless deserts, as it did for many less fortunate migrants. Instead, it was a comfortable 6.5-hour flight aboard an Emirates Boeing 777. We were searching for a better future for our children, and the UAE's ambition and inclusiveness made it the perfect choice.

Sure enough, there were the sceptics who claimed we were slightly unhinged, happily peppering their comments with "*delusional*" and "*crazy,*" with the casualness of armchair critics. But we were determined, only slightly deterred by the naysayers, and ready to contribute to this nation's mission. A mission that welcomes anyone willing to build and to become the best version of themselves, regardless of background, gender, or skills. Dubai, leading the way, has mastered the art of engaging its people, and we were (and still are, even more so) excited to be part of that experience.

When I give keynotes or workshops back in Belgium, I'm often asked about the most inspiring examples of engaged organisations. During one of my Aha moments, I decided to highlight Dubai as a prime example. Now, I'll be honest: this choice hasn't always gone over well with my audience. In fact, it's often met with raised eyebrows and the occasional side-eye.

It even sparks debates that sometimes derail the entire point I'm trying to make. One client deemed my example "*inappropriate*," brushing it aside as just "*bling bling.*" After some serious introspection, I had to ask: "*Should I keep using Dubai as an example?*" And after considering all angles, my answer was an unapologetic yes!!

Why? Because to highlight the influence of a marketing mindset on engagement, showcase tech innovation, and illustrate the twelve drivers of engagement, I honestly can't think of a better showcase. Dubai doesn't just talk the talk—it walks the walk. So, I didn't just stick with Dubai as a case study; I promoted it to a marquee example, backed by stories of local organisations and remarkable people who would convince even the most sceptical readers.

And that brings me to one final point that I discovered by living in this place (with or without the bling bling): The UAE is one of the most diverse places on the planet, with 195 nationalities living and working together. While Western organisations continue to grapple with diversity, Dubai seems to have discovered a formula that, though not without its flaws, brings some compelling results to the table. Studies show that diverse organisations—when managed well—are more likely to be engaged. As a strong advocate for Diversity, Equity, Inclusion, and Belonging, I'm rooting for Dubai to lead the way and teach the world a thing or two.

As I pen these final thoughts, I can't help but notice a world undergoing dramatic change—propelled by seismic shifts and powered by human-machine collaboration, set against a backdrop of regional tension. In this strange new reality, it dawns on me that tapping into the new world of work can only mean one thing. And that's keeping people and the value of human relations at the centre of the transformation agenda.

Now, more than ever, is the time to double down on investing in employee engagement. This isn't a burden for organisations alone; it's a shared endeavour. And it starts with YOU—whether you're leading from the front, working through the ranks, or just finding your footing. Ask not what your organisation can do for you—ask what you can do for your organisation. It's our duty to foster greater engagement within our team and in ourselves. Prioritising engagement not only amplifies productivity and profit; it enriches our professional and personal lives. It empowers us to connect more deeply with others and strive for our best selves.

Here's to shared success on this mission!

How to Read This Book

This book is a go-to guide for anyone in business who is committed to both professional and personal growth. I wrote it to give you a solid understanding of employee engagement and its value, backed by plenty of frameworks to help you put ideas into practice. I've found that theory really sticks when it's paired with real-world stories, which is why you'll find plenty of case studies and expert insights throughout these pages.

I know not everyone is an avid reader or academically inclined, so I've made sure there's something for everyone. For those who prefer visual learning, you'll find figures and boxed highlights. To keep the content as inclusive as possible, each chapter wraps up with a summary. And for those who are more into slogans and quick takeaways—I hear you! I've got you covered too, with quotes to keep things punchy. After all, who can resist a good quote?

Do you want to use this book in your daily work? Great! I've created a free workbook to help you do just that. It includes an Interview Guide and exercises for you and your team, complete with a handy list of questions for each engagement driver covered in the book. You can use them as a guideline in a face-to-face interview—whether informal or during a performance review—or in a group interview, in a one-to-many survey, or even in a broader quantitative survey, provided you use the right scoring scale and adapt it to a more closed-question format.

You can download the workbook by scanning this QR code.

PART ONE

❧

FOUNDATION

"Work is love made visible."

—*Kahlil Gibran—The Prophet*

No matter what phase your organisation is in—whether you're experiencing rapid growth, navigating a merger, undergoing a transformation, or wrestling with the integration of new technology to stay competitive—we're all operating in a complex and demanding world. The Fourth Industrial Revolution is in full throttle. We're in the thick of a new era of globalisation, where the pressure to innovate, digitise, and connect is relentless. New business paradigms and disruptive technologies are hailed as the golden tickets to growth and success.

But here's the reality check: all these strategic elements amount to little without the true cornerstone—the employees who make them happen. The difference between organisations that thrive and those that stumble is the strength of their workforce. As Jim Collins put it in *Good to Great, "Great vision without great people is irrelevant."*

To build a high-performing and productive organisational culture, employee engagement isn't just a nice-to-have. It's essential. More and more business leaders are catching on and becoming champions of this cause.

But before we rush to action, it's wise to take a moment and clearly define what we mean by engagement.

What's in a Name?

"Employee Engagement is about being fully present—
physically, cognitively and emotionally."

—*Paraphrased from William Kahn,*
Godfather of Employee Engagement

O ver the past decade, employee engagement has become the go-to catchphrase among experts of all stripes. Looking at my social media feed, it seems like everyone's suddenly a well-being guru or burn-out expert.

But let's face it. True engagement goes way beyond the surface-level perks, no matter how many yoga mats, fruit baskets, or pool tables you throw into the mix. I'm genuinely pleased to see this topic getting the spotlight it deserves, especially since well-being has been a cornerstone of our approach for years. Here's the kicker: we can't afford to narrow our focus to just one aspect of engagement. The challenge is much bigger than that. While many have jumped on the well-being bandwagon, it's crucial to understand that genuine engagement requires a wider and deeper approach.

At its core, employee engagement is about making your employees feel like they're an essential part of your organisation, like members of a close-knit clan. A tribe. Don't call it a family please, that's something else.[1] Engaged employees don't just show up to work; they're eager to give their best every single day. And the payoff? A happier, more productive workforce that takes better care of your customers. Delighted customers lead to satisfied shareholders, creating a cycle of success that everyone can rally around.

Employee engagement isn't just about employees giving their time and effort out of a sense of duty. Let's be honest, it's also about self-interest. People become genuinely invested when they see growth opportunities, receive authentic recognition, earn well, and see how their efforts make a difference. This principle holds true in every aspect of life—whether it's with community, friends, politics, or our jobs. When you combine passion for work with a strong organisational fit and belief in the company's goals, you get an unbeatable combination.

Professor William Kahn, often dubbed the "*Godfather of Employee Engagement*," was one of the pioneers in exploring the concept of workplace engagement in his 1990 article.[2] He defined **employee engagement as the simultaneous employment and expression of a person's true self in their work tasks, fostering connections both to the work itself and to others.** In simpler terms, it's about being fully present—physically, cognitively, and emotionally—while performing your role. When employees bring their authentic selves to their work, it leads to a deeper, more meaningful connection with both their tasks and their colleagues.

Since Dr Kahn's pioneering work, other experts have built on his foundation. Ray Baumruk introduced a succinct definition, describing employee engagement as **the emotional and intellectual commitment to the organisation**. This interpretation highlights the dual importance of the mind and heart in driving engagement.

Dilys Robinson offers a compelling perspective, specifying it as **a positive attitude held by the employee towards the organisation and its values**.[3] She emphasised that engaged employees aren't just aware of the business context—they actively collaborate with colleagues to enhance performance for the organisation's benefit. Robinson's view highlights that engagement is a two-way street, a dynamic relationship between employer and employee that demands effort from both sides.

I find myself perfectly aligned with Robinson's approach. Too often, in Anglo-Saxon literature, employee engagement is reduced to just another management tool—a method to boost productivity and polish the corporate image. But let's take a more holistic view. Employee engagement should be seen as a partnership between the employee and the organisation—an **Alliance** built on mutual trust. And it must be reciprocal. This isn't merely about keeping employees happy; it's about creating a ripple effect that starts within the organisation and extends outward, influencing everything from customer satisfaction (or better yet, customer delight) to attracting top-tier talent through strong employer branding. And the effects don't just stop there. The positive impact of genuine employee engagement can radiate outward, reaching the Board of Directors, investors, suppliers, industry partners, and even the broader ecosystem in which your organisation operates. Now that's a ripple worth making.

And while we're on the topic, there's another debate that's been gaining traction. The term *"employee experience"* keeps popping up and is often used interchangeably with *"employee engagement*," which only adds to the confusion about which term to use. This isn't just a matter of semantics; specialists can get pretty passionate about it. For example, management guru Jacob Morgan is a staunch advocate for the term *"employee experience."*[4]

Without diving too deep into the debate, let me share my perspective on the difference between these often-confused terms. As one of the original founders of Herculean Alliance, where we've been crafting powerful workforces since 1999, I'm all for delivering epic experiences. The company's DNA is deeply rooted in creating unique experiences, like Hercules Trophy or Pink Ladies Games. However, when it comes to this context and the link with performance, I prefer the term engagement. In this book, employee experience is defined as the sum of all interactions an employee has with their organisation. This includes everything from attracting talent, onboarding, and offboarding, to learning and development, those all-important *"Moments That Matter,"* and even alumni programs. Engagement, however, goes beyond just the employee experience; it connects to other critical aspects as well. You will find more details in Part IV, where we explore the drivers of engagement.

No matter how you slice it, engagement always blends a person's feelings about a situation with their work environment. As Don Phin puts it: **engagement is the story we tell ourselves about our work experience.**[5] Phin uses the word *story* because two colleagues with seemingly identical work experiences can have completely different levels of engagement. Yours or my engagement has a lot to do with how we feel in any given situation. Engagement is always a mix of a person's personality, nature, and age *(Nature)* and the experience or environment they're in *(Nurture)*.

Given this complexity, applying a *"one-size-fits-all"* approach to engagement is challenging at best. Engagement in a manufacturing environment looks very different from that in retail or an IT company. And let's face it: the motivations and backgrounds of a fresh graduate and a baby boomer are worlds apart. Engagement strategies must be as diverse as the workforce they aim to support.

An Inconvenient Truth

"Low employee engagement costs the global economy $8.9 trillion, accounting for 9% of the global GDP."

—*Gallup*

What is the current state of employee engagement globally? Since 2009, Gallup has been on a mission to crack the code of employee engagement, systematically gathering data from around the world. Their approach centres on three key aspects: Emotional Attachment to the Company, Commitment to Organisational Goals and Motivation for Discretionary Effort. These dimensions offer a clear window into the overall health of employee engagement within an organisation, providing invaluable insights.

According to Gallup's *State of the Global Workplace 2024* report, only **23% of employees** feel genuinely engaged with their employer.[6] You read that right—less than a quarter of the global workforce is truly connected to their jobs. However, these figures vary significantly from region to region, and even from country to country.[7]

State of the Global Workplace Report (Gallup)

The 2023 employee engagement rate remains stagnant compared to 2022, slightly improving from 2020 and 2021 (20% and 21%, respectively) and significantly better than a decade ago (14%) a far cry from the dismal 12% reported back in 2009.

Several studies consistently highlight a clear connection between engagement scores and key business metrics like customer satisfaction, profitability, productivity, and sales. But, despite being a top priority for many business leaders, employee engagement remains disappointingly low.

The sobering reality is that a staggering **62% of employees** report being disengaged, plus **15% actively disengaged**. The latter aren't just individuals who are unhappy at work—it's about those whose dissatisfaction actively undermines their company's goals. Often, they're psychologically detached from their work, and their negativity can be contagious, dragging down colleagues and sabotaging overall workplace morale.

Globally, employee well-being is slightly declining, from 35% to 34%. Talking about an inconvenient truth! And quite paradoxical too, especially given that job satisfaction is at an all-time high. So, clearly, the issue isn't with the content of the job itself.

The global slump in employee engagement can be traced to a mix of individual, organisational, and macroeconomic factors that have only become more pronounced since the pandemic.

Who Are They?

"For we walk by faith, not by sight."

—*2 Corinthians 5:7*

Engagement is all about passion and enthusiasm, much like diving into a beloved hobby, whether it's sports, cooking, or traveling. Three key signs epitomize true workplace engagement: Time flies by, and you barely notice that you're working. The job energizes you and builds your mental resilience. You feel genuinely excited, inspired, and proud of what you've accomplished.

Now, let's venture into the world of this extraordinary, yet increasingly rare, species, called the engaged employees, as if narrated by Sir David Attenborough in *Life on Earth*.

"Who are they? What do they do? And, most critically, what drives them?" Imagine Sir Attenborough's iconic voice guiding us as we uncover the intricate behaviours and environments that sustain their existence.

In true Attenborough style, you can almost hear him marvelling at these remarkable traits, highlighting the profound connection between this remarkable human being and their habitat.

Engaged employees transcend the average worker in their dedication. They are invigorated and inspired by their endeavours, eager to share their zeal. Their happiness radiates outward, creating a positive aura that lifts the entire organisation and extends its influence far beyond the office walls. Like a vibrant ecosystem, these exceptional individuals create a ripple effect, fostering a thriving and dynamic environment wherever they go. In essence, engaged employees truly are the lifeblood of an engaged organisation.

It's almost as if they've been sprinkled with a bit of magical pixie dust, boosting productivity and profits without any extra cost. That pixie dust is the elusive ***discretionary effort***. While this might sound technical, it's really about the freedom to choose between *"having to"* and *"wanting to"*—that intrinsic motivation to go above and beyond one's job description.

What discretionary effort looks like can vary wildly from one company to another. What does it mean to you? Is it staying late at the office, checking emails on the weekend? Or rather showing endless patience with a difficult customer? Maybe it's helping a colleague or sharing a brilliant cost-saving idea. The point is, it's different for everyone, and it needs to align with the company's culture and values to actually be effective.

But a word of caution—focusing too much on effort, even with the best of intentions, can lead to burnout and frustration. Employee engagement and discretionary effort are all about finding that sweet spot: too much pressure can demotivate, while too little can lead to mediocrity. It's a balancing act.

Characteristics of the Engaged Organisation

An engaged organisation is defined by several key traits that set it apart:

1. ***Purpose:*** *Employees feel a personal connection to the organisation's higher purpose.*
2. ***Empowerment:*** *They feel empowered to grow and shape the business.*
3. ***Belonging:*** *Every employee feels like they're an integral part of the community.*
4. ***Trust:*** *Mutual trust and support are the glue that holds everything together.*

In his book *Drive,* Daniel Pink points out a surprising disconnect between what science tells us and what many businesses actually do.[8] After 50 years of research into human behaviour and motivation, Pink argues that true motivation isn't all about money. Instead, it boils down to three key elements: autonomy, mastery, and purpose. Get these right, and both performance and satisfaction are likely to skyrocket.

Similarly, psychologists Richard Ryan and Edward Deci, in their ***Self-Determination Theory***, emphasise our inherent need to grow and feel fulfilled. According to them, we all have 3 fundamental psychological needs beyond the basics:

1. **Competence:** Feeling effective and capable in what we do.
2. **Autonomy:** Being in control of our actions and goals.
3. **Relatedness:** Feeling connected to others and experiencing a sense of belonging.

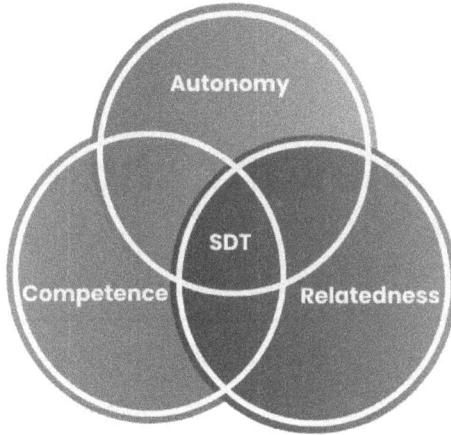

Figure 1. Self-Determination Theory (SDT) by Deci & Ryan

When these essential needs are met, employees are motivated, confident, and perform at their best. Autonomy includes the desire to feel psychologically free at work, choosing tasks they can support and value. Relatedness involves fostering positive relationships, feeling cared for by colleagues and superiors, and valuing others. Competence entails engaging in tasks where one excels, utilising talents, and making an impact on the world.[9]

More Relevant Than Ever

"It's now or never."

—*Conny Vandendriessche,*
HR Innovator, Founder House of HR

Employee engagement is more relevant than ever for these four reasons.

1. **Productivity powerhouse:** When employees are truly inspired, they show up ready to give their best. They don't dread Mondays and willingly put in extra effort without grumbling. What's even better is when intrapreneurship takes root. Triggered by an eagerness to learn, they push their own limits, manage the company budget as if it were their own money and ensure continuous innovation. An entrepreneurial culture is the big kahuna for many leaders.[10]

2. **Customer delight:** Engaged employees have a 50% higher focus on customer satisfaction, which translates into loyal customers and higher sales. It's the ultimate domino effect: engaged employees lead to happy customers, delighted customers keep shareholders smiling.

3. **Stronger brand:** Passionate employees don't keep the good vibes to themselves. They radiate them outward, creating a brand that is seen and felt. Whether it's prospects, customers, or potential new hires, everyone can sense that energy, and it draws them in like a magnet.

4. **Higher retention:** When you create a culture where employees feel heard, valued, and motivated, they're more likely to stick around. A culture of *"say, stay, and strive"* means employees are proud to talk about their workplace and are constantly looking for ways to exceed expectations.[11]

A high level of employee engagement is a key predictor of business outcomes, including customer satisfaction, productivity, and profitability, according to Harter, Schmidt, and Hayes in their Meta-Analysis on the relationship between employee engagement, satisfaction, and business outcomes.[12]

Show Me the Numbers

If you're reading this book, you're likely intrigued by the topic or convinced of high employee engagement's benefits. For those who find employee engagement elusive, here are study results illustrating its vital role in business models, demonstrating its importance beyond mere productivity.

The Numbers

- *A study by Harter and colleagues, shows that organisations with engaged employees see 51% higher productivity.*[13]
- *Research by Tower Watson indicates that companies with highly engaged employees report 9% higher shareholder returns.*[14]
- *Organisations with strong employee communication achieve 47% higher shareholder returns over five years.*[15]
- *Committed employees outperform non-committed ones by 20–28%.*[16]
- *Organisations with engaged employees show a 19% increase in operating income over a 12-month period, compared to a 33% decline in unengaged companies.*[17]
- *Employees who grasp how their work contributes to business performance are highly engaged.*[18]
- *Nearly two-thirds of employees perform at only 33% productivity due to unclear expectations.*[19]
- *80% of employees with high trust in management are committed, versus 25% with low trust.*[20]
- *Highly engaged employees are absent less, averaging 3.5 days/year.*[21]
- *A 5% increase in engagement correlates with a 0.7% rise in operating margin.*[22]
- *Highly engaged employees double the annual net income of disengaged companies.*[23]

Convinced by the Return on Investment? Excellent. Now, let's roll up our sleeves and dive into the real work. Yalla!

Forging an Alliance

Zi Gong asked: "Is there any one word that can serve as a principle for the conduct of life?"

Confucius said: "Perhaps the word 'reciprocity': Do not do to others what you would not want others to do to you."

In today's world, a job holds significant importance. It is more than a way to pay the rent. It defines our identity and what we aim to achieve in life. Sure, we all know that people work to cover expenses, support their families, and chase their personal dreams. Traditionally, companies have met these individual needs by offering employment, creating a straightforward employer-employee dynamic where the company holds the reins.

Once upon a time, companies could attract and retain talent by leveraging their brand power. But those days are long gone. Although it has softened slightly since 2023, the battle for talent is still on, with top performers being rather selective. Organisations are clearly evolving from mere workplaces to destinations where people genuinely want to be.

Reid Hoffman, co-founder of LinkedIn, champions the idea of forming an alliance with employees. When we rebranded our company from Herculean to the Herculean Alliance in 2019, we unwittingly aligned with Hoffman's vision, a serendipitous fit that perfectly captured our vision. Hoffman lays it out: In the past, you chose a field of study, applied to a respectable company, and climbed that corporate ladder. That progress was your lifetime achievement. Today, the world has changed. Companies no longer offer the stability of long-term employment. Employees have a buffet of options at their fingertips: from job-hopping to radical career shifts or even working abroad. And they're right to take advantage of these opportunities!

The challenge lies in the fact that many companies haven't caught up to this new reality. Instead of having open, honest conversations, they cling to the outdated notion of lifetime employment. The company says: *"We'll hire you, and you'll be here forever."* The employee nods along, *"Sure, I intend to stay forever,"* but both sides know this is a façade. This implicit conversation feels insincere and erodes trust.

Investor Chris Yeh calls it like it is: most career conversations are fundamentally broken. You've probably been in an interview and asked that classic question: *"Where do you see yourself in five years?"* The expected answer is something safe, like, *"I hope to have reached the level of manager or director by then."* Occasionally, a bold candidate might joke, *"I might have your job,"* and everyone would smirk. But what they're not going to say is, *"I'm not sure,"* or *"Maybe somewhere else,"* or *"Starting my own company."* So right from the first conversation, there's a bit of a fib. The truth is, that employee probably won't stick around forever, and that's the elephant in the room. Why not address it head-on? Why not talk about a mutual investment that pays off, long after the employee has moved on?

LinkedIn's former Vice President of Engineering, Kevin Scott, had a great approach. He would ask candidates, "*What job would you like to have after leaving LinkedIn?*" This question often caught people off guard, but it opened the door to honest conversations, building real trust and transparency.

Picture this: Employers and employees should see each other as allies. Survival in this landscape requires adaptability and a workforce of individuals who are ready to take risks, innovate, and try things that haven't been done before. But finding and keeping these people is the real challenge. That's where Hoffman's concept of the *Alliance* comes in.[24] It's a framework designed to attract, retain, and empower entrepreneurial employees. Those who push your business forward while also evolving their own careers.

In the Alliance, employer and employee should say, "*Look. We are in this boat together. We should be investing in each other. The world has changed, but together, we're going to build something remarkable.*" The company commits to investing in your lifetime employability—not to lifetime employment. Implying that, by staying, you enhance your economic standing, gain better opportunities, and shape your career path as you see fit. The employee, in turn, acknowledges that they may stay long or move on. But, either way, will make their time together transformative, making a real impact on the company's evolution.

This kind of honest conversations establishes a lifelong relationship. Just as universities have alumni, companies can tap into the big potential of their alumni network and cultivate this to their advantage. In an era where the network always wins, alumni can be powerful allies.

6

EX–CX–Growth

"The fastest way to get customers to love your brand is to get employees to love their jobs."

—*Tiffani Bova, Chief Growth Evangelist, Salesforce*

A strong **Employee Net Promoter Score** (*eNPS*) boosts the **Net Promoter Score** (*NPS*) of the company. A compelling statement for CEOs, sales managers, and marketers. And rightly so. Finally! The link between employee experience (EX) and customer experience (CX) is undeniable. High employee engagement leads to higher customer satisfaction, forming the equation **EX=CX**. Employee engagement fuels customer happiness, accelerating growth. Organisational growth boosts finances, motivation, and business momentum. Growth is good: it energises us, enhancing self-confidence and well-being at work and home. Growth is essential, especially when it's sustainable.

We call this the **Golden Triangle**: strategically linking EX, CX, and growth. A formula that prepares organisations for the future. A Gartner report called customer experience the new battleground for marketers.[25] Almost 90% of companies expect to compete primarily on the basis of customer experience and consider the employee role to be crucial in this. Blake Morgan's research reveals that 79% of employees at companies with high customer experience are very engaged, compared to 4% at companies with low satisfaction.[26] That's a game-changer.

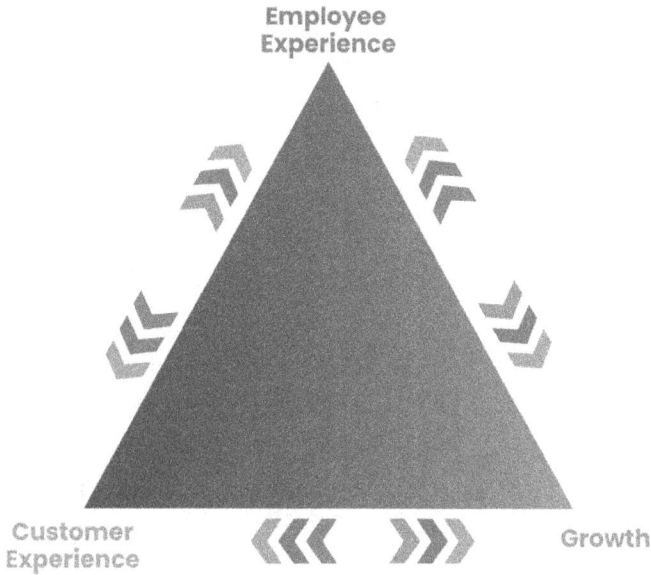

Figure 2. Golden Triangle

The powerful correlation between employee engagement and customer satisfaction isn't just theoretical—it has been put into action by leading global companies. A prime illustration is HCL, a 6 billion dollar leading global technology enterprise in India (and one of India's original IT garage start-ups). HCL has a central philosophy called *"Employee First, Customer Second."* It empowers over 77,000 employees to create real value for customers through engagement. *"Employee First"* is a management approach, proposed by HCL's CEO, Vineet Nayar. It aims to turn the organisational pyramid upside down and make management accountable to the people who create the value—the employees.

Nayar says: *"What we want at HCL is passion. We want people to be burning up with desire to pursue their interests. Fascinated by their assignments. Jumping out of their skins with excitement about what's next. Eagerly pursuing better solutions and new initiatives. We have found that the Employee First approach produces far more passion than any motivational or recognition program. Why? Because it proves that management understands the importance of the work being done by the employees in the value zone. It demonstrates that we are actively helping them in ways that make it easier for them to do their jobs. It shows that we trust them to do what needs to be done in the way they believe it should be done. And it shows that we respect them for the value they bring to the company."*

In a fascinating discussion with Yves Van Vaerenbergh, Professor of Marketing, we explored whether scientific evidence supports this link. Spoiler: it does! Dr Van Vaerenbergh confirmed that across industries, high employee engagement leads to better customer satisfaction. On an individual level, an employee's sunny disposition can't always save a bad service experience. But collectively, happy employees significantly impact customer experience.

Dr Van Vaerenbergh emphasizes the sequence: **happy employees create happy customers, who in turn boost employee commitment, creating a positive feedback loop.**[27] This cycle enhances employee motivation and self-esteem through customer praise. Conversely, dissatisfied customers can undermine employee commitment.

An interesting paradox here is the following. In the pursuit of maximising customer experience consistent across the entire organisation, we tend to standardise our processes.

This is to create consistency and clarity among employees in their interactions with customers. We want to ensure that every customer-facing employee knows exactly what is expected of them. But not to the point where the processes stifle the very individuality driving exceptional service. Efficiency and effectiveness are not the same thing. By eliminating personal touches, you might just eliminate the extra mile. And just like that—poof!—the magical pixie dust disappears.

Dr Van Vaerenbergh advocates for a more flexible approach, where a minimum set of rules provides guidance and loosens control, but where employees are trusted to use their judgement. It's a bit like Netflix's Culture Code, where founder Reed Hastings advises, *"Act in Netflix's best interest"* when it comes to expenses. Their five-word policy actually means employees are instructed to *"expense only what you would otherwise not spend and is worthwhile for work."* They don't have any limits, rules, reporting or tracking set in place, as they have proven to be a waste of time. For some leaders, this rule might be a lot harder than to manage by numbers...

Based on our own empirical findings, studies, and now also scientific research, this is the takeaway: **EX -> CX -> Growth**. It would have been perfect to complete the loop by stating that growth in revenue leads to happier employees. But unfortunately, in reality, this turns out not to be true. There is a limit to pushing the growth accelerator. Employees get tired and nerves get strained when growth comes too fast, too hard. That's why maintaining a continuous dual focus—on both growth and employee well-being—is critical.

Put Your Own People First!

"We are all obsessed with our customers. Are we that obsessive about the people who work for us?"

—Doug Baillie, Former Chief HR Officer, Unilever

"**P**ut *our own people first!*"—It almost sounds like a political slogan, doesn't it? And, in fact, it was. Back in the nineties, a right-wing political party in Belgium used it as a rallying cry. It was provocative, controversial, and it left a mark on the collective memory of many compatriots. But fast forward to the 21st century, and this once-contentious phrase could make for brilliant advice to any organisation still wrestling with the age-old *customer versus employee* dilemma.

"Treat your employees like your best customers." That was our mantra when we first founded our own company. We had a clear vision: our own employees would come first. A bold move, especially in an era when *"Customer is King"* was practically gospel. But our logic was simple: if our people weren't happy and healthy, how on earth could they make our customers happy?

Take, for example, our homegrown concept—the Hercules Trophy (and yes, in all modesty, it's the coolest corporate team challenge on the planet). We were determined to ensure that each Hercules crew member would embody our unique vibe, no matter where in the world we organised our events—be it Manhattan, Johannesburg, Madrid, Vilnius, or Abu Dhabi. But let me tell you, convincing hundreds of crew members—whom we saw only a few days each year—to fully embrace our specific DNA was like trying to explain that French fries are actually Belgian.

We were trying to crack the code on how to instil our specific care and happiness philosophy in this diverse group. We initially thought we could crack the code with the usual suspects like employee handbooks and inspiring videos. Spoiler alert: it didn't do the magic. And yet, maintaining a consistent total experience in all ten countries was non-negotiable.

So, we decided to turn the process on its head. We ditched the manuals and opted for something a bit more... intuitive. From the very first briefing with our local partners, we made it a point to warmly welcome each crew member into the Hercules family. Whether they were a local referee, security guard, hospitality crew, or janitor—we treated them like our top clients. Delicious food, kind words, personal attention, and of course, an invitation to join the party. Some thought it was a bit awkward at first. But soon enough, the results were undeniable. The hospitality and enthusiasm spread like wildfire, right through to our clients, who left with an unforgettable Herculean experience.

This approach, born from intuition and pragmatism, became our philosophy and was confirmed by Sir Richard Branson and Simon Sinek, who echoed the sentiment: *"**Happy employees ensure happy customers, and happy customers ensure happy shareholders. In that order**."*

What about Freelancers?

Who exactly do we consider our employees in today's ever-changing job market? The answer, quite simply, is everyone who contributes to an organisation's success, regardless of whether they're on the payroll or working from a café somewhere in the gig economy.

The traditional notion of employment is being shaken up by the rise of the gig economy, where short-term contracts and freelance work are no longer the exception but the rule. And no, it's not just the younger generation or the tech-savvy types jumping on this bandwagon. It's happening across all demographics and industries, from the bustling streets of Mumbai to the creative hubs of Lagos. The *"people first economy"* or *"gig economy"* is flourishing, with the World Bank estimating that the gig economy now makes up to 12% of the global labour market.[28]

The Gig Economy Spectrum

The gig economy encompasses various forms of freelance work, each with unique dynamics, challenges, and customer profiles. Here's how it breaks down:

- *Gig Economy: Think micro-tasks—designing a logo, translating a document—quick and efficient.*
- *Talent Economy: Predominantly in the creative sector, where freelancers bring their creative flair to longer-term projects.*
- *Knowledge Economy: High-skilled experts—like IT professionals, engineers, and healthcare specialists—offering their niche skills on a project basis.*

According to the Boston Consulting Group (BCG), gig workers find opportunities in this economy that allow them to leverage their skills in ways traditional jobs might not support.[29]

McKinsey highlights that independent workers are often highly engaged, thanks to flexibility, autonomy, and economic opportunity.[30] Overall, freelancers are optimistic about their future, with over a third expecting better opportunities within a year. Despite challenges like a lack of benefits and job stability, the flexibility and control they enjoy often leave them more satisfied than their traditionally employed counterparts. Freelancers often show an even higher level of commitment than the average employee. After all, they bring their talent and know-how as the most important asset and consciously choose a specific assignment in organisations.

Integrating freelancers into traditional work environments presents new challenges. Typically managed by procurement departments, freelance talent management should ideally be a joint effort between procurement and HR.

This approach recognises freelancers as human talent, making them feel like an integral part of the team. Enter the **Total Talent Management** (TTM) approach—a strategy that unites all types of workers under one cohesive plan, whether they're full-time, part-time, or freelance. This model aligns the entire workforce with business goals, valuing gig workers equally with permanent staff.[31]

Yet, companies often hesitate to include freelancers in team-building events, fearing it might blur the lines between employees and contractors. But here's a thought: involving freelancers in these activities can foster strong relationships and ensure they leave on a high note enhancing future collaboration prospects. Deloitte stresses the importance of integrating gig workers into the company culture by involving them in events and communications, which boosts both cohesion and agility. Additionally, providing freelancers with the same technology and resources as traditional employees enhances collaboration, performance, and innovation.

✋Case in Point

The Dubai Case—When Citizen Engagement Sets the Tone

There are plenty of companies out there that grasp the power of engaged employees to achieve customer delight. When I give a keynote on the subject, there's always that one person in the audience who asks, *"What's the most engaged company you've ever encountered?"* It took me a while before I realised that the best example I could give was right in front of me, staring into my face. It just required a bit of out-of-the-box thinking to consider a nation instead of a corporation. Are there any governments adept at engaging their customers, or rather, their citizens? Guess what? There is one. It's the UAE, with Dubai leading the charge. I know this firsthand—I've called this remarkable city home for quite some time now.

Dubai's story is nothing short of extraordinary. In just five decades, it has gone from a modest pearl-diving village to a dazzling global hub of tourism and trade. Dubai's population has skyrocketed to over 3 million—an impressive leap from just 20,000 in 1950. This transformation, often dubbed the *"Dubai effect,"* is something businesses and governments around the world covet.

Now, despite my credentials as an employee engagement nerd (a title I wear as a badge of honour), I find myself constantly learning from Dubai, the unparalleled maestro of citizen engagement and communication.

1. **Vision:** First, Dubai drew my family and me in with a compelling, crystal-clear vision. They've nailed the art of defining a purpose that engages people from every corner of the globe, all striving to be the best. Not in the region, but in the world, as Sheikh Mohammed explained in a 2007 interview with CBS. Explaining what he meant by number one in the world, he said, *"In everything: higher education, health and housing. Just making my people have the highest way of living." "And why do you want everything to be the biggest, the tallest?"* the reporter asked. His Highness challenged: *"Why not?"* The country's purpose is laid out in the UAE's Future Roadmap, a detailed plan covering everything from health and education to infrastructure and sustainability. It's no wonder millions of people have come to Dubai to be part of this shared dream.

2. **Leadership:** It is paramount. Dr Tommy Weir even dedicated a book to it, titled *"Leadership Dubai style."*[32] The Majlis, a cornerstone of Dubai's leadership approach, exemplifies this.[33] Before making decisions, leaders listen carefully to input from all corners—whether it's businesspeople, media, or the general public. UAE leaders focus on helping others achieve more than they ever dreamed possible. It's so much more than having a vision; it's about creating an environment where everyone can

succeed. For Dubai, that meant leveraging its prime location to become a global hub.

3. **Growth mindset:** Finally, the Dubai model thrives on a growth mindset. The Emirate ranks second among the world's top city destinations, drawing more visitors than Disney World or the Eiffel Tower. Its airport, DXB, is the busiest international hub on the planet. The leaders of Dubai are the epitome of a growth mindset: open-minded, eager to learn, and unafraid to take risks. They stick to their strategies. But they remain flexible in execution, always believing in the collective power of the country to shape the future. And yes, that includes its expats. *"Hello, Tomorrow"* isn't just a slogan here; it's a way of life.

Part I RECAP—The Foundation of Employee Engagement

✺ **Definition:** Being fully invested—physically, emotionally, and cognitively towards the employer.

✺ **4 Characteristics of an Engaged Organisation:**
1. Purpose
2. Empowerment
3. Belonging
4. Trust

✺ Employee engagement is essential for **organisational success:**
1. Productivity powerhouse
2. Customer delight
3. Stronger brand
4. Higher retention

✺ An **Inconvenient Truth:** Seventy-seven per cent of employees are not engaged, with 15% being actively disengaged. This disengagement costs the global economy trillions of dollars.

✺ **Employer–Employee Alliance:** Modern organisations should foster an alliance with employees based on mutual trust and investment.

✺ **Golden Triangle:** Employee experience (EX), customer experience (CX), and growth are vital for long-term success. Engaged employees create satisfied customers, driving organisational growth.

✺ **Freelancers** are an integral part of the workforce—and often highly engaged.

PART TWO

THE PEOPLE FUNCTION

"HR faces the choide. Reinvent itself or abolish itself."

—*Ignace Van Doorselaere,*
Former CEO Neuhaus

The pursuit of top talent is an enduring saga, forcing HR departments to continually broaden their horizons. Traditionally focused on hiring and firing staff, employee administration, and compensation, HR is now compelled to delve into leadership development, training, employer branding, sustainability, and diversity initiatives.

To thrive, HR must transcend its siloed operations, drawing inspiration from marketing and communications departments. The confluence of marketing and HR is logical given the modern need for businesses to cater to discerning consumers and critical job candidates alike. Marketers have adapted reasonably well in recent years. Now it's up to HR to come out of its shell. The worlds of marketing and HR have been flirting with each other for some time. Now it's time to get serious.

A growing number of organisations are currently blending HR practices with marketing tactics to display the organisation as a great place to work. Innovative companies are venturing to the next level. That of a data-first HR approach inspired by digital marketing and technology, allowing HR to transition into a comprehensive People department. This transformation demands new skills that balance the soft and hard aspects of HR harmoniously.

Ask the Expert ✑

Ignace Van Doorselaere, Former CEO Neuhaus

We all know it by now: people are the game-changers in companies. We don't need any more research to prove this. The compass needle pointing to the future is called the strategy. First and foremost, the *"what"* is essential; companies must make strategic choices to achieve long-term success. After all, strategy is about saying *yes* to segments, products, services, driving better outcomes and sustainable profitability. For these strategic choices to leap off the slides they are etched on, culture is indispensable. It's an ecosystem that grows within organisations and extends outward into partnerships with customers, service providers, agencies, and more.

I believe in performance ethics; a culture where performance is the ethical benchmark and is achieved ethically. Performance ethics view a company as a bridge connecting the customer interest pillar with the shareholder interest pillar, supported by the human energy that drives it. Indeed, people are the bearers of this energy. They collaborate to elevate the company and propel it forward. This shared focus binds them, akin to a soccer team striving for championships. The team members run because they want to, not because they are forced to. Wanting means enjoying the work, which is far more powerful than having to. Perceiving it not as mere toil, but as a meaningful life fulfilment. Fostering self-confidence, contributing, letting enthusiasm eclipse fatigue, gaining autonomy, feeling secure, having the right to take breaks, and simply enjoying what they do. That's the dream!

And just like the perfect marriage, the ideal business doesn't exist. But as long as the pursuit of improvement suppresses routine and indifference, everything will continue to thrive. What are the greatest adversaries of performance ethics? That's poor leadership and bureaucracy. The responsibility of leaders is immense, and their task is complex. Orchestrating hundreds or thousands of people to play with gusto and continuously receive standing ovations from full concert halls is no small feat.

It can go awry. Leaders must transcend the out-of-key notes with inspiration, optimism, and exemplary behaviour. The personality of leaders significantly influences the culture of an organisation. Their impact spreads swiftly, like a beneficial or harmful virus. Fortunately, leaders can often be replaced when negative signals or facts accumulate.

Culture, by the way, is not HR's responsibility but that of the management. How do we want to win? How do we handle downturns? Culture is tested when things get tough: "*It's not how you get into trouble but how you get out of it that defines the culture.*" How do people behave in our company? How do we communicate? Who must we let go for the greater good?

Bureaucracy is a trickier beast. A beast without a head or tail. It's omnipresent and self-perpetuating. Every two years, companies conduct exercises to reduce bureaucracy: staff departments, meeting cultures, and processes. It's all scrutinised. Usually, these exercises lead to disappointing results. The reason is simple: too many managers have been trained to monitor, to consult, do SWOTs, work out scenarios, and write procedures. Reducing bureaucracy is asking these managers to question their own existence; it is requesting them to commit professional suicide. That is why *"management"* has become a negatively charged word that isn't related to entrepreneurship or leadership. It is often at odds with it. Too many managers maintain themselves because they believe the frame has become more important than the painting. The painting is about content—the quality and commitment of people, the strength of the brand, the unique technology, profitability, satisfied customers, etc. The frame deals with all the systems, procedures, hierarchical structures needed to contain the painting. Without a frame, you get chaos. An excess of frame kills enthusiasm and drive. The art is the (im)balance.

This brings us to the core of this book: Drive and commitment. Parameters that are usually measured through employee satisfaction surveys. We all know the drill: we complete a well-designed questionnaire, which is analysed and segmented. The next step is to organise various workgroups to debate and draft actions. Then, the action list is implemented, or should I say: added to all the other existing action lists? Less than half of it is carried out because *"We just don't have the time, sir."* Then the next big thing, usually around the festive season: tis the season of the dreaded round of evaluation interviews! The company values, established after months of brainstorming, become a checklist. How did you score on team spirit, integrity, collegiality, and a positive mindset? I thought my last report with teacher comments dated from high school. But no, we have it here too. Annually. Two hours of talking, filling out, scoring, signing, training lists, and salary adjustments. Don't you do that at home too on New Year's Eve? *"Honey, how about an annual review of the family members? I've already posted the family values on the fridge."* And to make it absurd—you won't believe it—some companies even do career planning. *"The next five years are mapped out for you. If you want to be a divisional head by then, these are the positions to take on next. Let's add a few training courses here and there. Oh, and by the way: avoid making any enemies along the way."* Useless, if you ask me.

HR managers are often the architects of the frames and the frameworks. But shouldn't they be liberators of passion instead? How can we loosen things up, and free up some energy in the company? What makes people unhappy? What if I told you that the source of unhappiness is performance reviews, unfulfilled career plans, or poor follow-up on employee surveys? How can we increase autonomy? What achievements make us proud? What stories give people that sparkle in their eyes? Is there any weak leadership that is stifling our people? How to allow more flexibility? Who isn't giving their best, hindering the company, and demotivating colleagues? How can people take control of their path? Life's journey will fill it, rather than the career plan. HR's job should not be to focus on building the frameworks. But to help create a more beautiful painting! Too many systems lead to organisations where everything is right. Everything, except for the heart.

1

From Necessary Evil to Catalyst

"HR's job is not to be liked. It's to build the best company."

—*Laszlo Bock, Former HR Chief Google*

The most exceptional HR professionals? They're usually not HR-trained from the start; they got there because they felt the undeniable impact of human connection. That wasn't Ignace talking, but me. Yes, you can quote me on that. And every time I share this little nugget with business leaders, they grin and nod, as if I've just said out loud what they've always believed but never dared to voice.

Despite all the talk about the importance of HR and employee engagement, too many companies are just going through the motions. Their actions rarely match their words. Many still see HR as little more than a necessary administrative function, mainly there to manage payroll and push paperwork. It's no secret that HR doesn't always win popularity contests. HR is often tucked under the CFO's wing, treated as a necessary evil rather than the powerful growth accelerator it can be. In fact, frustration has grown so palpable that the Harvard Business Review recently ran a provocative cover featuring a bomb with a lit fuse and the headline, *It's Time to Blow Up HR (and Build*

Something New). The accompanying articles came with pointed titles like *Rethinking Human Resources, Why We Love to Hate HR*, and *A New Role for the CHRO*.[34]

Before you think I'm jumping on the bandwagon of HR critics, let me set the record straight. I have immense respect for the HR department. In fact, I'm their biggest fan. They're doing all they possibly can, often with limited resources. HR is the lifeblood of any business because they focus on what truly matters—people. And people, as we all know, are the heart of any organisation. There's no shortage of smart, capable HR professionals out there, quietly moving mountains as we speak. My mission? To shake things up and help them take the next big step—just like IT did in the 2000s and marketing in the 2010s. Honestly, I think this is the perfect time for HR to have its moment in the spotlight.

To understand how we got here, let's take a quick trip down memory lane. Back in the early 20th century, HR departments were born out of the need to handle growing piles of administrative tasks and navigate increasingly complex labour laws. Over time, HR's role expanded to include training, development, and performance evaluations, juggling the heavy burden of compliance with the demands of managing talent. This left HR with a bit of an identity crisis—on one hand, enforcing the rules and regulations, and on the other, trying to be the motivating force behind talent management. It's no wonder HR sometimes feels like it's dealing with split personalities!

HR has had to roll with the punches and adapt to changing work environments plenty of times over the years. But let's be honest, the COVID-19 crisis was a different beast altogether. It pushed HR into uncharted waters, presenting them with a whirlwind of new and unforeseen challenges while fast-tracking issues that were already simmering. No department felt these fundamental shifts more acutely than HR.

The pandemic forced HR to confront the most common challenges head-on, impacting everything from the organisation of work to the workforce itself, and the work environment we all had to adjust to overnight. It's worth taking a moment to refresh our memories on just how intense those early days were. During that period, HR leaders were handed a nearly impossible to-do list, with almost no time to check things off, from empowering employees to stay connected in a suddenly remote world, to resolving unforeseen illness and absences, and keeping up with rapidly changing safety measures and ever-evolving legislation. The COVID-19 crisis undoubtedly stands out as one of the most challenging periods HR has ever faced. But it's also a testament to the resilience of HR professionals that they managed to navigate these storms with such care.

2

The 1-Million-Dollar Question

"You're not responsible for your employees—you're responsible towards them."

—*Don Phin, HR Strategist*

Is **HR responsible for employee engagement?** Well, let me put it like this: Your duty isn't to take responsibility for your employees, but to support them responsibly.[35] Shouldering their responsibilities is a surefire ticket to burnout. Control over employees and their engagement? That's not in your wheelhouse—and trust me, you don't want it to be.

Back in the old manufacturing days, when work was all about repetitive physical tasks, the *command-and-control* method was king. Workers weren't paid to think, but to follow orders to the letter. Those days are long gone. The easily controlled employee is the last thing you need now because this type of worker expects you to carry responsibilities for them. In today's knowledge economy, trying to control employees just leads to micromanagement, stifling any initiative or decision-making.

Nowadays, in the age of engagement, your job is to create an environment where employees can truly thrive. It starts with clear-cut responsibilities. When people know what's expected of them, understand the skills required, and have the right tools at their disposal, the responsibility to perform and engage naturally flows to them. It becomes their accountability.

Employee engagement is a shared responsibility, not a burden that falls on one department alone. The CEO and the board initiate it, the HR team (or People department—if you prefer) owns it, managers drive it, and everyone—from the intern to the managing director—carries it forward. Employees don't need to sit around waiting for their boss or the organisation to swoop in and make their work lives better. They have the power to ignite positive change, find meaning, happiness, and engagement from within. In fact, they're better at engaging themselves than any HR program could ever hope to be.

> *Employee engagement is a shared responsibility: the CEO initiates it. HR owns it, management drives it. Every employee carries it.*

3

What If... HR Were a Bit More Like Marketers?

"The age of the consumer and the employee synergising is upon us."

—*Leena Nair, CHRO, Unilever*

"Recruitment needs to be faster, the onboarding process is uninspiring, internal communication is failing, and our people are not engaged, ..."

These are words spoken by Conny Vandendriessche, the leading lady in the European HR industry and co-founder of the recruitment agency House of HR. I had the pleasure of working closely with Conny for several years, and she rarely minces words when it comes to HR realities. She shared some valuable wisdom with me:

"HR professionals have known this forever: everyone in the organisation fancies themselves an HR manager, and they're not shy about sharing how they think things should be done. Marketers used to suffer the same fate, but with the rapid digital evolution of marketing, most of the armchair experts have gone silent realising that dashboards and online campaigns are a bit more complex than they thought.

The first thing Marketing and HR can tackle together is the rebranding of the term 'Human Resources.' We've long since moved past the days when employees were simply 'resources.' Today's (and future) employees are more like customers. If you want to attract them, give them a great experience, and keep them on board. Partnering with Marketing starts with defining your target audience. Who are you trying to attract? Where can you find these people? What motivates them to change jobs? HR often boils these answers down to bland job postings filled with bullet points on traditional job boards. But Marketing can help you position your company with compelling stories and eye-catching visuals in brilliant online campaigns.

The pandemic has perhaps given us the best opportunity yet to bridge the gap between these two teams. Together, they can create Internal Branding that exudes confidence and strength— Marketing doing what it does best behind the scenes, with the familiar, warm face of HR as its ally."

I couldn't agree more with Conny. Indeed, Marketing and HR are like siblings with different styles. Both are in the business of engaging people, building loyalty, and making a lasting impression. The main difference is in the focus, style, and methods.

If you put a typical marketing deck next to the average HR PowerPoint, you'd see a night-and-day difference. Marketing comes off smooth and confident, while HR often feels a bit more, well, apologetic. And that's exactly why we don't instinctively link the two. However, the line between Marketing and HR is getting blurrier by the day. You see it in the rise of hybrid marketing/HR roles and the shrinking gap between consumer and employer brands. Marketing is trying to present brands to consumers in the most authentic and impactful way possible. Meanwhile, HR's job is to take that sleek, polished external vibe and bring it inside to the people who make the organisation tick.

Given the growing similarities between customers and employees, it's no shocker that HR needs to borrow a few tricks from marketing's playbook.[36] HR should see itself as a marketing team, with colleagues as its customers. Marketing has mastered the art of understanding customers, creating simple yet powerful experiences that foster engagement and loyalty. It's HR's turn to replicate this for its people. When HR and marketing join forces, they shouldn't *copy/paste* existing marketing principles; they need to elevate them to match today's tech-driven world.

By embracing these competencies, HR can craft exceptional **human experiences**, gain a competitive edge, attract the right talent, and make engagement a central part of the business agenda.

Here are 3 key areas for HR to focus on:

1. *Strong brand: Traditionally, HR didn't exactly roll out the red carpet for in-depth marketing input, but that has changed fast. There's a growing recognition within organisations that blending the two domains has the potential to create a killer employer brand. More and more marketing pros are helping HR articulate a clear, compelling vision that attracts top talent, clarifies the organisation's DNA, and turns employees into passionate ambassadors.*

2. ***Evidence-Based Adjustments:*** *Data is king, and Marketing is still way ahead of HR on this front. Marketing can provide HR with insights and help craft engaging, inspiring stories. Setting up interdisciplinary teams from the get-go fosters empowerment, ownership, and strategic insight from both sides, ensuring collaboration becomes a recipe for success.*

3. ***Customer Insight:*** *Marketers invest significant resources into understanding their customers. What they think of the products, how to improve them, and how to meet expectations. Now, think of your company as the product: How do your employees see it? Are they in love with it? How did they first encounter it? Would they recommend it to others? What draws them in? Where are the skill gaps? Who are the top performers?*

4

On to the People Function!

> *"Just as the personnel department transformed into Human Resources in the 1980s and 90s, HR is now evolving into a data-driven 'People' function."*
>
> —*Unknown*

If HR teams can confront the new challenges and become the vanguard of change, they have a unique opportunity in the modern landscape. They must either prioritise their most significant asset for growth—their people—by placing them at the heart of their business strategy, or they risk stagnation and missed opportunities for success and expansion.

Since the beginning of the 21st century, HR has strived to cement itself as a robust internal business partner, with mixed outcomes. In many organisations, HR has not yet achieved equal footing in strategic planning. According to the HR Research Institute, mere 43% of firms regard HR as an equal partner in this process. In less than a third of organisations, HR's input is sought solely for talent-related matters during planning, while in 25% of cases, HR is excluded from strategic planning altogether. Only 29% of respondents rate their department highly in planning for the future beyond two years. According to Accenture over 50% of leaders and employees believe HR is lagging behind the evolving needs of the business.[37]

A 2024 study by the HR Research Institute reveals a troubling disconnect between what HR departments possess and what they require.

*Only **30%** of respondents believe their HR department effectively meets their organisation's strategic needs from an employee perspective. Conversely, **43%** rate their ability to fulfil the strategic needs of executive leaders as satisfactory. **97%** of respondents acknowledge the importance of HR's strategic activities to their organisation's success over the next three years. Yet only **51%** feel their department's strategic competencies are currently on par with their transactional capabilities.[38]*

This signifies an urgent need for HR departments to enhance their strategic acumen swiftly. In other words, large numbers of HR departments need to quickly improve their strategic capabilities.

It's likely to be a wild ride for HR. Not only will HR professionals need to forge more strategic departments, but they will also simultaneously need to cope with a wide range of other issues, including the impact of generative AI, skills shortages, changing demographics, geopolitical uncertainties, and shifting legal and cultural landscapes, among other trends.

These times present a unique momentum for HR to amplify its influence and develop new competencies. Just as the personnel department transformed into Human Resources in the 1980s and 90s, HR is now evolving into a data-driven "***People***" function. Increasingly, companies are renaming their HR departments to reflect this shift. Rightly so, because let's face it: The terminology *"Human Resources"* does not inherently convey a very people-centric approach...

The most successful organisations invest in their people as a core business philosophy. They leverage new technologies to attract and retain top talent, ensuring sustained growth. These organisations have mastered contemporary working methods, transitioning from low-value, manual policy processes to strategic teams that generate business value and cultivate significant employee experiences. By doing so, they keep their workforce motivated, engaged, and productive. These teams have adopted new competencies, roles, and responsibilities, such as people scientists, employer branding specialists, and people marketing roles. Companies that have embarked on this people-centric journey recognise it as a critical step toward thriving in the digital economy.

The imperative to focus on the human element has never been greater. As technology automates repetitive and routine tasks, the realisation of growth hinges on uniquely human traits—passion, creativity, and ingenuity—to deliver exceptional customer experiences. This shift underscores where humans excel over technology.

5

Reality Check

> *"Skills gaps are emerging as a critical challenge to business transformation worldwide."*
>
> —*WEF 2025 Future of Jobs Report*

Changing Needs

Profound changes demand different skills and constant adaptation. This necessity applies to HR and Marketing departments and every one of us. The World Economic Forum (WEF), in its *Future of Jobs Report*, underscores 10 crucial skills for the workforce, reflecting the rising importance of cognitive abilities, technology literacy, and socio-emotional skills.[39]

The Top 10 Skills According to the World Economic Forum's *Future of Jobs Report* 2023[40]

1. *Analytical Thinking*
2. *Creative Thinking*
3. *Technological Literacy*
4. *Curiosity and Lifelong Learning*
5. *Resilience, Flexibility, and Agility*
6. *Systems Thinking*
7. *AI and Big Data*

> 8. *Motivation and Self-awareness*
> 9. *Talent Management*
> 10. *Service Orientation and Customer Service*

Translating these trends into HR reveals two primary needs:

1. A rise in demand for computing and data analytics,
2. An increased need for human attributes such as critical thinking, creativity, and persuasion.

Accenture's *Brand Learning Report* indicates that HR managers feel they are lagging due to a shortage of specific skills, particularly commercial skills often found in marketing.[41] The main barriers to change identified are focus on too many priorities at once, lack of resources, insufficient knowledge to build a business case for change or the lack of vision or leadership within the organisation.

Closing the Skills Gap

To drive change and contribute to company growth, HR must address the skills gap. But how? By learning several competencies, recruiting non-traditional profiles into the traditional HR team, engaging external consultants (even if only temporarily) and partnering more intensively with other departments, including Marketing, Communication, and IT. For instance, HR can form cross-functional teams on a project basis or implement rotating functions to enhance skill sets.

Actions to Bridge the Skills Gap

1. *Cultivate More Tech Savviness*
   - *Engage fully in technology discussions without fear.*
   - *Dare to seek advice from IT employees and explore technology through webinars, events, demos, and vendor-provided resources (tools, training, and customer communities).*

2. *Foster Creativity*
   - *Challenge your team to experiment and innovate by encouraging flexibility and creative projects.*
   - *Establish a culture where failure is a learning opportunity and invite marketing staff to contribute fresh ideas and perspectives.*

3. *Develop People Analytics: Gradually Maturing as a Full-Fledged Discipline*
   - *Build literacy in data and analytics, essential for HR professionals.*
   - *No need to feel overwhelmed. Take it one step at a time, ensuring tools are linked to objectives and usability (cf. Part V).*

4. *Enhance Communication Skills*
   - *Centre storytelling around employees and collaborate with internal and external communications departments.*
   - *Utilise new tools like design and video to increase engagement.*

Deloitte's *Global Human Capital Trends Report* emphasises the role of HR in fostering a culture of continuous learning, leveraging technology for skill development, and building resilient HR teams. The report also highlights the need for HR to develop capabilities in AI, data analytics, and employee experience management to adapt to future challenges.

Part II RECAP—The Evolution and Strategic Future of HR

⁂ **HR's Long Journey:** HR has evolved, moving from administrative duties to a wider range of responsibilities. Despite its evolution, HR has often been viewed as a necessary function rather than a key driver of business success.

⁂ **Responsibility for Employee Engagement:** Shared, initiated by the CEO, owned by HR, driven by managers, and carried forward by employees themselves.

⁂ **HR and Marketing Synergy:** HR begins to adopt a marketing mindset, helping it improve internal branding, measure engagement, and present the company as an attractive workplace.

⁂ **3 Key Focus Areas for HR:**

1. Building a strong employer brand
2. Data and evidence-based adjustments
3. Customer insight applied to employees

⁂ **Next Big Step for HR:** The shift to a data-driven and strategic People function is essential to become a major strategic partner in business growth in the digital economy.

⁂ **4 Actions to Address the Skills Gap:**

1. Cultivate tech savviness
2. Foster creativity
3. Develop people analytics
4. Enhance communication skills

PART THREE

❧

THE SMELL
OF THE PLACE

"It's the smell of the place. And it's possible to create a specific smell in companies."

—*Professor Sumantra Ghoshal*

In a famous World Economic Forum talk, *The Smell of the Place*, Professor Ghoshal draws a vivid contrast between two environments: the oppressive, stifling heat of Calcutta in summer, where one feels drained and unmotivated, versus the fresh, energising air of the Fontainebleau forest in spring, which naturally inspires movement, energy, and initiative.

A shift in workplace culture is not just an abstract theory—it is a strategic choice that forward-thinking leaders can actively design and sustain. The "smell" of a workplace—its energy, norms, and emotional climate—shapes employee engagement far more than policies or incentives ever could.

Let's explore how workplace culture attracts, retains, and engages employees, showing that culture is not just an idea—it is the air they breathe. And just like air, leaders must take responsibility for its quality if they want to create an environment where people truly thrive.

1

Your Vibe Attracts Your Tribe

"We are completely at peace with the fact that we're not everyone's cup of tea."

—Lina Yousif, Head of People
& Culture at Media One Hotel Dubai

In the grand scheme of workplace dynamics, culture isn't an accessory; it's the main event. Most employees will tell you that culture is what keeps their engines running day in and day out. Culture and engagement are the best of allies—think Batman and Robin, but in a corporate setting. While it's not quite a cause-and-effect relationship, the two are tightly intertwined. A robust organisational culture lays the groundwork for high levels of employee engagement, like rich soil fosters a flourishing garden. Conversely, if that culture is lacking, you might find engagement withering on the vine.

I like to think of culture as the personality of a company. Now, here's the thing: it isn't something you can see, touch, taste, or even breathe. Think of it like a vibe, an energy that permeates the room—and it's absolutely contagious. It touches everything. Every organisation has its own unique culture, whether or not the original creators may no longer be on board.

This phenomenon is often likened to the *"hundredth monkey effect"*—the idea that once a critical mass of individuals adopts a behaviour, it becomes common knowledge. It spreads quickly and sticks, becoming a lasting part of how things are done.

There's no shortage of models to explain organisational culture, with Edgar Schein's *Onion Model* being one of the most popular. Picture it as an onion with three layers:

1. The **outer layer** is all about artifacts and symbols— think logos, architecture, or even the company's dress code.

2. The **middle layer** comprises norms, values, and rules of conduct—the ways the organisation expresses its goals, strategies, and philosophies.

3. At the **core**, you have assumptions—those deep-seated, often unconscious behaviours that are second nature within the company. They're tricky to spot if you're an outsider.

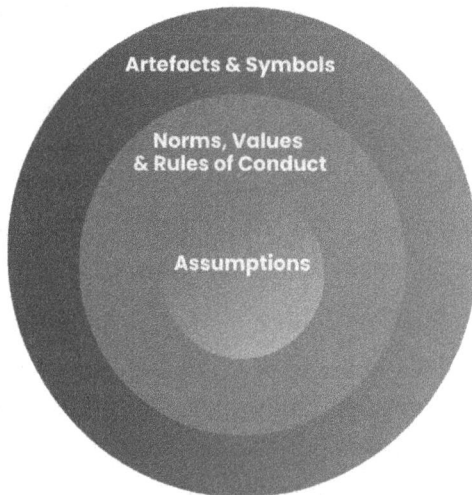

Figure 3. Onion Model by Edgar Schein

Robert Quinn provides a practical tool known as the *Organisational Culture Assessment Instrument* (**OCAI**), which is a bit of a Swiss Army knife for understanding culture. This model helps identify both the current and desired culture types within an organisation, whether it's family-oriented, innovative (adhocracy), hierarchical, or market-driven. Quinn's model offers insights into aligning leadership roles, effectiveness measures, and management approaches. The better these elements align, the smoother and more successful the organisation becomes.

From a practical perspective, think of organisational culture as the sum of the company's overall vibe and the intentional actions taken to shape and nurture that atmosphere. Culture influences everything—from how employees are treated and how products or services are developed to the way partnerships are formed, and the day-to-day work gets done. It's the invisible hand guiding how an organisation functions and evolves.

The most fascinating thing about culture is that's always there and everywhere, even if it's flying under the radar. Unlike the physical office environment, technology, or business processes, which cannot exist without being designed by the company, culture is more like the air your employees breathe. That's why handing it over to managers who live and die by their spreadsheets can be a bit of a gamble. Crafting a thriving culture isn't something you can just check off a list; it takes deliberate, ongoing effort.

Now, why does it sometimes *"click"* between employees and employers, and other times it's like mixing oil and water? A lot of it boils down to whether company values and personal values are in sync. We dive deeper into this in Part IV, where we talk about organisational values and principles as drivers of engagement. And let me say this: If you're not feeling as if you belong to a specific culture, it doesn't necessarily mean that it's bad. Or that you're the bad one. It just might not be *your* style. Or, as my teenage daughter would put it: "*You're just not vibing with each other.*" The silver lining? Culture is something that you as a leader, can always shape and refine. No matter where your organisation currently stands.

Good Culture—Bad Strategy

When I chat with CEOs, I generally notice a strong awareness of the importance of culture. With so much focus on this topic, it's no wonder Peter Drucker's famous line, "*Culture eats strategy for breakfast*," has become such a staple in business discussions. And probably it's devouring strategy for lunch and dinner too! Just ask WeWork, where a toxic culture threw a wrench into the business, despite a sound strategic vision.

Agreed, a top-down, rigid strategy might not cut it, but that doesn't mean you can skip strategy altogether. Instead, purpose, strategy, and culture need to work hand in hand to drive success. The question is: Can positive culture compensate for a flawed strategy? Hubert Joly, former chairman and CEO of Best Buy, highlights that traditionally, strategy has been considered the cornerstone to business success.[42] However, he emphasises that while culture plays a powerful role in bringing purpose and strategy to life, it cannot substitute for a fundamentally sound strategy. A strategy must be well-conceived and executable for the culture to be effective in supporting it.

Take Nokia, for example. In 2006, Nokia was the global leader in mobile phones, enjoying double-digit growth and ranked as the eighth most innovative company in the world by

Business Week. What could possibly go wrong? As it turned out, quite a lot. Despite fostering a collaborative and innovative culture, Nokia stumbled because its strategy couldn't keep up with the fast-evolving mobile phone market. The employees were engaged and committed, but the decision to stick with the Symbian operating system, even as Apple and Android were gaining ground, led to major setbacks.

Or look at Blockbuster. The company had a robust organisational culture, but its strategy failed to adapt to the digital streaming revolution—a critical misstep that led to its downfall. Other companies like Kodak, Sears, and Sharp Corporation serve as similar cautionary tales. A strong culture might drive great teamwork and execution, but if the strategy is fundamentally flawed or disconnected from market trends, the business is bound to struggle.

Culture played a key role in turning around companies like Microsoft under Satya Nadella's leadership. However, this revival wasn't solely due to culture; it was also because the strategy was realigned to fit the new cultural direction. Organisational culture never stands alone. The real magic happens when a strong strategy and a supportive culture work together in harmony.

2

The Culture Factor

"Culture is more often a source of conflict than of synergy. Cultural differences are a nuisance at best and often a disaster."

—Geert Hofstede,
Founder of The Culture Factor

Organisational culture is a topic that everyone loves to discuss and one that always captures attention, yet few can define it with clarity. Is it the sum of the individuals' cultures? Does it reflect the nationality of its leaders? Or does the organisation have its own DNA, regardless of who's working there? In reality, both organisational culture and national culture are deeply intertwined, especially in a globalised business environment. National culture influences organisational culture, and understanding this interaction is vital for managing diverse multiethnic teams effectively.

This is where The Culture Factor (formerly known as *Hofstede Insights*) comes into the picture.[43] The aim of the Culture Factor is to turn culture into a competitive advantage. A strategic asset, rather than a stumbling block. They do this by assessing and optimising both organisational and national cultures using tools like the *Multi-Focus Model*.

While there are various methods available to help understand cultural differences, such as Erin Meyer's popular *The Culture Map,*[44] which focuses on helping professionals navigate cross-cultural communication and management, The Culture Factor takes a deeper dive into the structural elements that shape both organisational and national cultures. It provides a framework to identify cultural gaps and to strategically align culture with business goals.

Organisational Culture tends to be more straightforward and precise to measure than national Culture. This is because, unlike nations, most organisations have clear objectives and requirements. Most of the activities within the organisation are designed to meet those objectives. While differences between national cultures are most apparent in the values, differences between organisations within the same nation can most clearly be seen in the practices of the organisations. This is also why organisational culture, unlike national culture, can be changed by changing those practices.

By the way, there is no one best organisational culture to aim for, because the best organisational culture is always contextual. The key thing to keep in mind is that the best organisational culture your organisation should aim for should be a culture that best supports your strategy.

When going deeper into analysing organisational culture, it becomes useful to make divisions between different types. The Culture Factor approach divides organisational culture into 4 key themes:

1. **Optimal Culture:** The ideal culture that aligns with an organisation's strategy, taking into account limitations such as rules, legislation, and the economic landscape.

It should be uniquely tailored to the organisation's context and not copied from others.

2. **Actual Culture:** The current culture within the organisation, which should be objectively measured using reliable methods to ensure accuracy in culture change efforts.

3. **Perceived Culture:** The culture as seen by individuals within the organisation. It is subjective and may not reflect the true culture, making it a less-reliable foundation for aligning culture with strategy.

4. **Ideal Work Environment:** A vision of the preferred organisational culture, based on employee preferences, which helps guide the development of the optimal culture but does not represent the current state.

The Multi-Focus Model on organisational culture is the result of a study on organisational cultures research which showed that a large part of the differences among the units could be explained by six factors related to concepts within organisational sociology. These six factors became the six dimensions of Organisational Culture.

D1	D2	D3
ORGANISATIONAL EFFECTIVENESS	**CUSTOMER ORIENTATION**	**LEVEL OF CONTROL**
Means-Oriented vs Goal-Oriented	Internally Driven vs Externally Driven	Easy-Going vs Strict Work Discipline

D 4	D 5	D 6
FOCUS	**APPROACHABILITY**	**MANAGEMENT PHILOSOPHY**
Local vs Professional	Open Systems vs Closed Systems	Employee-Oriented vs Work-Oriented

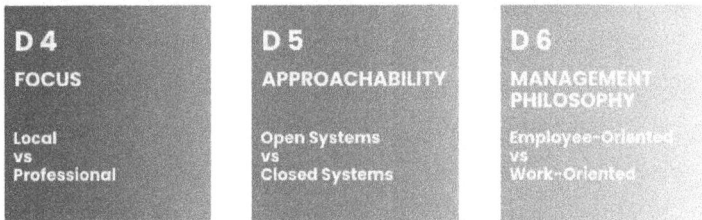

Figure 4. Multi-Focus Model—The Culture Factor

1. **Organisational Effectiveness (*Means vs. Goal Orientation*):** In a means-oriented culture, the focus is on how work is done. On the flip side, a goal-oriented culture is all about achieving specific internal goals, even if it involves taking some risks.

2. **Customer Orientation (*Internally vs. Externally Driven*):** An internally driven culture operates on the belief that the company knows best what's good for customers. In contrast, an externally driven culture prioritises meeting customer requirements, sometimes to the extreme, at the expense of a broader ethical perspective.

3. **Level of Control (*Easy-going vs. Strict Work Discipline*):** Easy-going cultures are fluid, with less predictability and more room for improvisation. Strict work disciplines, however, are the opposite: serious, punctual, and cost-conscious, leaving little to chance.

4. **Focus (*Local vs. Professional*):** In a local-focused culture, employees identify strongly with their boss or unit, with a short-term outlook and a strong push to conform. A professional culture, on the other hand, values the content of the job and the profession itself, often with a long-term focus.

5. **Approachability (*Open vs. Closed Systems*):** Open systems are welcoming, where newcomers are quickly integrated, and diversity is embraced. Closed systems are more exclusive, where acceptance isn't guaranteed.

6. **Management Philosophy (*Employee vs. Work-Oriented*):** In an employee-oriented culture, members of staff feel that personal problems are taken into account and that the organisation takes responsibility for the welfare of its employees, even if this is at the expense of the work. In very work-oriented organisations, there is heavy pressure to perform the task even if this is at the expense of employees.

But how does organisational culture interact with the national culture of individuals within the organisation? National culture, shaped by our upbringing, influences our values, behaviours, and emotional preferences—essentially, how we're programmed to navigate the world. The Culture Factor uses the 6D Framework to measure these differences between nations, which include dimensions like Power Distance, Individualism vs. Collectivism, and Uncertainty Avoidance, among others.

Ask the Expert 📝

Wassim Karkabi, Managing Partner at The Culture Factor MENA

"If culture can devour strategy for breakfast, leadership is just another item on its menu. Culture is most of the times stronger than leadership. Even founders can find themselves crippled by organisational culture. As they bellow commands to the crowds of the ranking pile of an organisation, they may find themselves that it's still not being achieved."

When it comes to culture, Wassim tells me that there are two types of organisations: Organisations that have purposefully gone out of their way to create a culture that is needed for them to succeed. And the other kind is the organisations that have fallen into a culture haphazardly. Because they're driven by the leader, or it has developed over time after having hired so many people from different places that came together and created an amalgamation of cultures. In both cases, it may work. Or not.

"The interesting part is when you try to identify what is good in that organisational culture, by taking it as some sort of a scientific measure. Utilising these positive elements to build upon it, in order for you to expand it even further to the advantage of the organisation. And to continue to do this over time. It's not just an exercise that you do once and then you stop: culture is an ongoing exercise as your employee base is never stagnant.

The problem with today's world is we are so worried about employee happiness and employee satisfaction, that some risk forgetting that a company needs financial success and high productivity. We kind of fall on our sword for the employee, but the majority of the employees aren't falling on their sword for the organisation. With that in mind, we are spending too much time worrying about that, rather than building the organisational culture needed to deliver on the business objectives. We must make people understand that if that doesn't happen, then there won't be a company for you to come to work for. So, if you don't build a strong organisational culture as a leader, then the collective programming will take over. If you don't build it, it will be built for you."

Strong organisational cultures are like the immune system of the human body—able to detect and respond to any new virus or bacteria that could disrupt the working organism. In a company, this might mean identifying and addressing the impact of hiring a disruptive individual. Such cultures act swiftly, with their collective programming zeroing in on potential disruptions. Like blood cells rushing to defend the body, they either integrate the new element into the system or expel it entirely.

A robust organisation (whatever its culture, good or bad) still has to have some sort of element of flexibility. It's able to pivot the culture dynamically, adapting to new situations as it moves forward. If it's not able to shift, then it will find itself being dysfunctional towards the strategy. Even though it may have been very functional in the past.

*"When you're actively working on changing the culture in your corporation, the biggest thing that you need to understand about **change, is that it cannot happen from the outside**. It can be guided by consultants and supported by tools. But it cannot be delivered by any external party. The actual work has to be done internally."*

Wassim also emphasised that successful organisations are those that can align their organisational culture with the diverse national cultures of their workforce. That can be especially challenging in organisations with an exceptionally diverse mix of nationalities, which is a hallmark of the UAE. He shared an insightful example from his work with Noor Bank, a prominent financial institution in the UAE.[45] Noor Bank faced the challenge of integrating employees from various cultural backgrounds into a cohesive organisational culture, which led to friction and misunderstandings.

The Culture Factor stepped in to measure both the organisational and national cultures at Noor Bank using the *Multi-Focus Model*. The assessment revealed significant gaps between the current organisational culture and the cultural preferences of the employees. For example, the bank had a more goal-oriented culture, but many employees came from national cultures that valued a more means-oriented approach. By identifying these gaps, Wassim and his team were able to help Noor Bank design a culture that respected the diverse national backgrounds of its employees while aligning with the bank's strategic goals. This involved creating a more inclusive environment where different cultural perspectives were not just tolerated but leveraged as strengths. The result was a noticeable improvement in collaboration, employee engagement, and overall productivity.

"It's about creating a culture that not only respects diversity but uses it as a strength," Wassim noted. *"By aligning Noor Bank's organisational goals with the cultural realities of its workforce, we were able to turn a potential challenge into a significant competitive advantage."*

3

Crafting Dubai: Culture Under Construction

"Tell me you live in Dubai without telling me you live in Dubai."

—*Instagram Catchphrase*

Whenever people come together, a culture inevitably forms. So, you might as well be intentional about shaping it. Can a genuine culture emerge when you have so many diverse people in one place? Absolutely. And if you need proof, just look at Dubai. I've been familiar with this Emirate for more than 15 years, and I've watched as it has cultivated its own very distinctive blend of cultures.

Is there something that differentiates Dubai from Abu Dhabi, Qatar, Kuwait, or Oman? Without a doubt. Each place has its own character and appeals to a unique breed of people. Dubai has its own *"smell of the place."* And it's not everyone's cup of tea. Some find it too dynamic, too loud, simply *"too much much."* But it is a vibe and that's exactly what gives it character, a culture that's becoming stronger and more defined every day.

Despite being a big fan of Dubai, I'm not blind to its imperfections. Navigating a multi-diverse work and life environment can be incredibly challenging. It's far from a walk in the park when even basic norms are interpreted differently. Take punctuality, for instance—what counts as "on time" can vary widely across nationalities and contexts. Dining etiquette presents another hurdle. For instance, many of our friends don't eat with a knife, which is practically a blasphemy in my culture. Then, there are the endless debates over what counts as spicy food, the ideal office temperature, and even what qualifies as great music at a party—a topic that sparks wildly different opinions. Driving styles on Sheikh Zayed Road offer another striking example, with each nationality bringing its own unique interpretation of the road rules. Every commute becomes a daily test of patience and tolerance—though, of course, swearing out loud is strictly off-limits! There's a reason why 2019 was declared the *"Year of Tolerance"* in the UAE by His Highness Sheikh Khalifa bin Zayed Al Nahyan…

While we strive to create harmony in such a varied environment, we also face the risk of becoming too vanilla or cliché in our approach to culture, blurring the unique edges in an attempt to please everyone. And let's be honest—while politically correct, that's downright dull.

I found that an excellent parameter of culture is humour. Just like New York City has developed its own brand of humour—a melting pot of different influences—we're seeing the same happen in the UAE. And it's something we all share a laugh over. We're even developing our own lingo that outsiders might grasp, but they won't fully get it unless they've lived it. Terms like *"Jumeirah Jane," "Chammaks," "Khalli walli,"* and *"shway shway."*[46] Or the popular memes like *"Tell me you live in Dubai without telling me you live in Dubai,"* perfectly capture this emerging cultural identity.

But it's not just the good times that bring people together. Tragedies can forge strong bonds too. 16th April 2024 is a date I'll never forget—the day when massive floods struck the UAE, Oman, and Iran. That morning, after a stormy, rainy night, my children and I stood on our terrace, watching in awe as gigantic, ominous green-brown clouds rolled in from the sea. It felt like a scene straight out of a sci-fi disaster movie, right before all hell breaks loose. My husband was out in the desert organising a leadership bootcamp with a client, and our worry was palpable. And with good reason. What unfolded that day was something we had never seen before. With 119 millimetres of rain (that's 1.5 times the typical annual amount), it was an event that etched itself into the UAE's identity. It also brought together the people of the UAE.

This moment of crisis reminded me of another, more than 60 years earlier: the Great Storm of April 1961, which Sheikh Mohammed bin Rashid Al Maktoum describes vividly in his book *My Story*. That night, a monstrous storm hit Dubai, and the British ship MV Dara suffered a catastrophic explosion, leading to a tragic loss of life. Sheikh Mohammed recounts how his father, together with a large number of residents sprang into action, rescuing 500 people. "*Although the winds had calmed, the aftermath of the storm hung over Dubai like a clear dark cloud for weeks. The toll of deaths and injuries were staggering. Every household had endured tragedy. Despite the harshness of the storm it showed the noble nature of the people of Dubai who came together in cooperation and support at a time of deep peril and distress.*"[47]

The 2024 floods, though not as deadly, had a spectacular impact on the city. Thousands were stranded, cars left behind, streets transformed into rivers, and homes and parking areas flooded, leading to extensive dialogues with insurance companies to navigate the aftermath. But what stood out for me personally was how people came together helping each other, sheltering strangers. Social media was flooded with videos of these acts of kindness. For weeks, restaurants handed out free meals, and those who lost their homes were taken care of. Humankind, as Rutger Bregman so aptly puts it, truly has a hopeful history.[48] It was one of those *"Moments That Matter,"* further shaping the identity of this young nation.

4

From Silo to Footprint

"We can change culture if we change behaviour."

—Dr. Aubrey Daniels

When we first founded Herculean Alliance, we took culture seriously. Seriously enough to measure it with our *Cultural Maturity Model* (*CMM*). Think of it as a corporate fitness tracker that gauges your organisation's cultural health on a scale from 1 to 5.

Figure 5. Corporate Culture Maturity

CORPORATE CULTURE MODEL
5 MATURITY LEVELS

3. PERFORMANCE CULTURE
- Feedback = food for champions
- High motivation
- Depending on leader

1. SILO CULTURE
- Solo players
- Low job satisfaction
- Self-interest prevails

4. WINNING CULTURE
- High engagement
- Organisation's success comes first
- High performance

2. PARTICIPATION CULTURE
- Collaborative atmosphere
- Job satisfaction
- No game-changers

5. FOOTPRINT CULTURE
- Epic culture
- Positive dissatisfaction
- Humble performers

Herculean Alliance

Figure 5. Corporate Culture Maturity

The 5 maturity levels are as follows:

1. Silo culture
2. Participatory culture
3. Performance culture
4. Winning culture
5. Footprint culture

The Culture Maturity model was originally based on the model used by former Olympic coach Alain Goudsmet of the Mentally Fit Institute.[49]

1. **Silo culture:** This organisation is characterised by solo players. Each person focuses solely on their own tasks, with little regard for what others are doing. The ego overshadows the collective interest, leading to an attitude of, *"I did my part; if something went wrong, it's someone else's fault."* Self-interest prevails over group interest.

2. **Participation Culture:** The atmosphere is much more collaborative, with colleagues genuinely enjoying working together and a pleasant sense of camaraderie. It feels a bit like a friendly neighbourhood sports league—people are happy to be involved, but there's no intense drive to reach the top. Job satisfaction is generally moderate to high, yet employees don't see themselves as game-changers. The idea of shaping the future feels more like wishful thinking than a tangible goal.

3. **Performance Culture:** Now we're getting somewhere! In a performance culture, feedback is viewed as food for champions. Motivation runs high, proactivity is the norm, and everyone knows the

game plan. Teammates are well aware of each other's strengths and weaknesses, and they're all in it to win it. Think of this as the team that's eyeing the podium, but don't believe in the first place yet. They still look at the leader to make it happen.

4. **Winning Culture:** This is where things get serious and the effects of high engagement kick in. In a winning culture, the organisation's success comes first. Team members feel like they're on the cusp of greatness, they can visualise this and are fully committed to making that happen. They grow themselves. When the going gets tough, team members pat each other on the back instead of pointing fingers. Engagement meets performance.

5. **Footprint Culture:** This is the pinnacle. In a footprint culture, the organisation doesn't just lead—it stands in a league of its own, with a history of remarkable achievements. The culture here is nothing short of legendary, shaped by team members who are positively dissatisfied and who possess a rare combination of humility and unyielding drive. This balance allows them to maintain their top position over the long term. Reaching this level of cultural maturity is the stuff of business legends and is rare.

🖐 Case in Point

"When Culture Is All You Have"
The Social Engineering of Culture
According to Frank

Not all leaders can afford a lengthy culture process. When Frank Van Massenhove stepped into the role of Chairman of the Belgian Federal Public Service Social Affairs in the nineties, he was faced with a department that was, to put it mildly, in dire straits. At the time, the department had become notorious for its inability to attract talent— only 18% of candidates who passed the government exam were willing to work there. It was not only a bureaucratic quagmire with 70% low-skilled workers, but also suffered from a severe image problem. Young professionals viewed the department's time-clock regime as outdated, and many believed their talents would go unrecognised.

In short, the department was a hard sell, even for the most idealistic job seekers. The environment stifled innovation, with proposals for improvements often ignored. Additionally, technological advancements in the business world left the government lagging, and budget constraints limited access to external consultants.

Despite these challenges, Frank saw an opportunity. He recognised that the key to revitalising the department lay in transforming its culture. He knew that real change had to start at the top, so one of his first moves was to select an entirely new executive committee. Frank brought in fresh talent from outside the civil service, assembling a team that was not only balanced in terms of gender but also brimming with new ideas and a willingness to challenge the status quo. This was no small feat in a sector where tradition often trumps innovation.

But Frank didn't stop at reshaping the leadership team. He understood that to create a lasting cultural shift, he needed to empower employees at every level. Enter the *"A-Team,"* a group of handpicked employees tasked with listening to their colleagues and gathering insights from the ground. Alongside them, a team that he named the *"Absurdists"* was charged with identifying and eliminating the bureaucratic red tape that had become synonymous with government work. Finally, the *"Contributors,"* a group of influential staff members, were given the responsibility of implementing the necessary changes. And the first initiatives began to bear fruit. After only three months, the culture began to change at the top and in middle management.

Now the main work could begin! Frank and his team devised a plan. In order to attract the right talent and make the government future-proof, the conviction grew that radical innovation was needed in their way of working. With this multi-layered approach, Frank began to dismantle the old ways of working. He introduced the concept of flexible work hours and remote working *avant la lettre,* 20 years before these ideas became mainstream. His philosophy was simple: *"Work at Home. Home at Work."* By giving employees the freedom to choose where and when they worked, he not only improved their work-life balance but also boosted productivity. The result? A 121% increase in productivity, all while employees spent less time commuting and more time with their families.

One of the first predetermined milestones was digitisation, whereby all files had to be digitised. In those days, that meant making every document available online and thus having it scanned. Frank decided to bring in a group of low-skilled workers and give them an important role in the *"Great Digitisation Process."* Read: the ungrateful task of scanning documents all day long. Unfortunately, the large scanning machines were located in the basement of the building, an environment that isn't exactly conducive to job happiness. Fortunately, Frank and his A-Team decided to move the digitisation team and their machines to the top floor of the tallest government building they could find. At least, the employees could scan with a fantastic view of the Brussels skyline. Moreover, they reduced the number of scanning hours to 5 hours a day. A gesture that was greatly appreciated by the team. And guess what? Despite the reduced number of hours, the number of scans performed per day remained just as high.

The results of his initiatives were nothing short of transformative. The department, once seen as a bureaucratic backwater, became a model of efficiency and employee satisfaction. Engagement levels soared, absenteeism dropped, and employees began to take the initiative to improve processes and workflows. For example, the turnaround time for a project involving disabled citizens was reduced from 18 to 3 months, thanks to the proactive suggestions of employees who realised that digital files could be shared simultaneously with all stakeholders.

Frank abolished the traditional meeting culture, empowering employees to call meetings only when necessary, which saved time and increased productivity.

Expertise was no longer imposed from above; instead, employees, who had the best knowledge of their tasks, set key performance indicators (KPIs) and determined how to achieve goals.

Frank's leadership style was as much about fostering a supportive culture as it was about driving results. He believed that a good leader takes responsibility when things go wrong but gives credit to the team when things go right. This approach not only earned him the respect of his employees but also cultivated a culture of ownership and accountability.

Moreover, Frank's approach to leadership was not just about top-down management. He established a feedback culture where employees could appraise their superiors, an initiative that further strengthening the organisation's trust and mutual respect. This participatory model became so successful that other government agencies attempted to replicate it, though often with less success. Frank was quick to note that such a model cannot be imposed from the top down; it must be built by the people within the organisation.

What made Frank's achievements even more remarkable was the fact that he accomplished all of this with limited financial resources. His ability to drive significant change in a typically rigid environment earned him the title of Government Manager of the Year. A merited accolade for a leader who transformed not just a department, but contributed to the very culture of government work.

Part III RECAP—The Impact and Dimensions of Culture

✹ **Your Vibe Attracts Your Tribe.**

✹ Culture eats strategy for breakfast, but can't compensate for a flawed strategy.

✹ **The Culture Factor** helps turn culture into a competitive advantage by aligning it with business goals. It assesses and optimises organisational and national cultures for better strategic alignment.

✹ **6 Dimensions of the Multi-Focus Model:**

1. Organisational effectiveness (*Means vs. Goal Orientation*)

2. Customer orientation (*Internally vs. Externally Driven*)

3. Level of control (*Easy-going vs. Strict Work Discipline*)

4. Focus (*Local vs. Professional*)

5. Approachability (*Open vs. Closed Systems*)

6. Management philosophy (*Employee vs. Work-Oriented*)

✹ **The Culture Maturity Model:** A tool to measure and improve an organisation's cultural development, described in five levels: Silo, Participation, Performance, Winning, Footprint.

PART FOUR

❧

DRIVERS AND KILLERS OF ENGAGEMENT

"It is not the destination so much as the journey."

—*Captain Jack Sparrow*
(Pirates of the Caribbean)

To truly grasp what drives employee engagement—or lack thereof—we need to explore the various factors that shape it. We've identified 12 key drivers that can significantly influence engagement, both positively and negatively. Since the pandemic, drivers like well-being, leadership, and belonging have firmly moved to the forefront. In the pre-pandemic era, the lack of flexible work was a major obstacle—a challenge we've all worked hard to address. But these are just one piece of the puzzle. Engagement is also shaped by personality, compensation, teamwork, inclusion, and even sustainability. All of these elements play a crucial role in how committed your employees feel.

None of this should be surprising if we consider Maslow's hierarchy of needs. While it's a well-known and sometimes overused model, Maslow remains relevant in this book because it provides a clear framework to understand the full spectrum of human motivation—and, by extension, engagement.

His hierarchy bridges basic survival needs with higher aspirations, providing an excellent foundation for understanding what drives employee engagement and why these drivers vary across socioeconomic, regional, and industry contexts. In terms of employee engagement, meeting these needs is vital. After all, it's difficult to be fully engaged at work if you're constantly worried about making ends meet or job security, particularly in uncertain times.

Figure 6. Maslow's Hierarchy of Needs

The first need is **survival**—ensuring basic needs are met, which is often a primary concern for lower-wage, entry-level employees. Improving their engagement may be as simple as offering a pay rise. **Security**, on the other hand, is about long-term stability and job retention. Clear job expectations help fulfil this need; when people know they're performing well, they feel more secure. **Belonging** is a deep, tribal instinct. In today's world, part of that sense of belonging is derived from an organisation's culture and brand. Then comes **self-esteem**, or the *"What's in it for me?"* question. This is particularly important to your top performers. Neglect this need, and you risk losing them to competitors. However, recognising and boosting their contributions can unlock even greater productivity. Finally, we reach **self-actualisation**. When employees find meaning in their work, they become deeply engaged. This is where the greatest commitment lies, and it presents a golden opportunity for leaders to help employees discover the meaning of their daily work.

Here are the 12 key drivers that shape engagement, in no particular order:

1. Purpose
2. Organisational Values
3. Leadership
4. Teamwork
5. Learning & Development (L&D)
6. Well-being
7. Employee Journey
8. Compensation and Benefits
9. Working Environment
10. Flexible Work
11. Corporate Social Responsibility (CSR)
12. Diversity, Equity, Inclusion, and Belonging (DEIB)

Understanding and addressing these drivers (or killers, if not managed well) can transform how engaged your workforce feels. Nurturing these drivers is more than ticking boxes—it's building an environment where your employees can truly thrive.

1

Driver 1. Purpose

"If you want to build a boat, don't drum up your men and women to gather wood, divide the work, and give orders.

If you want to build a boat, awaken the desire in their hearts to long for the vast and endless sea."

—*Antoine de Saint-Exupéry*

Why do some employees go the extra mile, while others simply clock in and out? A major factor is belief in the company's mission.

When employees see their company's purpose not just as a corporate mantra, but as something that resonates deeply with their own values, they don't just show up. They invest themselves fully, bringing energy, loyalty, passion. But here's the catch: our measurements reveal that this vital connection often falls short.[50] Employees frequently find their company's *raison d'être* blurry at best. **People lose their way when they lose their why.**

While many corporations possess extensive know-how, few have really considered their *know-why*. Why do they do the things they do? What is their significance in their customers' lives? What would the world lose if they vanished tomorrow?

Just as marketers build bridges between what the outside world desires and what the company offers, HR and the leadership team must become the architects of connection, forging powerful links between the company's greatest strengths—its expertise, its stability—and the real, human needs of its employees and customers. Healthy marketing does this by answering the question, *"How can I make our company's strengths relevant to our customers?"* Whether those customers are end consumers or business-to-business clients, it all boils down to understanding their needs, struggles, and how the company can add value.

The magic of a strong purpose lies in articulating it with both clarity and inspiration. When a company's purpose is clear, it guides decisions and sparks innovation, and a shared sense of mission. While often internal, a company's purpose serves as a guiding compass. Sometimes, it becomes a public-facing slogan or baseline. A memorable example is DEME, the international dredging company. Marketing agency Duval Branding worked with DEME to unite all 20 companies under a shared purpose, logo, and identity. The aim was to find a common purpose for all companies, with a common logo and corporate identity. The quest led the Duval team to the engine room of a massive ship off the coast of Dubai, pumping up silt. With a thoughtful gaze over the blue Arabian Gulf, the captain remarked, *"Actually, we're making new land."* Bingo! The purpose, elevated to baseline, became: *DEME. Creating land for the future.* This powerful purpose unified the companies under one brand, and it transformed how employees viewed their work. No longer did they have to tell their aunties at a family party that they *were "digging up mud off the coast of some country."* But instead *"building land for future generations."* A captivating mission that was widely embraced and fired up the imaginations of those eager to join DEME.

Does your company have a compelling purpose? Can you sum up what you do in one inspiring sentence that resonates with customers, employees, and stakeholders alike? Or are you stuck in a dry, technical description of your products and services catalogue?

A well-formulated purpose is more relevant today than ever. Talent Acquisition Managers, especially, should take note of the reverse interviews frequently conducted by the Gen Z generation. These candidates want to know what the company does for society and its sustainability policy. They're asking, *"Why should I make an effort to come to the office every morning?"* If HR thought more like marketers, this inner search for meaning would be at the top of their agenda and be clear for everyone.

🖐Case in Point
"The Human Touch in Finance: Inside Maybank's Purpose"

To appreciate the power of purpose, consider the story of Maybank. Officially known as Malayan Banking Berhad, Maybank is not just Malaysia's largest bank but also one of Southeast Asia's financial titans. I had the privilege of speaking with Shameem Farouk, Human Capital Director, who offered fascinating insights into how Maybank's purpose drives both strategy and employee engagement.

Maybank's motto is *"Humanising financial services."* This has become more than a catchphrase—it's a mission that has shaped the bank's identity and operations. In Malaysia, where respect for hierarchy is deeply rooted, the challenge is making an organisation agile. In a society where titles hold significant weight, the pressing question for Maybank was: *"How do you create a culture where ideas can flow freely, and everyone—regardless of rank—feels empowered to contribute?"* In the aftermath of the 2008–2009 financial crisis, the answer took shape. *"Humanising financial services"* was an ethos that permeated every corner of the organisation. It became their way of doing business.

But the COVID-19 pandemic pushed this commitment to an entirely new level. With small and medium-sized enterprises (SMEs) struggling to survive and government relief efforts falling short, Maybank didn't wait for instructions. Driven by a shared sense of purpose, employees took matters into their own hands. In just three weeks—an incredible feat for any large organisation—they developed a platform that connected merchants with providers, bypassing bureaucratic hurdles and offering real, immediate solutions. The entire organisation, from the boardroom to the frontlines, was united by a purpose that transcended individual roles or corporate hierarchy. In that moment, humanising financial services became the lifeline.

But Maybank's story doesn't end there. The bank has consistently looked for ways to live out its mission in innovative and forward-thinking ways. A recent example is their launch of a credit card that tracks carbon emissions, allowing customers to understand—and reduce—their environmental impact. A testament to Maybank's growing commitment to Social Responsibility beyond financial duties.

The story of Maybank illustrates a powerful truth: when a company's purpose is real—when it's lived, breathed, and embodied by its people—it can achieve extraordinary things.

2

Driver 2. Organisational Values

"Hire, fire, and reward on values."

—*Unknown*

We've all been there. You know how it goes: a job candidate looks perfect on paper, ticks all the right boxes, and aces the interview. You think you've found the ideal fit! But just a few months in, disappointment hits. They're a complete misfit!

What happened? The recruiter missed the hidden but crucial question: *"Do our values align?"* And that's where things went wrong.

Typically, candidates undergo assessments to gauge their knowledge, skills, and personality. But what often slips through the cracks is whether their personal values match with those of the company. When things go south between an employee and an employer, it's usually due to a value mismatch. It's not a matter of right or wrong, but of how much importance each party places on specific values. The chemistry just wasn't there. When values don't align, company culture takes a hit. Misalignment leads to conflicts, demotivation, and even high turnover, draining both morale and resources.

Values might seem intangible, but they're highly practical. **Values define who we are—and who we are not.** They help us identify people who share our core values, leading to better hiring decisions. Values dictate how employees behave, especially in unclear situations or when nobody is watching. When you understand what your company stands for, your work feels more fulfilling, and the business becomes stronger. Clear values are essential for productivity and success; without them, it's tough to replicate desirable behaviours or eliminate unwanted ones.

HubSpot created a handy Company Values Glossary, with 50 examples and terms to help companies discover their core values.[51] If you scan the most frequently cited values from, say, the U.S. Fortune Global 200, you'll notice the same ones pop up: accountability, teamwork, respect, innovation, customer focus, and trust. Admittedly, these core values can sometimes feel like clichés: corporate jargon that gets stuck on repeat. It's even joked that you could swap the *"mission statement & values"* frames between company boardrooms, and no one would notice. Because they feel like a generic form of aspirational internal marketing that nobody remembers.

Truth is: Organisational values cannot deliver on their promise if nobody remembers them. Many organisations have five or more values, which might explain why employees struggle to remember them. That's why I advise them to limit core values to four because that's the usual number people can remember. To fix the problem, companies are typically advised to double down on communication. They mention the core values everywhere they can, in reports, meetings, and internal announcements. The hope is that, with enough repetition (and some gamification or fun), the core values will eventually be drummed into everyone's skull. But employees cannot be expected to remember a laundry list of generic, taken-for-granted assumptions if they aren't lived.

Over the past twenty years, we've seen values shift to be more people-oriented, with a greater focus on emotion rather than pure logic. This trend shows a more relational and sustainable dynamic, reflecting the shift to a new kind of leadership.

Some companies make their values more memorable by bundling them into an acronym. For instance, Australia's QANTAS uses *"FLY"* (*Friendliness, Loyalty, Yielding Service*), while India's Tata Group uses *"LEAD"* (*Leadership, Empathy, Accountability, Durability*) and South African bank ABSA chose *"RISE,"* a combination of *Respect, Integrity, Service, Excellence*.

Using distinctive language can also make values stick. Instead of *"Service,"* Toyota says, *"We go the extra mile."* I also love how the American platform Lattice describes their approach: *"We wanted to make values that were more than our cultural foundations - they're more about our cultural ideals, of our company standards that we strive to reach."*[52] Their values are: *"Chop wood, carry water/Clear eyes/Ship, shipmate, self/What's next?"* Accent Jobs has nailed it with values like *"be a friend"* (to clients, candidates, colleagues), *"stay gutsy"* (embracing boldness and learning from mistakes), and *"go pro"* (maintaining professionalism and continuous learning). These phrases are anything but dull—they're unexpected, emotional, and inventive.

But the real issue isn't whether core values are catchy or original. Universal human values like honesty or integrity don't change much over time, so there's no shame in sticking with the basics. It's whether they resonate and truly reflect who you are

111

and how your organisation becomes unique by the way it lives and breathes these values daily.

Interestingly, more and more organisations are moving away from the word *"values"* altogether. Shawn Pope and Arild Wæraas encourage organisations to go for something more creative and tailored, like tenets, precepts, adages, or axioms. A sports team may devise *"rules of the game,"* a tech company a *"source code,"* or a restaurant a *"recipe for success."*[53] Other possibilities might be a motto, or a mantra that offers simplicity and communicability. Such formats will make a more lasting impression by striking a balance between familiarity and novelty, stimulating the brain in new ways.

Other organisations prefer to use **principles**. I'm particularly fond of the *"Ricoh Way,"* the corporate philosophy of Ricoh Company, which is built on two fundamental principles: the *"Spirit of Three Loves"* (*"love your neighbour, love your country, love your work"*) and the Founding Principles (customer-centricity, innovation, and sustainable business practices). These guiding principles foster a strong culture of integrity, teamwork, and excellence.

They offer more practical guidance and aren't interchangeable because they're rooted in the company's DNA. Principles describe not only what you will do but also what you won't do. Family businesses are more likely to have principles by nature, with an unwritten code of conduct in place for generations. Writing these down is highly recommended, as they provide a reliable touchstone for decision-making.

A notable example of living and breathing values can be seen in Lotus Bakeries. One of Lotus Bakeries' core principles is: *"Never compromise on taste."* You might think, *"That's pretty obvious; it's about food."* But at Lotus Bakeries, this principle goes much deeper. The entire operation is dedicated to achieving that perfect lotus speculoos cookie.

When Lotus opened its biscoff factory in the United States, a dedicated team travelled to fine-tune the baking process. Local production was only greenlit after experts from the factory in Belgium—where the original speculoos recipe was perfected—confirmed that there was no discernible difference in taste between the American and Belgian versions. This was no easy feat, especially considering the differences in ingredients like dough and butter between the U.S. and Europe. Today, a team from Belgium continues to support their American counterparts, ensuring that the signature Lotus speculoos taste remains consistent worldwide. This unwavering dedication to taste is a key factor in Lotus's global success.

Another manifestation of this uncompromising approach is seen in their stance on sugar. While many sugar substitutes are available, none have yet met Lotus's standards for taste. Rather than compromising and cutting back on sugar, the company holds its ground, keeping recipes pure and responding to health concerns with smaller portion sizes. The message couldn't be clearer: *"Never compromise on taste."* From day one, every new employee at Lotus understands that this is what the company is all about.

3

Driver 3. Leadership

"If you want to lead, then learn how to follow."

—*Jon Snow (Game of Thrones)*

"**A** *re you a manager, or a leader?"*
The former Managing Director at my first job would challenge us with this question, his tone heavy with expectation—there was no mistaking which role he valued more.

Within the Western business context, hierarchy often distinguishes between bosses, managers, and leaders, with leaders seen at the apex of effectiveness. But once you've worked in different regions, you quickly realise it's not quite so black and white. Whether it's better to be a manager, a leader, or a boss depends on many factors: the context, the team's needs, and your own strengths and goals.

Each role serves a distinct purpose, and the effectiveness of each varies, depending on the situation at hand:

Bosses are frequently caricatured as old-school command-and-control figures, exerting power through their titles and, at worst, displaying oppressive behaviour. Yet, let's not be too quick to dismiss the *"boss"* entirely. A boss who combines directive authority with a touch of effective management can provide clarity, direction, and even inspire a team—if they lead with fairness, empathy, and a genuine concern for their employees' well-being.

Managers, positioned in the middle, sometimes get a bad rap for being reactive, clinging to the status quo, or indulging in micromanagement. But the reality is, being a manager is essential when the focus is on maintaining efficiency, ensuring tasks are executed to plan, and managing resources effectively. If you're naturally organised, skilled in planning and execution, and focused on operational goals, then being a manager might be the right fit.

Leaders, on the other hand, are often glorified. Those who, through sheer charisma, set the direction, define goals, and ignite the passion in their followers. At its core, leadership is about inspiring change that resonates deeply with others. Leadership qualities are essential when the focus is on motivating a team, setting the vision, fostering innovation, and driving transformation. If you have strong interpersonal skills, being a leader is highly effective, especially when rallying people around a common cause.

The most effective individuals in positions of authority don't stick rigidly to one of these roles. Instead, they blend the best elements of all three. They are leaders who can efficiently oversee operations, managers who can inspire and guide, and bosses who create a positive and productive working environment.

Regardless of their official title, leaders aren't always born. They can also be made. While certain intrinsic qualities provide a head start, the right context is equally crucial in developing leadership abilities. Some people, like entrepreneurs, create that context for themselves, while others might find it through guidance or even sheer luck. Then there are the rare few who exhibit what is known as contextual leadership, where they adapt their style to suit any situation. This is an exceptional trait that few possess by nature.

Leadership has a profound influence on engagement, whether in politics, social settings, or the business arena—and perhaps more so now than ever before. If you asked me to list the most inspiring leaders I've encountered, I would hesitate. I've seen leaders of all forms and shapes across different aspects of life, sometimes in the most unexpected places.

Business literature reveals more than twenty leadership styles—servant, autocratic, transformational, visionary, affiliative, democratic, and so on. So, what stands out in exceptional leaders? Several qualities: They put people first, communicate clearly and frequently, tell stories that resonate, and are in tune with their team's emotional landscape. True leaders don't just create followers; they cultivate other leaders.

Among the many attributes attributed to great leadership, one stands out above all: trust. Trust is the bedrock on which all effective leadership is built. So, let's talk about trust!

"The first duty of a leader is to define reality, the last is to express gratitude, and in between, the leader must become a servant."

—*Max De Pree, Former CEO,*
Herman Miller

Trust as Powerhouse for Leadership

Trust is the cornerstone of effective leadership. If your team doesn't trust you to lead them where you claim you'll take them, or if you lack faith in your team's ability to get there, true leadership falters. Trust isn't passive; it requires active effort, continuous dialogue, idea exchange, and above all, empathy. As they say, trust takes years to build, moments to destroy, and forever to rebuild. A leader must always be mindful of how, what, where, and when they communicate, as these elements can make or break trust.

And when the going gets tough, trust demands decisive action. Whether it's navigating budget cuts, layoffs, or any other challenge, leaders must step up. In service industries such as advertising, where the only real assets are the talents of your people, swift leadership is crucial. When business is booming, you need more staff; when it slows, you may have to let some go. These rules are brutally unforgiving. Weak leaders delay tough decisions, worsening the problem. The odds of quickly replacing a significant client are slim, and a lack of timely leadership can endanger the entire organisation.

The Trust Equation

Let's dive a little deeper in the research. Steven Covey, author of *The Speed of Trust*, highlights the significant impact trust has on outcomes with his equation: **Results = Trust (Strategy × Execution)**.[54] Teams with high levels of trust consistently outperform those with low trust. Trust acts as an exponent that can dramatically amplify or diminish outcomes. High trust accelerates progress, reduces costs, and boosts performance across all areas. As Covey puts it, *"High trust is a dividend, while low trust is a tax."*

But what exactly is trust? Can it be measured, and how can you influence it? According to the Cambridge Dictionary, trust is *"the firm belief in the reliability, truth, or ability of someone or something."* It is the confidence that someone is good, honest, and will not cause harm, or that something is safe and dependable. Synonyms include confidence, faith, and belief.

Trust is fundamentally relational; it's about connection and perception—both with yourself and others. This means that just because you believe you are trustworthy (which is certainly a good starting point), it doesn't imply others will perceive you as such. *"Say what you do and do what you say"* is a solid foundation for building trust, but it's not sufficient on its own.

Charles Green offers a more comprehensive framework with his Trust Equation: **Trust = (Credibility + Reliability + Intimacy) / Self-orientation.**[55]

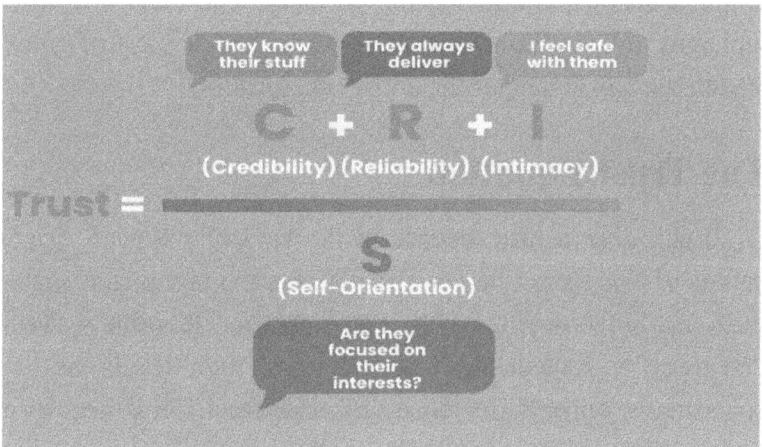

Figure 7. Charles Green's Trust Equation

The Trust Equation has one variable in the denominator and three in the numerator. Increasing the value of the factors in the numerator increases the value of trust. Self-orientation, which sits alone in the denominator, is the most important variable in the Trust Equation.

- **Credibility** is about the words we speak. For example, *"I trust what she says about intellectual property; she's very credible on the subject."*

- **Reliability** concerns actions. For instance, *"If he says he'll deliver the product tomorrow, I trust him because he's dependable."*

- **Intimacy** is the sense of safety we feel when sharing something. You might say, *"I can trust her with that information; she has never breached my confidentiality, and she wouldn't embarrass me."*

- **Self-orientation** refers to a person's focus. Specifically, whether their focus is primarily on themselves or the other person. You might hear, *"I can't trust him on this deal because he's more focused on his own gains."*

It's like in a sales process: A seller with low self-orientation is free to completely focus on the customer, which is quite rare among typical salespeople. The irony in selling is that you succeed more when you stop trying to sell. When you focus solely on honestly helping others, they trust you more and are more likely to buy from you.

The Trust Equation encapsulates the most common dimensions of trust in everyday business interactions. Note that these dimensions are almost entirely personal, not institutional.

While companies may be described as credible and reliable, it's the people within these companies who embody these traits. Intimacy and self-orientation, however, are nearly always about individual relationships. Trust in business and sales requires strong *"scores"* in all four variables of the Trust Equation: high credibility, reliability, and intimacy, paired with low self-orientation.

"Leadership is the art of getting someone else to do something you want done, because he wants to do it."

—Sun Tzu, The Art of War

Trust and Employee Engagement

In an insightful Harvard Business Review paper, Paul J. Zak examines the influence of trust on employee engagement.[56]

His findings reveal that employees in high-trust companies experience 74% less stress, have 106% more energy at work, demonstrate 50% higher productivity, take 13% fewer sick days, exhibit 76% more engagement, report 29% higher satisfaction with their lives, and suffer 40% less burnout compared to those in low-trust companies.

Zak identified **8 management behaviours** that foster trust:
1. Recognise excellence
2. Induce challenge stress
3. Give people discretion in how they do their work
4. Enable job crafting
5. Share information broadly
6. Intentionally build relationships
7. Facilitate whole-person growth
8. Show vulnerability

Ultimately, trust is cultivated by setting a clear direction, providing the resources needed to succeed, and then stepping back. It's not about being lenient or lowering expectations; rather, high-trust companies hold people accountable while treating them as responsible adults.

Two Legs of Leadership

Finally, great leadership is also about striking a balance between two essential components: love and demands. Leadership coach Joe Sejean's concept of *"The Two Legs of a Great Leader"* underscores the importance of nurturing team members with genuine care, while also setting high expectations to drive performance.[57]

The *"Loving Leg"* involves showing authentic appreciation for employees, creating a respectful, inclusive environment that boosts engagement. However, leaning too heavily on this leg can lead to complacency and a lack of urgency, potentially undermining performance.

The *"Demanding Leg"* emphasises pushing team members toward excellence by setting challenging goals and encouraging growth. While this approach can foster high achievement, an overemphasis on demands can create a culture of fear, stifle creativity, and increase turnover. The key to effective leadership lies in mastering the use of both legs, adapting to the needs of the situation, and maintaining a dynamic balance that drives performance while nurturing team morale.

Joe suggests that true leadership is not about finding a static middle ground between love and demands but about dynamically adjusting one's approach based on the context and the individual needs of team members.

Management by Fear

It's disheartening to see that, even today, some companies are still ruled by a crippling fear of hierarchy. Employees are often more concerned with *"What will my boss think?"* rather than exercising their own judgement. It's like a throwback to the court of French King Louis XIV, where courtiers twisted themselves into knots to stay in the Sun King's good graces. Flattery and bootlicking were just part of the daily routine.

This fear of falling out of favour trickles down, creating a culture where impossible demands are the norm. And, as they say, *"The fish rots from the head down."* Fear, unsurprisingly, paralyses people and squashes any hope of success. If fear-driven companies manage to survive, it's often because they're swimming in cash, publicly traded, or sitting on a monopoly.

And let's be honest, many organisations still use fear as their go-to management tool. Sometimes deliberately, sometimes out of ignorance. Leaders who expose mistakes for all to see, belittle their teams, or humiliate others might think they're getting results, but they're building a house of cards.

I still hear about business leaders who are okay with short-term successes, even when those results are driven by fear. Whether they're screamers or masters of quiet, cutting insults, they seem to believe the ends justify the means, no matter the human cost. What's worse, some executives willingly ignore this behaviour for the sake of hitting targets, disregarding the sky-high turnover and crumbling collaboration.

It's no surprise that such leaders often end up surrounded by a team of martyrs or hardened individuals who have become desensitised to the toxic environment. Using threats might get someone promoted or even land them a job. After all, who wouldn't want a results-driven leader? But by the time the damage is recognised, and the organisation starts crumbling from the inside, it's often too late. The toxic habits have taken root, and changing these leaders becomes a near-impossible task.

Is this hitting home? Have you ever worked in an environment like that?

5 Reasons Why Management by Fear Fails[58]

1. It Impairs Cognitive Functioning: Fear clouds judgement, making it difficult for individuals to think clearly and make rational decisions. When people are afraid, creativity dwindles, innovation stalls, and spontaneous initiatives are quashed, all of which are critical to a thriving workplace.

2. It Breeds Resentment and Retaliation: When employees feel cornered or threatened, they may disengage, becoming part of a silent majority that does just enough to avoid conflict but never goes beyond the bare minimum. This lack of initiative can be a direct consequence of fear.

3. It Reflects Insecurity: Leaders who manage through fear often do so to mask their own insecurities. This approach reveals a lack of confidence in their own abilities, leading them to rely on intimidation rather than inspiration to maintain control. Ultimately, this survival tactic comes at the expense of the very people they should be motivating.

4. It Triggers Fight or Flight Responses:
When fear is the primary management tool, it triggers a fight or flight response in employees, creating unnecessary barriers to success. In such a state, employees are prone to mistakes, whether through a lack of clear thinking or as a deliberate act of defiance against their managers.

5. It Erodes Team Commitment:
Managing through fear alienates employees, driving a wedge between them and the company's objectives. A lack of commitment manifests in various ways: some may disengage completely, showing up but no longer contributing proactively, while others may actively seek to sabotage efforts, undermining the team's success.

Towards a Fearless Organisation

This fear-based approach stands in stark contrast to the principles laid out in Amy C. Edmondson's *The Fearless Organization*.[59] Edmondson argues that a **culture of psychological safety** is the real foundation of sustained success.

In a fearless organisation, employees are encouraged to speak up, take risks, and innovate without the looming dread of repercussion. For companies to truly thrive, fear tactics must go. Instead, they should create a culture where openness and mutual respect replace intimidation and silence. And yes, it can be done! After all, true progress happens when people feel safe to think independently and share their best ideas.

The COVID-19 pandemic is often referred to as the culmination point of a leadership crisis. To me, it's a powerful catalyst and a litmus test in one, exposing cracks in traditional leadership while giving rise to new leaders. I'm referring to those whose potential might have gone unnoticed in ordinary times, regardless of their roles or titles.

Perhaps one day, we'll view the pandemic as the dawn of a new era, one where we can discover the leadership qualities that reside within each of us. And what better place to cultivate this potential than within the supportive cocoon of a team?

4

Driver 4. Teamwork

---

*"When people are financially invested, they want a return.
When people are emotionally invested, they want to
contribute."*

—Simon Sinek, Author & Motivational Speaker

From what we've explored, it's fair to say that trust may be the fuel for leadership, but it's the engine that powers true teamwork. Think of a fast-paced team sport, like basketball. Professional players often pass the ball almost blindly, fully confident that a teammate will be there to catch it. You run, jump, push your limits, and trust your teammates not to drop the ball.

It's no coincidence that trust is foundational to Lencioni's renowned *Five Behaviours of a Cohesive Team* Model.[60] Patrick Lencioni speaks less of predictive trust—*"I know how my colleague will react"*—and more of vulnerable trust. It's the willingness of team members to expose their vulnerabilities and embrace open, candid exchanges.

A vivid illustration of this trust can be found in elite military units, like the Navy SEALs in the USA.[61] Each aspiring SEAL endures *"hell week,"* a gruelling period of hardship and sleep deprivation that pushes them far beyond their limits. That trust only deepens as they train together, to the point where SEALs trust each other with their lives. Notably, leadership within such teams is fluid—any member can step up to lead when needed.

Naturally, the extreme conditions of SEAL training foster an exceptional bond. But how do you translate this to the business realm, where the stakes aren't life or death? To cultivate unity and trust within a team, 3 elements stand paramount: safety, vulnerability, and purpose.

1. **Safety:** Imagine starting a new job. Feeling safe within your new team is crucial. But this doesn't happen automatically. Our brains are wired to be cautious around strangers, attuned to potential threats, and deferential to hierarchy—traits that once helped our ancestors survive. The first step in building trust, as Daniel Coyle explained in *The Culture Code*, is creating a safe environment.[62] It's up to the team to ensure everyone can be themselves, express their thoughts, and make mistakes without fear. Safe teams are easy to spot: they share more, joke more, and even interact physically, like with a pat on the back or a reassuring touch.

2. **Vulnerability:** The word vulnerability still sounds cringe in the ruthless business world. Yet it's essential. Can you admit a mistake to your team and work together to fix it? Only by acknowledging and discussing our errors can we prevent repeating them. Leaders set the tone: by showing vulnerability, they pave the way for others to follow.

3. **Purpose:** Without a shared goal, a team is just a collection of individuals. Perhaps a fun posse, but they

won't experience the thrill of achieving something truly remarkable together. Every team member needs to be intimately aware of the team's purpose, which should be translated into clear, measurable objectives.

This may all sound logical, but I invite you to take a moment to reflect on your own organisation. **Does everyone know the top three priorities for this year? The sales targets? How do their roles contribute?**

People who are uninformed rarely cooperate. Don't forget to include them in your story, communicate regularly, and be transparent. Information is the key to action, and there are three levels to consider: *"nice to know," "need to know,"* and *"must know."* While you may assume that certain groups don't require specific information, never underestimate the importance of the *"nice to know"* tier. Though seemly trivial, this level of knowledge fosters a sense of belonging.

People inherently crave involvement: they want to be in the action, not stuck on the sidelines. This sense of inclusion is essential for true commitment to team goals. So, don't just tell your employees where things stand. Solicit their input, listen to their opinions, and then act on them.

If you want people to cooperate, inform them. Want them to be committed to your goals, engage them. And if you want them to contribute actively and creatively, inspire them.

Inspired individuals transcend their limitations, becoming a better version of themselves. They get inventive, finding new ways to achieve objectives. Inspiration can come from many sources: through leading by example, storytelling, sharing knowledge, expanding their horizons via workshops, encounters with industry icons, or creating experiences that push people out of their comfort zones.

Inspiration and creation are closely intertwined, often forming a self-reinforcing cycle. Creation involves crafting something new or reimagining the existing. These innovations are often inspiring enough to rekindle team motivation and spark further creativity. It's a powerful, continuous momentum—and a beautiful thing to witness.

Ask the Expert 🖉

Yves Vekemans, Founder at Herculean Alliance

The clichés "Teamwork makes the dream work" or "There's no I in team" may sound hollow—until you've been part of a breakthrough team. The kind that transforms a company's culture and revolutionises customer satisfaction. Then you'll feel it in every cell of your body.

Creating Breakthrough Teams

A team of teams: isn't that the ultimate dream of every ambitious leader? The concept, championed by a famous general with a centrally controlled army, was designed to compete in a new world with an army of small, nimble teams.[63] Make no mistake: your competitors are no longer monolithic entities.

Imagine an environment where teams decide their direction within the organisational framework. Individuals alternate between leading and contributing, all while moving towards the company's long-term purpose, like the natural flow of a birds' flock. These teams exhibit agility, operating not just for the company, but with an eye on customers and societal impact. They form and dissolve as needed—not as stagnant silos that cripple traditional departments. Diversity thrives, with every skill necessary residing within one cohesive unit.

These teams are catalysts, spreading cultural change like wildfire, creating a footprint culture where *"positively dissatisfied"* individuals are driven by a relentless pursuit of excellence. Picture a culture where even after achieving world-class success, the team is already asking: *"What could we have done better? How can we reach higher next time?"*

But let's be honest: it's easier said than done. How do you build a breakthrough team? Too often, success is attributed to a charismatic leader who seems to navigate team dynamics purely on intuition. Some managers might turn to the latest bestseller for answers. But personal anecdotes, while valuable, still lack the theoretical foundation for sustainable success.

This is where things can go off the rails. Charismatic leaders may rely on their aura, but team coaching is an artisanal craft that requires dedicated practice. Strong team leaders work tirelessly with their teams, always humble and ready to serve within a carefully maintained framework. They deflect credit back to the team, always asking: *"How can I help each individual become their best self so the team can thrive?"*

I'm a firm believer in *The Orange Revolution* by Adrian Gostick and Chester Elton.[64] This is how I apply the three pivotal pillars: **WOW, *Open Communication,*** and ***Cheer Each Other to Victory*** in my team mantra:

WOW

Are you striving for a goal that transcends the individual? A target only achievable through collective effort? A long-term, impactful ambition that aligns with your organisation's purpose? Do you visualise this goal daily? The kind of goal that makes you jump out of bed each morning and fall asleep each night reflecting on what you've learned? Leaders, alongside their teams, set audacious goals—seemingly impossible, yet achievable if everyone commits to personal growth in a supportive environment. Call it your *North Star Vision* if you like.

Open Communication

Communication is often reduced to talking. But to achieve WOW, storytelling is indispensable, and everyone on the team must master it. Look at Satya Nadella, who in his book *Hit Refresh*, illustrates how storytelling can transform the culture of an entire multinational.[65] In a team of ten, nine are listeners while one speaks. Thus, the listening skills of the majority are far more crucial than the oratory prowess of the leader or the extroverts dominating the meeting. True leaders listen deeply, connect the dots, and bring unspoken stories to the surface. They ensure the team remains attuned to the customer, learning from them. Even when the learning is painful.

Cheer Each Other to Victory

Encouragement isn't just about giving compliments or writing thank-you notes. That's the easy part. It's about praising a team's collective achievements and recognising individuals who are growing or struggling.

Making it clear you believe in someone during their self-doubt is ten times more impactful than complimenting a star performer. This is a common stumbling block for companies. Are mistakes viewed as learning experiences? Can people joke about their own setbacks?

This is the heart of Carol Dweck's *growth mindset*. Let it inspire you, like Nadella, to take bold action.

5

Driver 5. L&D

"I am the master of my fate. I am the captain of my soul."

—*William Ernest Henley*

In today's unpredictable world, it's no longer feasible for organisations to dictate every move their people should make. Instead, companies must equip their teams to think critically and adapt, making them aware of the changes, understanding how they impact both life and business, and providing the skills necessary to thrive amidst constant transformation.

It's crucial to recognise that many of the skills young people are currently learning in college are quickly becoming obsolete. This means organisations will soon be recruiting for jobs that don't even exist yet. It's not just a matter of filling the skills gap we've discussed before—there's also the challenge of skills uncertainty, as highlighted by Jacob Morgan in the *Future of Work.*[66]

As AI and automation continue to reshape the world of work, there is an urgent need for companies to reskill and upskill their workforce. Generation Z, which will make up 30–35% of the global workforce by 2030, is highly committed to learning.[67] This generation is increasingly drawn to companies that prioritise continuous learning and personal development.

Raised with instant access to online courses, YouTube, blogs, Wikipedia, and TikTok, Gen Z (aka *The Zoomers*)[68] actively seeks to develop their skills. They crave opportunities to enhance not only their technical expertise but also their soft skills, such as self-confidence, integrity, interpersonal communication, and critical thinking. On top of that, they share their experiences on platforms like Glassdoor and Comparably, allowing them to either attract their peers or warn them to stay away.

According to the *Mercer 2024 Global Talent Trends Report*, 70% of companies view learning as a top priority, recognising that the skills in demand today may not be relevant tomorrow. So, how can employees—both potential and current—thrive in this dynamic environment?

By learning how to learn. Focusing on continuous learning allows companies to ensure their employees remain competitive and capable of adapting to new roles as they emerge.

Of course, it all starts with the right attitude: the willingness to learn, to stay curious, and to question the current state of knowledge. With the *growth mindset* as the foundation, the necessary skills and qualities can be cultivated. And where does this growth mindset begin? With awareness. This is the first step in creating a Learning Culture—one that not only makes employees aware of the need for continuous learning but actively encourages it.

"Engaged employees are those who continually seek feedback and opportunities to grow. They understand that personal development is key to professional success."

—Marshall Goldsmith (What Got You Here
Won't Get You There)

The Learning Organisation

Building a learning organisation is about more than surviving. It's about thriving. Companies that make learning central to their culture tap into a fundamental human desire for growth and development. Employees who adopt the Gen Z learning attitude are the backbone of future growth. Engaging them through L&D initiatives is key to retaining top talent.

Key Characteristics of the Learning Organisation

1. A Curiosity-Driven Culture: Employees are encouraged to ask questions, explore new ideas, and challenge the status quo. This curiosity fuels innovation and keeps the organisation agile in the face of change.

2. Leadership Support: Leaders play a critical role in fostering a learning culture. They lead by example, making learning a priority and encouraging their teams to do the same.

3. Shared Knowledge: Knowledge is not hoarded but shared openly across the company. This ensures that everyone benefits from the collective wisdom of the group.

4. Continuous Feedback: Feedback is viewed as a gift. Employees receive regular, constructive feedback that helps them grow and develop in their roles.

5. Flexible Learning Opportunities: Learning isn't confined to formal training sessions. It also happens through mentorship, peer-to-peer learning, and on-the-job experiences. These inclusive learning opportunities are very valuable in a neurodiverse environment.

But how do you build a learning organisation in practice? Start with your people! What else?

5 Steps to Get Started:

Step 1. Ignite a Growth Mindset: Spark curiosity throughout your organisation by encouraging employees to embrace challenges as stepping stones for growth. Like a real Carol Dweck. Shift the narrative from *"This is too hard"* to *"What can we learn from this?"* If Microsoft's CEO Satya Nadella could change the mindset of 200,000+ employees from *"know-it-alls"* to *"learn-it-alls,"* you can do it too!

Step 2. Involve Your Employees: Ask what they want to learn and where they see the skills of tomorrow. This not only helps identify learning gaps but also empowers employees to take charge of their development. Bet you'll be amazed at how much knowledge is already present within the group.

Step 3. Create Learning Ambassadors: Create a breeding ground with employees who are passionate about learning. These ambassadors spark curiosity and drive the learning culture by sharing their insights, demonstrating the benefits, and encouraging others to follow suit. Over time, more team members will step up as learning ambassadors.

Step 4. Embed Learning into Daily Work: Instead of relying on large, sporadic training sessions that shut down entire departments, incorporate small learning moments into daily routines. Nudging, you know. This could be as simple as discussing a new concept during a team meeting or watching a short video during a coffee break. Think about gamification and playful learning—acquiring knowledge doesn't have to be dry or overly academic.

Step 5. Leverage Technology: Leverage the power of cutting-edge technology to unlock personalised learning experiences. This includes online courses, mobile learning apps, or AI-driven personalised learning paths. Companies like Siemens and Unilever use AI-powered platforms to create personalised learning paths for employees. This approach has significantly improved training relevance, engagement, and retention while fostering a culture of continuous learning.

In a world where AI is rapidly reshaping the landscape of work, L&D has emerged as a key driver of employee engagement. It's more than staying relevant. It's thriving in an environment where the only constant is change. A learning organisation isn't a luxury; it's a necessity.

How can commitment to growth and learning be translated into real-world success? One company that exemplifies the power of L&D in action is Radisson Hotel Group.

✋ Case in Point

Radisson's Room for Growth: The L&D Advantage

Learning and Development can significantly elevate employee engagement, turning a workforce from merely functional to exceptional. Radisson Hotel Group serves as a prime example of how a strong learning culture can drive engagement and help an organisation overcome challenges.

Harpreet Singh Chhatwal, Vice President of People & Culture for MEA, SEAP, & SA at Radisson Hotel Group, explained to me how the company has leveraged L&D to emerge stronger.

Radisson, one of the largest hotel chains globally, operates over 1,100 hotels in more than 120 countries, employing a diverse workforce. The company's approach to employee engagement is anchored in its seven cultural beliefs.[69] These beliefs (deliberately termed as such rather than values) underscore their commitment to a dynamic, action-oriented culture. This ethos is central to their strategy, driving everything from daily operations to long-term decision-making.

The pandemic posed significant challenges to Radisson, particularly in attracting and retaining talent within the highly competitive hospitality industry. With low margins and less-than-competitive pay, Radisson had to innovate to stay ahead. They realised that, to bounce back, they needed to focus on strengthening their learning culture. In September 2023, Radisson introduced a career map that celebrates successful careers within the company. This initiative was part of a broader effort to profile and highlight employee achievements.90% of the audience joined the platform—a clear indicator of its rapid success.

One of the standout achievements in this area is the Radisson Academy, the online learning platform that offers a comprehensive range of courses with engaging gamification elements, making learning enjoyable and interactive. Additionally, Radisson offers in-person business cases, ambassador-led storytelling sessions, and a train-the-trainer approach to disseminating knowledge effectively.

This platform encompasses learning modules for all levels: VPs, Directors, Managers, etc. at the offices and General Managers, Hotel Head of Departments, and line employees at the hotel level.

Radisson's commitment to learning goes beyond providing resources. Individual managers are empowered through a framework, rather than leaving engagement to the manager's interpretation. This structured approach ensures consistency and fairness, where every employee can thrive.

Harpreet also strongly believes in self-assessment: employees are encouraged to take responsibility for their own development, offering tools to assess their skills and identify areas for growth. This self-driven approach is complemented by the company's strong focus on peer learning and support from supervisors, ensuring that learning is a continuous, collaborative process.

This learning ecosystem is now a key part of Radisson's Employee Value Proposition (EVP). By providing employees with the tools and opportunities to grow, Radisson has created an environment where learning is integrated into the cultural fabric. Harpreet calls it *"Abilitude,"* a smart combination of Ability and Attitude.

The emphasis on continuous learning has visibly enhanced employee engagement. It has also led to high levels of employee enablement—well above the industry benchmark—and elevated customer satisfaction, earning Radisson well-deserved recognition in the industry, like being awarded the *Global Best Employer in Travel & Leisure* by Forbes.

Career Development

Imagine showing up to work every day knowing there's no room for growth. How long could you stay motivated? The Universe is probably sending you signs that it's time to consider a change!

A lack of growth opportunities is consistently one of the top reasons employees decide to leave their jobs. In fact, according to Randstad, it is the primary reason for employee turnover.[70] Most professionals have a natural desire to progress in their careers, yet some find themselves in roles where advancement seems out of reach. This lack of perspective can be incredibly demotivating. The challenge for managers is to recognise and nurture the potential.

Take, for instance, a cashier in a retailer. It's a role that can be mastered relatively quickly, which raises the question: *"How long should an employee remain in that position?"* While some managers might be content to keep a team member in a role as long as they're performing well, this approach doesn't consider the ambitions of those who are hungry for more. Feeling stuck in a dead-end job is the last thing they want!

As a manager, consider these proactive steps to help high potentials see a promising future within your organisation:

- Start by clearly identifying potential career paths and documenting them in a career ladder.
- Have open, honest conversations with your team about these opportunities—don't leave them guessing or waiting for them to approach you. For some, initiating a conversation about their career trajectory can be

intimidating, and they might hesitate out of fear of making assumptions.

- Paint a vivid picture of the possibilities within your organisation. Let employees see the road ahead, not just the lane they're in. While some employees may excel in their roles for a few years, they may need to move on to continue their career growth. If you don't offer the next step, they have no choice but to look elsewhere.

Career Development at LVMH

At LVMH (Louis Vuitton Moët Hennessy), one of the most iconic luxury brands, career development is a core part of their brand DNA.

Their THINK Retail programme is focused on nurturing individual aspirations, ensuring that employees' growth aligns with the future of the company. It provides those from the retail side with the opportunity to pursue their professional aspirations.

By understanding the employee interests, LVMH ensures that skills match with future demands. L&D is considered more than an investment. It has become part of the evolution of their brands, leading to the creation of LVMH House, the global learning and development centre.

Additionally, the Métiers d'Excellence programme—an apprenticeship programme designed to train the next generation of creative and craftspeople across their Maisons—has been collaborating with Tiffany & Co. to instil trainees with artisanal excellence and savoir faire.[71]

Few employees today expect to spend their entire careers at one company, with the average tenure being around four years. However, you can extend their loyalty by helping them see a clear path for growth and then supporting them as they advance along that path. Investing in a culture that prioritises upskilling and career development enriches the employee experience and solidifies the organisation's reputation as a place where careers are built—and futures are made.

✋Case in Point
Highflyers: How Etihad Develops Talent from the Ground Up

At 30,000 feet, success goes beyond reaching point A to point B. It's also cultivating a culture of excellence where every employee feels empowered to grow. At Etihad Airways, L&D fuels that journey, playing a pivotal role in shaping organisational culture.

During my conversation with **Andrew Stotter-Brooks**, former Vice President of Learning and Development at Etihad Airways, it became clear just how transformative L&D can be. Brought into the company to challenge traditional approaches, Andrew has been instrumental in redefining how Etihad trains, develops, and engages its workforce.

Etihad Airways, headquartered in Abu Dhabi, is a national flag carrier with a significant focus on developing local talent. The airline has over 20,000 employees and serves more than 60 countries, making it a major player in the global aviation industry. Within this context, Andrew and his team were tasked with ensuring that the workforce was not only skilled but also highly engaged.

One of the standout initiatives introduced under Andrew's leadership was a structured learning framework designed to guide employees through five career levels, from entry-level roles to senior executives. This framework encompasses eight key knowledge areas, including coaching, impact, and team management. As employees progress, the complexity of learning increases, equipping them with the skills they need to advance their careers while remaining aligned with Etihad's broader mission.

This structured approach brought clarity to career development, eliminating ambiguity and ensuring that employees understood what was expected of them at each stage. By providing clear pathways for progression, a sense of purpose and empowerment was fostered across the organisation. The results speak for themselves: Etihad has achieved a remarkable employee engagement score of 76%.

For Andrew, L&D is not simply a tool for professional development, but the very heart of employee engagement. He believes learning should be accessible, relevant, and directly connected to the company's long-term objectives. At Etihad, this philosophy has been embedded into daily operations, making L&D a key driver of the company's success.

What sets Andrew apart as a leader is his human-centred approach to leadership and learning. Beyond his work at Etihad, he has been an influential figure in the wider L&D community in the Middle East, hosting podcasts through *Weird Human*. His approach is innovative and empathetic, focusing on empowering individuals to unlock their potential. His recent transition to a new role as Chief Learner at ADNOC Group, one of the world's leading energy producers, is a testament to his forward-thinking vision.

A memorable insight from Andrew was his reflection on the common phrase from employees, *"I'm just a (cabin crew, operator)..."* He told me how this phrase deeply saddens him, as it diminishes the value of people's roles within the organisation. Andrew believes that every role is critical to the company's success, from the barista serving coffee to the pilot flying the plane. This belief is central to his L&D philosophy, where the goal is to ensure that every single employee feels seen, valued, and integral to the larger system.

6

Driver 6. Well-being

"A lot of times, we are angry at other people for not doing what we should have done for ourselves."

—*Rupi Kaur (Responsibility)*

POV: *You're sitting at your desk, exhausted, craving a break. But instead, your company schedules a mandatory lunch talk on well-being. The topic? The importance of taking regular breaks. By the time the session is over, you realise that you've missed your lunch. Later, you scroll through Instagram, only to see your company's post proudly showcasing their dedication to preventing burnout. "Maybe they should have used "Ironic" by Alanis Morissette as the soundtrack for their reel," you mumble.*

Don't you think? Well, I think that it smells like a classic case of *"well-being washing"*—a practice that has become all too common. Organisations make superficial gestures towards well-being while neglecting the real issues.

A study by the Institution of Occupational Safety and Health found that 51% of employees believed their employer was guilty of this at some point. Picture green juice, ping-pong tables, or well-being walks. While they sound nice, these gestures fall flat when employees face unaddressed issues like unrealistic workloads, workplace bullying, or looming deadlines. Glossy social media posts don't make up for genuine support. For those genuinely struggling, these surface-level perks can feel like salt in the wound, leading to disillusionment and frustration.

What Holistic Well-being Looks Like

Spoiler: It's not yoga pants! Back in 2012, when we first set out to implement corporate well-being programmes, we quickly realised we were only scratching the surface, and that the journey ahead would be long and complex. Since then, there's been commendable progress in raising awareness and bringing once-taboo subjects like burnout to the forefront. Introducing coaching as a standard offering is one such advancement. But despite the strides made, one common pitfall from the early days of well-being persists: an overemphasis on physical health.

While physical well-being is crucial, focusing solely on it is too narrow. This approach often alienates significant portions of the workforce. Sure, fitness enthusiasts will participate in physical challenges regardless of company initiatives. But what about those who aren't as active? Bet they will feel misunderstood or excluded. True well-being is more complex, with different layers. That's why we advocate for a holistic approach—one that sees individuals as whole beings, blurring the lines between personal and professional life.

By the way, let's drop the word *"work-life balance"* once and for all. Once a cornerstone of well-being strategies, the concept is heavily outdated. It suggests a divide between the two. In reality, our personal and professional lives are inextricably linked. Work is life, and life is work. What we need now is an integrated approach that embeds well-being into the rhythm of work itself. The pandemic accelerated this shift, pushing companies to rethink how work fits into life—and how well-being can become part of the fabric of daily operations.

So, how can one achieve a more holistic state of being? As an individual and as an employee? The answer lies in the pursuit of **5 pillars** based on personal balance:

1. **Mental Balance:** Managing stress, anxiety, and insecurities, filtering the constant influx of digital information, and focusing on personal growth are all vital to maintaining mental equilibrium.

2. **Physical Balance:** Regular physical activity is essential, but it should be at a pace that respects your body and life circumstances, especially in a world where sedentary jobs and hectic lifestyles dominate.

3. **Nutritional Balance**: A healthy, realistic diet tailored to individual needs is key to sustaining energy and overall health. Let food be thy medicine.

4. **Social Balance**: Human connection is at the heart of well-being. Interactions with colleagues, friends, and family, along with alignment between personal and organisational values, are essential for a fulfilling life.

5. **Financial Balance**: Financial well-being means having the confidence and ability to meet both daily expenses and future financial obligations, freeing up mental space for personal and professional growth.

These five pillars must coexist in harmony. Focusing too much on one area at the expense of another can be detrimental. For instance, pursuing physical fitness while neglecting mental rest or social connections can undermine overall resilience. Financial stress, if left unchecked, can impact both mental and physical health. A flexible approach that allows employees to

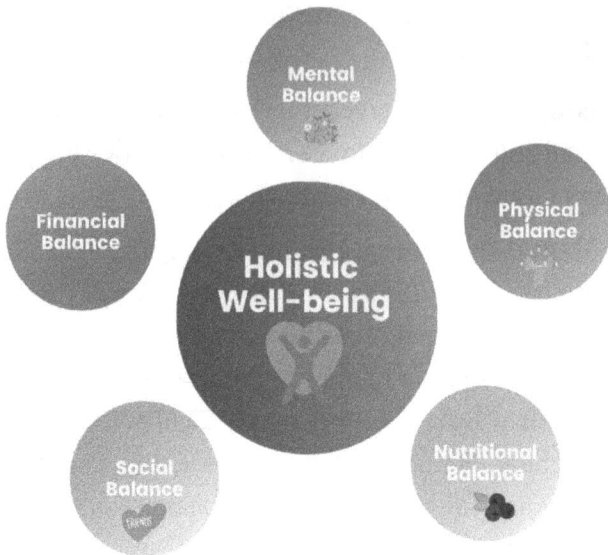

Figure 8. Holistic Well-being

focus on the area that resonates most with them sets them on a path to both personal and professional growth.

"When employees are in debt financially, they are very unlikely to be engaged at work, always on the lookout for another opportunity that would pay more."

—*Ali Khaled Al Hashmi,*
Former SVP & Head of HR, Union Bank

A Pillar in Crisis

Among these pillars, mental well-being deserves particular attention. The global decline in mental health has reached crisis levels, with United Nations Secretary-General António Guterres warning that we are spiralling out of control. Although it may seem paradoxical that mental health is deteriorating in an era of unprecedented progress and prosperity, it is a reality we must confront.

The *Gallup State of the Global Workplace 2024 Report* paints a sobering picture. It reveals that well-being has declined, particularly among younger workers.[72] Forty-one per cent of employees worldwide experience significant stress, and 20% report feeling lonely on a daily basis. Remote workers, in particular, face new challenges when it comes to maintaining well-being in a digital-first world. A report by Claro shows that, while 70% of workplaces celebrated mental health awareness days, only a third of employees rated their organisation's mental health support as good or outstanding.[73]

In recent years, we've been bombarded with alarming reports highlighting the surge in depression and anxiety, especially among Gen Z. This generation has come of age in an era defined by school closures, remote work, and economic uncertainty—factors that have taken a serious toll on their mental health. Gen Z and young Millennial employees are missing the equivalent of a day's work every week due to mental health struggles, new research has shown.[74]

Against this backdrop, I find Gen Z a remarkable generation. What stands out most is how deeply this generation cares about their mental health and well-being, and how vocal they are on the subject. The Forbes Business Council even describes them as the first generation to be this committed to mental health and to speak so openly about it.[75] Several factors contribute to this, starting with an increased awareness of mental health and well-being.

While Gen Z has yet to fully prove itself in many areas, when it comes to this topic, I think they have shown wisdom beyond their years. Their commitment to breaking down stigmas could very well inspire other generations to overcome their own fears of addressing mental health openly. These young adults have grown up with celebrities like Billie Eilish, Ed Sheeran, Selena Gomez, and Shawn Mendes, openly discussing their mental health challenges. This openness has normalised the conversation for millions of young people, empowering them to speak up about their own experiences.

Companies are taking note. An article from Johns Hopkins University stresses the importance of creating stigma-free workplaces that integrate mental well-being into the fabric of the business.[76] But Gen Z wants more than just awareness; they seek tangible support like access to therapy or mental health tools, and the ability to take mental health days without facing judgement.

And the challenge remains significant. According to data from Korn Ferry, many employees feel uncomfortable accessing mental health resources or even discussing their well-being with managers, despite working in companies that claim to take mental health seriously. The stigma seems to be especially pronounced among office workers who are paid to use their minds. *"They're naturally worried about being perceived as diminished,"* says Ron Porter, Senior Client Partner at Korn Ferry.[77]

The Society for Human Resource Management indicates that nearly half of HR professionals don't feel comfortable discussing their own mental health at work, and 26% don't feel at ease asking for mental health resources.[78] Alarming numbers, especially when we consider that they're supposed to be the gatekeepers of well-being programmes. If HR professionals, who should ideally be the most knowledgeable and receptive to mental health benefits, are hesitant to engage, it highlights a much larger issue. In an ideal world, they would lead by example, modelling an open attitude towards mental health benefits. Yet, in practice, they often harbour concerns about privacy and confidentiality.

This unease suggests deeper organisational issues that go beyond just stigma. Concerns about how mental health disclosures might be handled, and fears that even accessing mental health services could lead to unintended consequences. As a result, both employees and HR professionals often avoid engaging with mental health resources altogether, afraid of being labelled. This reluctance creates a culture of silence, where the very programmes designed to support well-being are underutilised or sidelined.

Well-being = Profit

Apart from being a moral obligation, investing in employee well-being is also a smart business strategy. A Deloitte report highlights that for every dollar invested in employee well-being, companies see a return of five dollars. The World Health Organisation (WHO) suggests that the return can be as high as 14 times.

Fostering a culture of well-being doesn't have to come with a hefty price tag. What's needed is a shift in mindset. By focusing on healthy habits and rethinking the way work is structured, well-being can become a natural part of organisational culture. This shift, coupled with inspiring leadership, is key to motivating employees, helping them flourish, and fostering long-term loyalty.

However, there is often a disconnect between what employers and employees perceive as effective well-being measures. A report by Winckworth Sherwood found that while 37% of employers believed that employee benefits such as yoga, resilience training, and healthy lifestyle seminars were effective, only 26% of employees agreed.[79] In contrast, 50% of employees favoured good work itself as a means of promoting well-being.

To make meaningful change, it's crucial to understand what your employees actually want. When was the last time you asked your team for feedback on health and wellness benefits? Are they comfortable accessing these benefits without fear of stigma? If not, it's time to rethink your approach. For instance, consider your sick day policy—does it include time off for mental health? If not, it may be time to expand your policy.

I also don't believe that corporate well-being is really eligible for outsourcing. While Employee Assistance Programmes (EAPs) are valuable, they do little for prevention. The challenge is to create emotionally healthy environments proactively. Everyday actions, from managers and leaders, often have more impact and are more cost-effective than well-meaning programmes.

Just like engagement, well-being is a **shared responsibility**. Employees must take ownership of their personal well-being and make conscious choices, while employers must create an environment that supports and inspires growth, offering resources, information, and inspiration to help employees thrive. All without being patronising.

Managers, in particular, are pivotal. They are the ones who understand their teams' unique needs and can foster an environment that supports their well-being. However, Gallup research shows that many managers themselves are disengaged, which negatively impacts their teams. Unsurprisingly, engaged managers are more likely to lead engaged teams, which is critical to improving both well-being and performance.[80]

As business psychologist Melanie Katzman points out, we can learn from the evolution of corporate social responsibility (CSR) departments: until well-being goals are considered integral to a company's success, they will remain on the margins—an add-on to work rather than the work itself.[81]

7

Driver 7. Employee Journey

"Recruitment IS marketing. If you're a recruiter nowadays and you don't see yourself as a marketer, you're in the wrong profession."

—*Matthew Jeffrey, Global Head of Sourcing and Employment Brand, SAP*

From the first handshake to the farewell party, the employee journey is filled with opportunities to create lasting impressions. Whether someone is a job candidate, a current employee, or a proud alumnus, their experience with your organisation shapes how they feel about your brand. Experiences, after all, are what make us human and what makes life so exciting.

So why not invest the time and energy to create moments that matter? For this too has an impact on your people's loyalty.

The employee journey consists of 4 key phases:

1. Attracting Talent
2. Onboarding
3. Moments That Matter
4. Offboarding

Phase 1: Attracting Talent

Recruitment is *le moment suprême* in the employer-employee relationship. The crucial moment when you either hook a great candidate or watch them swim away. Attracting top talent goes far beyond posting job ads. It's about creating an experience that immediately captivates candidates and makes them think, "*I want to work there!*"

How can you up your recruitment game? Well, let's start with a few tweaks:

1. First, **presence.** Think about the first impression your organisation leaves on job candidates. What do they see when they look you up on LinkedIn, Glassdoor, or Indeed? Are your job postings telling a compelling story, or do they sound like the fine print of a mobile phone contract? Engaging candidates starts long before the interview—make sure your online presence is top-notch, with employee testimonials, videos, and opportunities for growth.

2. Second, **clarity.** Don't be afraid to be explicit about what you expect. If you're after high performers who are willing to give their all, say so! Forget the sugar-coating and make it clear that mediocrity has no place in your team. A striking example comes from ex-Executive Vice-President Ignace Van Doorselaere's book *The Road to Infinity*, where he discusses the recruitment process for top positions at the Brazilian company that later merged with the global brewery AB InBev. The criteria were straightforward: First, was the candidate intelligent? This was assessed through their education and degree. Second, could they handle

155

setbacks? Resilience was key, as candidates needed the grit to push through challenges until they succeeded. Finally, had they experienced poverty? Understanding the value of money and being willing to fight for every Brazilian real was considered essential.[82]

3. Third, **consistency**. Ensure your recruitment approach is consistent across all channels, including job fairs. Standing out is key—whether that's with an eye-catching booth, hiring a special barista serving extraordinary coffee (what else?), a fortune teller, or anything that reflects your brand's personality. Communicate your company culture in the most vivid way possible, e.g. using the latest footage to show your colleagues in action, highlighting the real atmosphere at work, or with video testimonials from employees sharing their experiences. The goal is to get creative and make your recruitment efforts truly memorable and authentic.

IKEA nailed this with their *Career Instructions* campaign— tucking job ads into their flat-pack furniture instructions. The perfect blend of brand identity and recruitment. L'Oréal's approach to talent acquisition is equally creative and forward-thinking. Through its long-running *Brandstorm* competition, L'Oréal invites students from around the world to solve real business challenges, fostering a spirit of innovation and entrepreneurship.

As their former Marketing Director Hadi Kamouh insightfully noted during our conversation, *"L'Oréal has always prioritised personalities over diplomas, seeking unique profiles rather than standard competencies. Despite receiving over*

1.3 million unsolicited applications annually, HR managers continuously seek out atypical talents. We look less for pedigree than the atypical profile, the one who can handle paradoxes."

🖑 Case in Point

A Fine Point on Talent: BIC's Culture-First Hiring Process

The French manufacturing company BIC, renowned for its globally recognised stationery products, lighters, and shavers, maintains a highly selective approach to hiring new employees. Named one of Time's *World's Best Brands of 2024* and listed by Newsweek as one of the World's *Most Trustworthy Companies*, BIC exemplifies a unique blend of global reach and family-business ethos.

With a workforce exceeding 13,000 and products available in over 160 countries, BIC fosters an entrepreneurial culture grounded in its core values: Integrity, Responsibility, Teamwork, Sustainability, Ingenuity, and Simplicity. Known for its *"roll up your sleeves and get the job done"* mindset, the company attracts self-starters, problem solvers, and innovative thinkers.

BIC's thorough hiring process involves extensive input from future team members and various colleagues, ensuring that new hires align with the company's culture and values. Every voice in this process is valued, playing a pivotal role in the final decision.

Peter Van den Broeck, Senior Vice President for the Middle East and Africa, explains: *"It's true that joining the BIC family isn't easy, but once you're part of the*

157

organisation, you're treated as one of us. This careful approach has reduced employee turnover to just 2%. We are deeply committed to prioritising the health and well-being of our people, going above and beyond to support them and celebrate our unique culture. When our team feels supported, we achieve more together.

Our organisation, particularly in the Dubai office, is highly diverse, and I'm personally passionate about fostering Diversity and Inclusion, ensuring everyone can bring their true selves to work. There's little room for big egos here. By staying true to our mission 'At BIC, we bring simplicity and joy to everyday life'—and upholding our values, we continue to attract the right people."

Phase 2: Onboarding

"We want to create an environment where every employee can bring their whole self to work and not just make a living but also live a life."

—*Indra Nooyi, CEO, PepsiCo*

You never get a second chance to make a first impression. That holds true for onboarding too.But does it really matter if the rest of the employee journey is going smoothly? Absolutely! That's why it's crucial to ensure that a new hire remembers their first day as a genuinely warm welcome. Preparation is key, so it's essential to send a message a few days before onboarding starts. Deloitte, for instance, takes a thoughtful approach by sending a survey to the candidate while they are still wrapping up their previous role. Additionally, they create a detailed plan for the first day, covering everything from the moment they walk through the door to the end of their workday.

Iconic toy company Lego offers a great example of how to make onboarding both fun and hands-on. New employees receive a *Welcome Box* that includes a Lego set they need to build as part of their introduction. This not only helps break the ice with new colleagues but also immerses them in Lego's playful and creative culture from the very start.

Small, thoughtful touches can really make a difference. Consider providing a welcome card, a personalised coffee mug, or even decorating the new hire's workspace. Organise for as many members of the management team as possible to stop by for a brief chat to welcome them. If they're unavailable, a pre-recorded personalised video message can serve as an excellent alternative. Think carefully about the impression you want to create.

If you're committed to continuous improvement, think about introducing an entry interview. While exit interviews are common, why not begin with an entry interview? After all, isn't it just as important to understand why a new employee ultimately chose to join? You could ask questions like, *"What are you most looking forward to?"* or *"What was the main reason you chose to work with us—was it the role itself, the salary, the location, friends or family, or something else?"* Even if similar questions were asked during the hiring process, revisiting them now, when the pressure is off, might reveal fresh insights. Not only will this provide you with valuable feedback, but it also creates a surprising experience for the new hire.

Phase 3: Moments That Matter

Throughout our careers, we experience countless significant events that shape the course of our lives, even if we don't often stop to reflect on them. These are the *Moments That Matter*. Consider the life-changing experiences of having a child, going through a divorce, dealing with a toxic colleague, or the sudden death of a team member, ... As the lines between work and personal life become increasingly blurred, our brains don't make a clear distinction between the two. They leave lasting impressions, marked as milestone moments in our memories.

Moments That Matter are the most meaningful and impactful points in an employee's journey, the ones that stick with them long after the moment has passed. Recognising these moments shows that you consider your employees as complete individuals. They give organisations an excellent opportunity to personalise their approach and truly bring their culture to life.

Jacob Morgan identifies 3 types of *Moments That Matter*.[83]

1. **Specific Moments:** These are major milestones in an employee's life, moments with deep personal significance. Think of events like buying a house, losing a loved one, receiving a promotion, or experiencing their very first workday. While these events are unique to each individual, they happen regularly within an organisation. As an employer, it's essential to respond to these moments in ways that align with your culture.

2. **Ongoing Moments:** The day-to-day interactions that shape the ongoing relationship between colleagues or with management. They might not always be immediately obvious or easy to define, but they profoundly influence the overall employee experience. Examples could include when a colleague takes credit for your work, a micro-aggression, or when you receive unexpected praise after delivering a successful project. These moments aren't planned; they occur organically throughout the working relationship.

3. **Created Moments:** These moments are planned and require some degree of organisation. Think of teambuilding events, innovation challenges, project kick-offs, or hackathons. These initiatives are designed to make employees feel valued or to address a specific business need. In our experience, Created Moments are most powerful when they are clearly defined and occur regularly, becoming key reference points for the team. They give employees a chance to step outside the normal business context and connect with each other in a more meaningful way.

Creating unforgettable moments with colleagues forges bonds that last a lifetime. This is something we have always held very close to our hearts with the company I co-founded, Herculean Alliance. In fact, it's our very guiding principle. For over twenty years, we have been helping hundreds of companies in ten countries, creating lasting memories through our unique formats, including *Hercules Trophy, Pink Ladies Games, BRAVOS! Employee Engagement Awards*, and bespoke events.

Herculean Blueprint for Moments That Matter

Here are the key ingredients of our secret Herculean recipe that consistently deliver results, no matter where in the world it's applied:

1. Communication and Thorough Preparation: Ideally, this should start digitally, allowing you to build anticipation across different audiences and measure outcomes, both before and after the event.

2. Bringing People Together Physically: We strongly advocate for the phygital *approach: a blend of physical experiences and the digital element that allows for more objective measurements. An entirely digital event, without a real-world link, can't yet achieve the same level of connection. To truly resonate, you need to bring people together in person.*

3. Action: At the very least, include some form of physical activity. It doesn't need to be intense exercise, but if you can encourage movement, those happiness-boosting endorphins will flow. Happiness is a super powerful catalyst for connection!

4. Plenty of Good Food and Drinks: We place great importance on this—blame our Burgundian nature. You don't need to break the bank, but make sure the food is tasty and there's more than enough to go around. You want to avoid any sense of stinginess, as food shortage is often the only thing people will remember! Also, cater to the diverse needs of your team by offering vegetarian, gluten-free, and halal options. It's a small gesture but one that earns you extra appreciation.

5. Gamification: *If you really want to get to know your people, organise a competition. In some,* the homo ludens—*the playful human—might be hidden, but once unlocked, be ready for a highly engaging spectacle. And remember Plato's timeless wisdom:* "You can discover more about a person in an hour of play than in a year of conversation."

6. Celebration: *Celebrating as a team is essential for building cohesion. It doesn't mean everyone has to be dancing on tables, but marking achievements together fosters a sense of unity.*

7. A Healthy Dose of Humour: *Humour breaks the ice, opening the hearts and minds of your audience in a way logic can't. People who laugh together, work together.*

We've organised events across a diverse range of nationalities, spanning Arab, Asian, American, European, and African cultures, and we've learned a lot from each experience. No matter the differences, one thing always stands out: the universal need for connection. These moments are vital for team cohesion and bonding. They become milestones in the collective memory of employees, recalled fondly for years, often with a twinkle in their eyes.

"Happiness is only real, when shared."

—*Christopher McCandless*
(Into The Wild)

Phase 4: Offboarding (and Beyond)

As valuable as it is to leave on a high note, let's face it: not having to say goodbye at all is the best outcome. But when it's time for an employee to move on or you decide to end the collaboration, doing so with grace and style is essential.

Employees leaving (whether voluntarily or not) can cause significant damage if the exit isn't handled properly. While a solid exit strategy doesn't completely eliminate the risk, it can certainly minimise the fallout. Potential hires often scour the internet for reviews, before applying. A company that treats employees with respect from start to finish demonstrates a genuine commitment to the human touch, rather than just paying lip service.

That's why it's crucial to have a standardised offboarding process. Not only does this help streamline operations for the organisation, but it also ensures you can focus on the departing employee as a person, the role they're leaving behind, and the team that remains. By taking the time to understand why employees are leaving, you can uncover valuable insights. After all, someone with one foot out the door is often much more open to share their views on the organisation, management, and job.

Exit interviews, while not revolutionary, are far more common than you might think. In fact, according to a study by the *Society for Human Resource Management* (SHRM), 61% of organisations use exit interviews as part of their feedback loop.[84] These conversations offer a unique opportunity to gain quick, candid insights into organisational dynamics. It's like a shortcut to identifying areas that need improvement, straight from the source. *Harvard Business Review* even found that 80% of turnover is due to issues companies could have addressed.[85] By analysing patterns from these interviews, you can pinpoint recurring problems and spot systemic issues that might be flying under the radar.

How you say goodbye also sends a clear message to those who stay. Employees watch how departures are handled and, consciously or unconsciously, adjust their behaviour accordingly. A thoughtful, offboarding process not only leaves a positive impression on the departing employee but also reassures the rest of the team. Plus, former employees who leave on good terms are more likely to remain advocates for your brand. They might help you find new talent or tap into their networks to support your business.

Looking at it positively, strong offboarding can open doors for future opportunities. Leaving the door ajar benefits both parties. One may become a client of the other, and let's not underestimate the power of a glowing recommendation. And who knows? That departing employee may one day come back with fresh ideas and new experiences. *Boomerangers* often re-enter the company more smoothly than new hires and can bring a wealth of outside knowledge to the table. Steve Jobs' famous return to Apple is the ultimate example of a boomerang success story, but there are countless other cases where returning employees have helped boost growth and innovation.

If your company finds a way to tap into this, it can provide a significant competitive advantage. Perhaps you've noticed how many LinkedIn groups exist for former employees of specific companies? Many of these have been set up spontaneously by enthusiastic ex-colleagues, filled with interesting information but not officially connected to the company. What a missed opportunity! As a leader, it's up to you to take the initiative. Why not organise an alumni event or host regular meet-ups? Reach out to them … they're waiting for you!

8

Driver 8. Compensation & Benefits

"I have never seen a bag of money score a goal."

—*Johan Cruyff (Football Legend)*

What role does Compensation and Benefits play in engaging employees? Another million-dollar question!

Benefits and rewards are a cornerstone of any organisation's *Employee Value Proposition* (*EVP*), standing alongside the more intangible elements. A well-crafted EVP is like a tailored suit—it represents the unique package that an organisation offers to its employees in exchange for their skills, talents, and experience. This proposition is vital for attracting, engaging, and retaining top talent.

Comp & Ben act as tangible proof of the organisation's commitment to its people. They reinforce the idea that employees are valued, encouraging a deeper connection to the company. When aligned with the needs and aspirations of employees, they don't just meet basic expectations; they create a sense of fairness and appreciation—essential ingredients for long-term engagement and loyalty.

I'll admit, assessing the impact of Comp & Ben on employee engagement can feel like chasing your own tail. From our own surveys, predominantly in Western countries, these elements don't emerge as top drivers of engagement. However, it would be overly simplistic to dismiss their importance. After all, how many people do you know willing to work for free? While compensation may not always be the most exciting factor in the engagement puzzle, it remains a very significant conversation topic in every workplace.

To dig deeper into the issue, I looked at a myriad of sources. But the studies on this topic can be quite contradictory, to say the least. Depending on which report you read, Comp & Ben either rank as one of the most important factors in job satisfaction or they barely scrape the list. For example, the SHRM ranked pay as the second most important factor affecting overall job satisfaction.[86] According to Korn Ferry's *Workforce 2024 Global Insights Report*, having a generous compensation package makes employees more likely to stay put. The same report states that salary is the second reason most employees choose to accept a new job in 2024.[87] Meanwhile, a study by job site Indeed places salary right at the bottom of what employees say drives their happiness at work.[88] Three studies with wildly different conclusions.

Could it be that compensation is, as Frederick Herzberg's theory suggests, a **"hygiene factor"**?[89] In other words, if a certain salary level isn't met, it tends to have a demotivating effect. However, once this threshold is surpassed, a higher salary doesn't necessarily lead to greater satisfaction or engagement. That tipping point is personal for each individual, marking the moment they feel valued. Anything above that? A much-appreciated bonus, but not a dealbreaker for motivation.

We previously discussed Netflix's *Culture Code*. This code explicitly states that, alongside its range of perks and rewards, the company is committed to paying its employees well.[90] This approach is common across all organisations that take employee engagement seriously. After all, it's hard for someone to feel truly valued if they believe they're being underpaid.

To shed more light on this, I turned to two experts: Sabine Schellens, Director of HR & Organisation Development at Aquafin, and Karin Van Roy, CHRO at Arvesta—both of whom have served as jury members for the *BRAVOS! Employee Engagement Awards*. Their insights offered fresh perspectives on the ever-complicated role of Comp & Ben in keeping employees motivated.

Ask the Expert 🖎

Sabine Schellens, Director HR & Organisational Development Aquafin, the wastewater treatment company

"While compensation alone may not be the magic bullet for engagement, we'd be wrong to underestimate its impact on how people feel about their jobs—and themselves."

The Role of Compensation & Benefits in Employee Engagement

According to Sabine, there's a clear link between how employees are compensated and their sense of self-worth. Sure, research might tell us that benefits aren't always the primary driver of engagement but ignore them at your peril. When the paycheque doesn't align with expectations, employees are likely to become disengaged, and, as Sabine

168

puts it, *"That's a slippery slope no organisation wants to be on."*

To prevent this, she stresses the importance of crafting a compensation strategy that achieves two things: keeping current employees happy and attracting the right talent. In her view, any reward system must be tailored to the market you operate in. After all, a *one-size-fits-all* approach is a sure way to lose the plot.

Compensation for the Job vs. Appreciation of Personal Fulfilment

When creating and implementing transparent compensation systems, it's important to recognise that employees interpret these in a personal way. Sabine points out that many employees see their pay as a reflection of their worth and how they approach their job. That's why remuneration isn't just a number on a pay slip; it influences overall satisfaction in ways that aren't always easy to quantify.

Take job classification systems, for example. The system may seem objective: roles are assigned weight based on parameters like budget responsibility, hierarchy, or strategic vision. The higher the weighting, the better the pay. Although this system is designed to be objective and independent of the individual filling the role, many employees strongly associate their personal worth with the weighting of their job and its corresponding compensation. And if that value doesn't align with their self-image? Well, it's no surprise they'll be less than thrilled. In fact, Sabine notes, that when employees feel strongly identified with their roles, a perceived under-valuation can seriously damage their engagement.

Perceptions of External Equity vs. Internal Equity

Dissatisfaction with compensation systems can also stem from a perceived tension between two realities: external equity and internal equity. Some reward systems are designed to align with what the market pays for a particular job (*external equity*). However, employees might view this as unfair if the internal relationship between roles within their own company differs from market averages (*internal equity*).

Belonging is a crucial factor for engagement at work and is equally important for an individual's well-being in their personal life. Compensation partly determines who we connect with, and who we consider part of our social circle. For organisations, structuring Comp & Ben systems means not only defining financial rewards but also considering the broader implications for employees' private lives. If an employee feels dissatisfied with their pay, it can lead to frustrations that spill over into their personal life.

Compensation as a Key Factor in Satisfaction

When designed well, Comp & Ben systems need to be well-considered, stable over time, and transparent. If you want employees to feel good about their pay, make sure they understand how the system works. Not just when they're hired, but throughout their career. Clear communication is the key to avoiding the all-too-common grumbles about fairness or transparency.

Sabine's takeaway? Comp & Ben may not be the sole driver of employee engagement, but their impact is undeniable. The link between pay and personal identity runs deep, and if you're serious about employee satisfaction, it's a factor you can't afford to overlook.

Ask the Expert ✍

Karin Van Roy, CHRO at Arvesta, European market leader in agriculture

"Without explicitly aiming to drive engagement, one thing is certain: if pay isn't right, it can have a powerful disengaging effect. I'm a firm believer that wages should simply be 'in order,' full stop."

Of course, what it means to be in order can vary widely from person to person. Inge's example from Netflix illustrates that, for them, remuneration is a key differentiator—paying well goes beyond simply paying fairly.

Every company has its own reward strategy, and while it's important to have some flexibility to hit specific goals, consistency is the key. You've got to measure your approach against the market. What are your competitors offering? One size never fits all, but you do need a consistent approach. Your compensation strategy must align closely with your business strategy, guiding the direction you want to take and influencing the outcomes you aim to achieve. To make sure you're staying on track, regular internal assessments are essential. Ask your employees how they feel about their compensation package. Would they consider leaving for a competitor offering something similar? Checking these points yearly keeps your strategy fresh and relevant.

Giving someone a raise purely to motivate them? I'm not convinced that's a long-term solution. Sure, it might provide a short-term boost. But if it's too dramatic, the employee might start questioning why they weren't being fairly compensated in the first place. That's why transparency around pay is so critical for engagement. People generally understand that there will be pay differences, and that's not usually the issue. The problem arises when those differences seem unfair or stray outside the boundaries of the compensation policies you've communicated.

So, where does remuneration truly impact engagement? You may have the most fantastic HR programmes: rich with experiences, development opportunities, rewards, etc. But all of that can unravel quickly if pay isn't handled right. Lose your employees' trust over something as fundamental as pay, and that distrust can spread like wildfire, undermining everything else.

In short, compensation needs to be accurate and in line with what was promised. While it may not always serve as the biggest motivator, it's the foundation of trust. And trust, as we know, is essential for any healthy workplace. If that foundation isn't solid, dissatisfaction sets in fast, and from there, it's a steep downhill slide.

We can't discuss the Comp & Ben without touching on rewards and benefits.

As part of our ongoing conversation on customer and employee engagement, I also spoke with Julie Barbier-Leblan, founder and CEO of Merit Incentives, the rising engagement technology company operating across the UAE and KSA. With both of us sharing a background in law and a deep passion for fostering engagement, we explored her perspective on the evolving role of rewards in the workplace and the impact of technology on employee satisfaction.

Ask the Expert 📝

Interview Julie Barbier-Leblan, founder and CEO of Merit Incentives

"The future of employee rewards lies in the integration of AI and real-time analytics, offering hyper-personalised and timely incentives. As technology advances, it provides even greater freedom of choice, allowing employees to customise their rewards."

How do you see the effect of employee rewards and incentives on employee engagement?

"Rewards do not just reinforce a specific action—they can transform the entire pattern of behaviour. A study from the Zuckerman Institute at Columbia University sheds light on the 'credit assignment problem' in the brain, which explores how rewards reinforce certain sequences of actions.[91] The key takeaway is that it's not just the reward itself that drives behaviour, but the clarity on which action specifically deserves credit within that sequence.

For example, rewarding an employee by saying, 'Great work on that project' is good, but telling them, 'Great work on that project, specifically your exemplary research and analysis' is far more effective. It makes clear which actions earned the reward, encouraging them to repeat those efforts. Dopamine not only signals a reward but also guides us on the behaviours that lead to these rewards, rapidly evolving our behavioural structures.

While continuous reinforcement is effective for learning new behaviours, intermittent reinforcement (where rewards are delivered after some, but not all actions) proves to be stronger in maintaining long-term behaviour. This method fosters habit formation, where the action itself becomes a reward, rather than a task to achieve an external reward."

Have you noticed a shift in the approach to employee incentives and rewards over the past few years?

"Yes, there has been a noticeable shift towards immediate, digital, and personalised rewards, driven by advancements in technology. Many companies are now incorporating wellness and work-life balance perks into their reward systems, recognising that holistic approaches to engagement are becoming more essential. Employees today seek more freedom of choice and instant gratification, expecting personalised rewards that cater specifically to their needs and preferences."

Do the same incentives appeal to both customers and employees?

"Customer loyalty and employee engagement are rooted in the same fundamental principles: recognition and reward. Customers are recognised for their loyalty through

rewards, just as employees are rewarded for their efforts and performance. Both are driven by value.

The effectiveness of any incentive relies on the perceived value it offers. If the reward doesn't resonate with the recipient, whether they are a customer or an employee, the loyalty or engagement generated will be weaker."

In your view, how do compensation and benefits influence employee engagement? If given a choice, do you think employees would prefer cash over other incentives or rewards?

"The preference between cash and non-monetary rewards largely depends on the economic climate and individual circumstances. In times of economic instability or recession, employees tend to prioritise hygiene factors like compensation, cash bonuses, and job security. Cash can be crucial for long-term financial planning or for covering immediate utilitarian needs like groceries or transport.

In contrast, in a flourishing economy, where financial stability is less of a concern, employees are more receptive to non-monetary rewards, such as recognition, growth opportunities, and benefits that go beyond a competitive salary.

Offering a freedom of choice—allowing employees to select the rewards that matter most to them—creates a more engaging rewards ecosystem."

How do you see the future of employee rewards and benefits?

"The future of employee rewards lies in the integration of AI and real-time analytics, offering hyper-personalised and

timely incentives. As technology advances, it provides even greater freedom of choice, allowing employees to customise their rewards. For example, Merit's Points Exchange (PX) platforms enable users to transfer earned points across different loyalty programmes, enhancing personalisation. In addition, sustainability is becoming more important, with companies now offering eco-friendly rewards and incentives for environmentally conscious behaviour.

Technology has become the core medium for engagement and rewards. With smartphones central to our lives—used for everything from making purchases to communicating—engagement must be a mobile-first experience. The integration of mobile wallets for instant reward redemption is a game-changer, enhancing both employee and customer satisfaction."

✋ Case in Point
The Power of Ownership at Nedap

When most companies talk about compensation, the conversation tends to circle around salaries and bonuses. But at Nedap, they've realised something much more powerful: true engagement isn't built with pay checks alone.

Nedap, a technology company founded in 1929 in the Netherlands, specialises in creating innovative solutions across various sectors, including healthcare, security, livestock management, and retail. The company's guiding principle, *"Technology for Life,"* reflects its commitment to developing technology that enhances productivity and success in the workplace. The focus is on meaningful innovation—solutions that make a tangible difference in people's daily lives.

Nedap places a strong emphasis on openness, autonomy, and a strong belief in the potential of its people. With over 1,000 employees, the company fosters a work environment where people are given the freedom to shape their work, fostering a sense of ownership. This environment is designed to cultivate leadership at all levels, where the quality of ideas outweighs hierarchical status.

As Maarten Van Cauwenberghe, Managing Director MEA, puts it, *"The company believes in 'people before technology,' emphasising that understanding and nurturing human potential is key to innovation. At Nedap, we don't tell you what to do or how to work. We trust our people to make the right decisions."* This trust-based approach allows employees to take the lead in their roles, fostering a strong sense of responsibility.

A cornerstone of Nedap's approach to employee development is Nedap University, an internal academy that offers tailored learning opportunities. From its headquarters in Groenlo, NL, the company provides a range of programs that help employees advance their skills and grow within the organisation. This commitment to continuous learning not only benefits individual career development but also drives the company's ability to innovate.

Alongside this, Nedap's Employee Participation foundation, allows employees to own a stake in the company. This initiative gives employees the opportunity to purchase shares, making them direct stakeholders in Nedap's success. By aligning personal and corporate goals, this ownership model fosters deeper engagement and a shared sense of purpose.

Maarten continues, *"We believe that when people feel they truly belong, they don't just work for the company— they work as part of it."* This ownership model serves as an effective form of compensation and strengthens employee motivation and loyalty, driving the company forward with a committed workforce.

Through these initiatives, Nedap demonstrates how a thoughtful approach to Comp & Ben can significantly enhance employee engagement. By empowering employees to take ownership of their roles and the company's future, Nedap is proving that when people truly feel they belong, they can become partners in innovation.

9

Driver 9. Work Environment

"People make buildings, and buildings make humans."

—C. N. Raghavendran, Architect

Your office speaks before you do. If I walked into your company today, what would I hear? Not from the people, but from the space itself. Most companies give little away—just a sterile front desk and a polite smile. But every square metre of your workplace is speaking, whether you're listening or not. And here's the thing: it's telling a story about engagement. The question is: Are you telling the right one?

Are you in the midst of a major transformation? Make it visible! Nothing to be ashamed of. Let your workspace be the canvas that showcases who you are and where you're going. Fill the halls with quotes that inspire, images that reflect your journey, and strategic goals that remind your people of the bigger picture. Your office should say, *"We're not just here to work—we're building something meaningful, and you are part of it."*

A Business Card and a Workplace

Your office is like a business card you can't tuck away. It's always out there for the world to see. Over the years, we've learned how the design and atmosphere of an office can deeply influence both client and staff. Clients notice, employees live in it.

First impressions are powerful. Clients form opinions within seconds of stepping through the door. In marketing, this is known as the *primacy effect*. An aesthetically pleasing building acts as a silent ambassador for your values and professionalism, creating a halo effect where the quality of the space enhances perceptions of your overall services. A sleek, modern environment signals innovation and efficiency, while a disorganised, cluttered one? Well, that tells a different story.

The right environment quietly builds trust and influences everyone who walks through the door, whether they're there for a meeting or for the long haul. Your office shapes the employee experience too, every single day. A well-thought-out space provides psychological comfort, fostering loyalty and commitment.

Strategic Tool for Engagement

If designed with intention, an office environment can drive engagement. Clean, well-organised spaces naturally make people feel good. When employees feel supported, whether through ergonomic setups or flexible workspaces, they're more focused and productive.

Brand alignment is equally crucial. When the office reflects the company's values, it deepens employees' connection to organisational goals. This alignment transforms the physical workspace into a powerful tool for reinforcing engagement.

A global Steelcase study reveals that nearly 90% of workers are dissatisfied with their work environment.[92] The study also shows a direct link between workplace satisfaction and engagement. Employees who have control over their physical space—whether it's choosing between private areas for focus or open spaces for collaboration—report significantly higher levels of engagement. This highlights a huge opportunity: design spaces that empower your employees and engagement will follow.

A well-known approach is *Activity-Based Working* (ABW), a concept pioneered by Dutch consultant Erik Veldhoen in the 1990s. An activity-based way of working goes beyond simply building a great workspace or cutting costs. It's about fostering collaboration, empowerment, leadership visibility, and connection. ABW promotes the mutual relationship between productivity and enjoying one's work. It recognises that different tasks require different environments, and even the same employee may need various spaces throughout the day. This variety encourages both autonomy and engagement.

According to the ABW model, culture, technology, and physical space are inextricably connected. A holistic workplace strategy is built on these three interdependent elements:

- *Bricks*—the built environment
- *Bytes*—digital platforms and virtual space
- *Behaviours*—culture, rituals, and rhythms of work

181

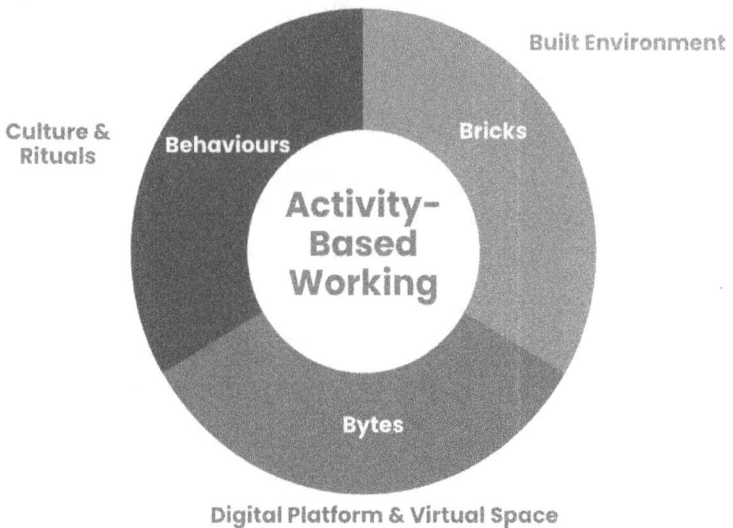

Figure 9. Activity-Based Working

The right balance of these elements varies by workplace. For example, in a hybrid setup, physical space may take a back seat, making a behaviour-first approach essential.

ABW categorises activities into 3 main types:

1. **Individual Work:** tasks that require deep focus
2. **Collaborative Work:** group activities like dialogues, presentations, or brainstorming
3. **Other Activities:** such as relaxation or more technical tasks

Each activity type is best suited to a specific environment or physical space and is best supported by certain behavioural mindsets. Leaders are encouraged to ask, *"What do people, regardless of job title or expertise, need?"* and then trust employees to choose the spaces that support their work.

Achieving this, however, requires a shift in mindset across leadership, teams, and individuals.

So, what do these workspaces look like in practice? According to CBRE, the world's largest commercial real estate services firm, the top priority is **productivity and comfort**, recognising that not all tasks require the same kind of workspace.[93] The goal is to provide a variety of settings that employees can choose from, depending on the nature of their work at any given moment.

Variety of Settings

- *Individual Workspaces & Focus Rooms: Dedicated spaces for solo tasks, ranging from traditional desks to private focus rooms. Some employees prefer quiet, closed-off spaces for deep concentration, while others thrive in shared, busier spaces. Offering a variety of options meets diverse needs.*

- *Collaborative Spaces & Open Lounges: Flexible areas designed for teamwork and informal collaboration, featuring everything from movable furniture in closed rooms to open lounges with comfortable seating. These spaces encourage spontaneous interactions to spark creativity.*

- *Huddle Rooms & Project Rooms: Small, private meeting spaces for quick, ad hoc gatherings or focused group work. These are ideal for project teams needing a dedicated space to discuss ideas.*

- *Café Areas & Open Workspaces: Inspired by coffee shops, these spaces offer casual seating for work or informal meetings over a cup of coffee. By blending social interaction with productivity, they foster stronger working relationships.*

- ***Conference Rooms, Pitch Rooms, & Private Lounges:*** *Formal meeting spaces for board meetings, client pitches, or large-scale collaboration. Equipped with modern technology, these rooms are versatile enough to cater to various needs.*
- ***Quiet Nooks & Phone Booths:*** *Small, soundproof spaces designed for privacy, allowing employees to focus or make calls without distractions, providing a valuable retreat when needed.*

🖐️ Case in Point
Fire Poles, Big Ideas, and Hot-Air Balloon Meetings: Welcome to FHH

Leading companies like Google, Airbnb, or Spotify understand that unconventional workspaces can spark creativity and fuel productivity. By moving away from the traditional office setup, they set the stage for innovation and engagement.

Fine Hygienic Holding (FHH), a distinguished family-owned business founded by Elia Nuqul in 1958, is one such company. As a global leader in wellness and hygiene products, serving over 80 markets worldwide, FHH embraces this philosophy with its dynamic and innovative office designs. With headquarters in both Jordan and Dubai, and a workforce of over 3,000 employees, FHH has created an environment that stimulates creativity, promotes well-being, and fosters a strong sense of belonging.

I had the privilege of visiting their Dubai office in Jebel Ali Free Zone (JAFZA), just a day after CEO James

Michael Lafferty was named one of Forbes Middle East's Top 100 CEOs. And I was struck by the authenticity and vibrancy of their workspace, which beautifully reflects the regional heritage, core values, and dedication to well-being of the employees.

Having visited many impressive offices in the past—complete with all the bells and whistles for employee comfort—I can say that FHH's office stands out for its authenticity. In some places, the cool features feel like mere showpieces, hardly ever used. But at FHH, everything feels like an integral part of their way of life. The entire office isn't just authentic—it's genuinely lived in, a place where you can see the company's culture in action. The office boasts unique elements like a skateboard ramp that spans 40 meters along the length of the building, encouraging a dynamic and engaging work environment. When I asked James how often he uses the fireman's pole connecting the first and ground floors, he casually mentioned, "*at least once per day.*" This wasn't just for show—I visited on a Friday during the school holidays and noticed several children in the office, all of whom greeted James like he was their favourite uncle.

The office includes a well-equipped gym, reflecting James's commitment to health. And when employees need to recharge, they have access to rooms that are used multiple times a day for yoga, meditation, and prayer. It's a practical, no-nonsense approach to well-being that fits seamlessly into the workday. For those up for a challenge, there's even the Fine Push-up and Suitcase Challenge: "*Can you beat the Boss?*"—adding a playful yet competitive element to the office culture.

185

James himself is a dynamic leader with a unique background as a fitness and Olympic coach, which he seamlessly integrates into his leadership style. He actively encourages his team to embrace a healthy lifestyle, offering coaching videos on how to work out, but always with a gentle touch. As he points out, *"It's your life,"* making it clear that while wellness is promoted, it's never imposed or patronising. His dynamic personality and forward-thinking leadership style have clearly left a mark on both the company and its physical environment. During our conversation, I couldn't help but feel inspired by his energy and vision (though I was also reminded that I really should go to the gym more often!).

The office design goes beyond aesthetics, embedding the company's values into the very fabric of the space. The reception area, with its Bedouin tents and modern majlis seating, nods to the company's Jordanian roots, while custom-designed vintage wallpaper featuring the old Fine logo adds a touch of continuity. The Fine Story Wall on the ground floor offers a straightforward, visual timeline of the company's growth from its early days to becoming a recognised leader in the FMCG industry. And while the design of each office mirrors the headquarters, it's far from cookie-cutter. Some offices even swap the fireman's pole for a slide, because why take the stairs?

One standout feature of the Dubai office is the hot-air balloon-themed informal meeting room. This creatively designed space is intended to inspire out-of-the-box thinking and provide a casual, relaxed environment for meetings. The balloon theme adds a whimsical touch, making it a true highlight in their innovation-driven office design.[94] The offices also feature uniquely themed meeting rooms, such as a yellow-themed room with light bulbs on the table to encourage new ideas, and another room with a large vault door and maze graphics to instil a solution-seeking attitude.

It's no surprise that whenever FHH invites a job candidate from leading organisations like P&G to visit the office, it's almost always a win. They see firsthand the vibrant, welcoming, and innovative environment they could be part of. Visiting FHH's office was a chance to see how a company can truly live its values, from top leadership to daily operations. The environment is vibrant and deeply rooted in their culture, but with enough modern twists to keep things interesting. If FHH is anything to go by, the future of work looks pretty bright. And maybe just a little bit more fun.

Rethinking KPIs

Leaders today need to stop counting hours and start counting impact. It's time to shift from merely monitoring presence to actually measuring results. In an era where workspaces are becoming more flexible, clinging to old-school KPIs that track inputs—like hours worked or physical presence—feels increasingly out of touch. Instead, the focus should be on what really matters: **output** and **outcome**.

Output looks at the quality and timeliness of the work delivered. The real question becomes: Are employees hitting deadlines and delivering top-notch work, no matter where they're based? **Outcome**, on the other hand, goes beyond the immediate tasks, focusing on the ripple effect of that work, particularly in terms of customer satisfaction. This focus on outcomes fosters a more engaged workforce, as it reflects the real value employees bring to the table.

A compelling example of this shift is ISS, a key player in facility management, with roughly 9,000 employees. Their services, from cleaning to reception and catering, may not be central to their clients' businesses, but they are critical for keeping everything running smoothly. As ISS looked ahead to the future of work, they realised it was time to rethink the way they aligned their managed services with outcome-based KPIs.

In the old world, companies paid for input. Take cleaning services: a contract might state that 20 meeting rooms need to be cleaned daily, whether they were used or not. With hybrid working and four-day workweeks becoming more common, ISS pivoted to an output-focused approach. Now, rooms are cleaned based on actual usage, boosting efficiency. But ISS took it one step further, zooming in on outcome, asking: *"Were the rooms spotless and fit for use? Was the temperature comfortable? Was the space available when needed?"* In other words, getting involved in the activity-based organisation and ensuring that the entire management of the rooms is optimised. This is what ISS is doing today.

This shift from input to outcome is a game-changer. It transforms how companies interact with their employees and service providers. But it also requires a leap of faith. Trust and autonomy are key, giving employees the freedom to manage their work in a way that prioritises results over rigid processes.

The Power of Space

Engagement is a multifaceted challenge, influenced by countless factors, and the workplace is one that often gets overlooked. Yet the design of your physical space plays a crucial role in shaping how employees feel, behave, and connect with their work.

A well-thought-out workspace goes beyond the pure aesthetics—it's an interconnected ecosystem that empowers employees by giving them the flexibility to choose how and where they work. When employees feel supported by their surroundings, it amplifies their performance, satisfaction, and overall connection to the organisation.

In other words, your workplace can either be a silent ally or a missed opportunity.

Ask the Expert ✍

Nuria Muñoz Arce, founder Habitarmonia

"Biophilic design transforms workspaces into restorative sanctuaries, where nature's essence enhances well-being, productivity, and connection."

Navigating the concrete jungle daily often makes us long for the natural world. Biophilic design serves as a bridge, seamlessly connecting the cityscape with the lush landscapes we instinctively crave. Rooted in the concept of Biophilia, this design philosophy is more than an aesthetic choice. It goes back to practices observed in ancient civilisations and weaves elements like water features and gardens into the very fabric of our buildings, enriching our living spaces with the vitality and diversity of the outdoors.

I spoke with Nuria Muñoz Arce, founder of Habitarmonia, the Spanish company dedicated to integrating biophilic design into personal and professional spaces, focusing on how natural elements can enhance well-being and foster a deeper connection with the environment.

To reduce biophilic design to merely placing a potted plant in the corner is an oversimplification. It's a mindful approach to creating spaces that embrace the essence of nature through specific, intentional biophilic design principles. It encompasses a wider spectrum, like sensory experiences (sounds, smells, textures, sights), spatial patterns (mimicking natural forms in design layout), non-living natural materials (wood, stone, water, bamboo, or even recycled materials), and dynamic processes (changing elements like dynamic lighting).

Several studies confirm that biophilic enriched environments can significantly impact brain activity, reducing stress and burn-out and enhancing cognitive function, leading to higher productivity and a reduction of absenteeism. Moreover, experiments involving biophilic design in learning environments revealed amplified focus and lower stress levels as evidenced by brain imaging results.[95]

These studies have been confirmed by workplace strategist Dr Nigel Oseland. In his book *Beyond the Workplace Zoo*, Dr Oseland advocates for human-centric office design, that considers psychological comfort and facilitate natural human interactions.[96] Elements that are often overlooked in traditional office setups.

Nuria underscores that transforming your workspace is attainable for all budget levels. It doesn't hinge on extravagant spending but on strategically utilising resources. Companies should assess their existing environments for opportunities to make subtle yet impactful enhancements. Simple modifications such as introducing indoor plants, optimising natural light, using natural materials, and enhancing air quality through better ventilation can significantly improve the work atmosphere.

Biophilic working spaces can become restorative environments for employees.[97] Especially when aligned with the specific organisational culture and company values, as emphasized by Nuria. *"Therefore, the (interior) architect should always ensure that the design of the workplace happens in co-creation with employee representatives and cultural ambassadors,"* Nuria states.

More and more companies are looking for holistic, sustainable business practices that nurture both people and the planet. Given the profound impact of well-considered biophilic environments on workplace dynamics, employee satisfaction, and productivity, this design philosophy is very likely to become a strategic component of future workplace design.

10

Driver 10. Flexible Work

"Work is not somehere you go, but something you do."

—Unknown

The New Normal

Prior to 2020, flexible work was a common complaint, though employers were often reluctant. Then, a global crisis compelled a rapid shift, transforming *when, where*, and *how* we work almost overnight. Suddenly, companies had to pivot, adapt, and learn new ways of functioning. While the world didn't ask for this crash course in flexible working, it's hard to argue it wasn't necessary. In fact, it was long overdue.

Flexible work has a profound impact on employee engagement, and it's different from the broader conversation about the workplace and working from home (WFH). Your approach to flexible working can shape your employer brand and determine how you're perceived. What kind of company do you want to be? Remote-first? A hub for collaboration and in-person interaction? Or a bit of both?

Whatever your choice, be clear in communicating it, because your stance on flexibility is a major draw for today's talent, particularly younger generations. Many of Gen Z began their professional careers during the pandemic. Foosball tables and pizza Fridays aren't going to get this generation into a cubicle now. They're prioritising the balance between work and personal life from the start and are comfortable setting boundaries. For them, flexible work isn't a perk—it's a given. In today's job market, flexibility has shifted from being a *nice-to-have* to a *non-negotiable*.

But where does flexible work stand now? And how can we make hybrid working *actually* work, avoiding the pitfalls of disengagement? What role does leadership play in this?

Let's revisit the Gallup report on the *State of the Global Workplace*. We learned that only 23% of employees are engaged at work. But if you dig deeper, the numbers tell an interesting story. Employees who work remotely up to 20% of the time are the most engaged. It seems this balance—collaborating in the office while enjoying the privacy of working solo—hits the sweet spot.

A survey by Owl Labs in early 2024 highlighted that **16% of employees** globally are fully remote, while a staggering 62% are working in a hybrid setup.[98] Only **22%** remain in the office full-time. The stats speak for themselves: there's a **clear preference for hybrid working**.

We're only human after all. Different employees have different needs. New hires, recent graduates, and those who thrive on social interaction may need more face-to-face time for guidance and mentorship. Similarly, some employees struggle with time management, and the discipline of a physical office can help them stay on track.

The Future Is Flexible

At the beginning of 2020, the buzzword of the moment became *hybrid*. Some boldly declared the death of the office, while others demanded a full return to in-person work. Yet these polarised views fail to capture the diversity of workstyles and organisational cultures.

In *Beyond Hybrid Working*, Andy Lake presents a more nuanced vision of flexibility, arguing that flexible working isn't just about remote work; it's a spectrum of possibilities.[99] Lake identifies several forms, from flexible working to agile working, smart working, and hybrid working. Flexible working is actually an umbrella term, and in many countries, there is a legal right to request it. This right may apply to flexible working hours, remote work, or a combination. Companies have even coined their own terminologies: *"The Way We Work"* and *"WorkWise,"* for instance, to describe their approaches.

Lake advocates for Smarter Working, where flexibility becomes the default, without requiring formal requests. *"Smart Working is about transformation—actively pursuing benefits by working in smarter ways, rather than being driven by individual employee choices. Ideally, it provides a framework in which individuals and teams can make choices about the most appropriate times and places for work, while balancing individual preferences wherever possible."*

While Activity-Based Working is often applied within buildings, Lake extends the concept of ***Smart Working*** beyond the office. Advances in technology have made it easier than ever to work from anywhere. Success, however, hinges on a strategic, company-wide approach. An interdisciplinary team, involving HR, IT, Property, and Finance, should lead the way.

Smart Working boosts productivity—provided a strategic and comprehensive approach is adopted. It's less likely to succeed if employees merely continue doing the same work in different settings. A key point is that more people can work flexibly than is often assumed. Therefore, it's crucial to understand that it's less about roles and more about tasks. And work with teams to assess how time- and location-specific their tasks are.

To embed a Smart Working culture, Lake suggests starting with the *CAN Test*: *Challenge the Assumption of Necessity*. It questions the *where*, *when*, *why*, and *how* of performing tasks. He provides numerous examples of this, such as the assumption that face-to-face must mean physical presence, and that this always leads to better outcomes. He also explores the obstacles to implementing Smart Working, including changing systems, providing training for both staff and managers, and developing new ways of thinking.

✋ Case in Point

Marriott: Rethinking Flexibility in an In-Person World

Not all industries lend themselves to remote work, yet the demand for flexibility is universal. One company that has successfully navigated this challenge is the global hotel chain Marriott, where adaptability has taken on a different meaning in a predominantly in-person industry.

Ty Breland, Chief Human Resources Officer, sheds light on how the company navigated shifting expectations during and after the pandemic, especially regarding flexibility.[100] While Marriott operates in an industry where many roles, like housekeeping and front-desk services, are firmly tied to physical presence, Marriott employees began questioning: how could flexibility apply to roles?

Breland stresses that, while remote work isn't feasible for many hotel-based positions, the company has prioritised intraday flexibility, allowing employees to manage their shifts around personal needs. Whether it's adjusting schedules for medical appointments or school pick-ups, this approach empowers employees to feel more in control of their time. A small shift with a big impact, showing that flexibility is about adapting work to fit life.

To extend this, Marriott introduced a blend of full-time and part-time positions, catering to specific needs, such as parents looking for shorter hours during school times. This strategy has not only strengthened employee loyalty but also boosted performance, including cleanliness and guest satisfaction.

Another innovative move was launching the "*iJobs*" programme, where employees rotate between different tasks throughout the day, adding variety and keeping work fresh.

The result? Higher levels of engagement across the board. Marriott's experience demonstrates that flexibility isn't solely about working from home but about empowering employees to have greater control over their schedules and responsibilities in a way that benefits both them and the business.

It's the Manager

Hybrid work assumes strong team cohesion. In my view, corporate policies on flexible work must leave room for teams to decide how to organise themselves internally.

Enter the middle manager, the unsung hero of the hybrid workplace. I apologise for not giving them the attention they deserve until now because they're instrumental in attracting and retaining talent. Far more than their higher-ups or HR, they have the power to craft individualised working arrangements that suit their teams.

Hybrid leadership is a skill—and it doesn't always come naturally, not for executives or managers.[101] Team leaders and managers must be trained to become coaches, adapting their leadership style to fit the hybrid context.[102] This will help them understand what works best for each team member, determine the optimal ways and timings for collaboration, ensure accountability within the team, and help everyone become the best version of themselves.

*So, the question is: "**Are your managers ready to lead in a flexible world?**"* Because the future of work isn't just hybrid —it's human.

Organisational Health Lessons from Remote-First Companies

High performance in a hybrid environment doesn't just happen by chance; it's built on a foundation of clear values, transparent decision-making, and deliberate work practices. According to McKinsey, hybrid work can be a healthy model— if done right.[103]

Striking the perfect balance between flexibility and performance isn't always easy. But there are seasoned pros in this game who have been doing it for years. Remote-first companies—those that embraced full-time remote work long before it became a necessity—offer invaluable insights on making flexibility work while staying focused on the big picture.

So, what can we learn from these highly distributed organisations? Even before the pandemic, remote-first organisations were miles ahead in operational discipline, which helped them foster high performance. These companies, often ranked in the top quartile of McKinsey's *Organisational Health Index*, prove that outstanding organisational health isn't limited to traditional, in-person setups. In fact, the largest and most mature remote-first companies consistently score in the top decile, surpassing more traditional setups.

What sets them apart? They excel in work environment and motivation, with leadership playing a critical role in their success through consultative and supportive practices. Operationally, these companies are experts at removing ambiguity. They don't rely on guesswork: clear expectations, consistent meeting protocols, and asynchronous work practices allow seamless collaboration across time zones.

In other words, this operational discipline ensures that everyone knows what's expected, how to get it done, and how their efforts tie into the company's broader goals. Clarity, like a strong Wi-Fi signal, is the key to making remote work run smoothly.

6 Priorities for Hybrid Organisations

For companies looking to replicate this success in a hybrid model, McKinsey offers six priorities for sustaining a flexible workplace while maintaining top-tier organisational health.

1. **Remove Ambiguity:** *Establish clear working practices, role definitions and meeting protocols, embracing asynchronous work wherever possible.*

2. **Reset Performance Expectations:** *Ensure fairness between on-site and remote employees by creating clear, standardised performance goals, so no one feels disadvantaged.*

3. **Be Transparent:** *Develop a single source of truth (like a handbook) that outlines rules and norms, fostering consistency across the organisation.*

4. **Intentional Work Locations:** *Help employees understand when and why they need to be onsite, fostering collaboration for key moments while being equally intentional with remote work.*

5. **Foster Trust and Support:** *Create a work environment grounded in inclusion, belonging, and trust, with visible, supportive leadership.*

6. **Test and Learn:** *Regularly assess what works, make data-driven decisions, and foster a culture that sees failure as an opportunity for growth.*

The success of fully remote organisations offers a blueprint for hybrid companies. By embedding these six practices, hybrid organisations can foster collaboration, drive performance, and enhance their organisational health. That's how hybrid work becomes less of a balancing act and more of a well-oiled machine.

Ask the Expert ✍

Andreas Creten, Founder at madewithlove

"Hybrid work requires more discipline."

While remote work has become a necessity for many, we've had years to fine-tune how we operate, and believe me, it's not all pyjamas and video calls. Being a remote-first company has been part of our DNA from the very start. We didn't stumble into this; we designed it that way. Our team, made up of software engineers scattered across the globe, is built on the principle that geography doesn't matter—talent does.

One of the first things we learnt, often the hard way, is that communication is king. Poor communicators struggle in remote settings. To thrive remotely, you must make your work visible to your colleagues. Those who master this skill will reach a whole new level of effectiveness.

You also need to adapt your communication style, shifting from synchronous (real-time) interactions to asynchronous ones. Your colleague won't be able to glance over your shoulder, so it's essential to document progress and decisions using the right tools. By filtering out instant communication, we allow for greater focus and deeper work. Since you're not asking questions in real time, you're forced to think more carefully about how to articulate your queries. And often, that clarity reveals a different angle, sometimes eliminating the need to ask the question at all. The result is fewer interruptions during the workday, allowing for sustained, deeper focus. This, in turn, leads to improved productivity across the board.

Let's talk about meetings for a second. We've all experienced how draining it can be to sit through virtual meeting marathons all day. In the remote world, meetings can feel flat, lack depth, and drain energy fast. That's why we have strict meeting hygiene: start with a clear agenda, stick to the time, and end with concrete action points. It's all about making every minute count. These are practices that should apply to in-person meetings as well. Jeff Bezos, CEO of Amazon, takes this to an extreme: each meeting begins with silent reading time for the preparation, followed by a memo outlining the decisions that need to be made. No PowerPoints allowed.

For ideation, the creative process of shaping ideas and solutions, we handle things differently. If you've ever tried to recreate the magic of a whiteboard brainstorming session over Zoom, you know it's not quite the same. So, we flipped the process. I ask everyone to come fully prepared with ideas already thought through. We start by having each person present their solution—this way, even the quieter voices get heard. After everyone's had their say, we debate and decide. It's simple and effective: meetings are for decisions, not discussions.

Remote work also demands more rigorous processes. At madewithlove, we had to nail down clear guidelines for everything from working hours to running personal errands. It might sound like overkill. But without these frameworks, you end up with chaos. Crystal clear processes let us switch smoothly between office and home. No confusion, just work.

Years ago, we discovered some remote work wisdom in *Remote: Office Not Required* by Jason Fried and David Heinemeier Hansson. It quickly became our go-to guide for making distributed teams click—both for our employees and, let's not forget, our clients. The book gave us a blueprint for seamless collaboration across time zones, and we've never looked back.

So, whether you're thinking of going fully remote or embracing a hybrid model, do yourself a favour and crack open some literature on the subject. Trust me, your future self (and team) will thank you.

11

Driver 11. CSR

> *"Economic growth must go hand in hand with social responsibility."*
>
> —*Sheikh Khalifa bin Zayed Al Nahyan,*
> *Former president of the UAE*

Do Well by Doing Good

We all share a bit of a soft spot for the idea of making the world a better place. People love being part of something bigger than themselves. It gives meaning to their day-to-day grind, knowing they're contributing to something more lasting, more significant. This taps into the same motivation we saw with our first engagement driver—organisational purpose. And when we zoom in on *Corporate Social Responsibility* (CSR), that sense of purpose gets supercharged. Employees who feel they're not just benefiting the company, but society at large are more motivated, loyal, and productive. I often call CSR the jewel in the engagement crown.

The United Nations defines CSR as a *"management concept whereby companies integrate social and environmental concerns in their business operations and interactions with their stakeholders*." Put simply, it's about finding a balance between making money and doing good for the planet and people.

CSR isn't a shiny new concept. The roots go way back to the 1950s when economists like Howard Bowen and William Frederick first raised eyebrows by suggesting businesses had social responsibilities. This came in response to moral questions arising from the professionalisation of management and the emergence of giant corporations.

Fast forward to the 2000s, and CSR became more mainstream. There has been an increasing focus on corporate sustainability and reporting. Today, 90% of the world's largest companies publish CSR reports: a far cry from the 30% that bothered in the late 2000s.

A common question is the difference between **CSR** and **ESG** (Environmental, Social, and Governance), the framework that's fast becoming the darling of investors. While CSR may serve as an internal framework, ESG gives investors a way to measure sustainability and hold companies accountable. Experts even say ESG is edging out CSR as the go-to measure of sustainability in the corporate world.[104]

Still, CSR isn't about picking favourites. The truth is, when companies get CSR right, everybody wins. The business makes a positive impact, and employees feel engaged, motivated, and proud to work there.

CSR 2.0

CSR (or ESG—if you prefer) has been on the agenda for decades. But let's be honest: results have been a mixed bag. Dr Wayne Visser, in *The Age of Responsibility*, describes the different stages companies have gone through (or are going through) to reconcile doing good and doing well.[104] He charts the evolution of CSR over the last century, from defensive approaches to charity, to a marketing-oriented CSR and finally strategic forms of CSR. In this latter stage, CSR policies are linked to the company's core business.

What is needed, says Visser, is **CSR 2.0**. That's where sustainability is embedded into a company's very DNA. It's about overhauling processes, products, and business models to be radically sustainable. This next-generation approach hinges on five key principles: **creativity, scalability, responsiveness, glocality** (think global strategies with local adaptation), and **circularity**. If businesses don't evolve in this way, Visser warns, we won't succeed in tackling the pressing climate, social, and ethical crises we face.

And here's where HR can really shine. When CSR is tightly interwoven with employee engagement, it becomes a potent tool for motivation and connection. Once business leaders have their *Aha* moment, they start to see how CSR can cross-pollinate with engagement, fuelling even more enthusiasm.

🖐Case in Point
DHL's Commitment to Sustainability

A strong example of commitment to sustainability comes from global logistics and courier company DHL Global Forwarding. DHL has committed to ambitious environmental goals, including achieving zero emissions by 2050. And it's not just about fulfilling corporate responsibility; it's a strategic imperative that aligns with global trends and is embedded in DHL's operations, ensuring that the company remains at the forefront of the logistics industry while also playing a significant role in addressing global environmental challenges.

DHL's commitment in the UAE to making a positive impact goes beyond environmental goals. DHL transcends standard corporate social responsibility by organising *"Kindness Week,"* a special initiative dedicated to supporting refugees and people with disabilities. This initiative was started by CEO DHL Global Forwarding for the MEA region, Amadou Diallo. The DHL's team works with an organisation called *"Enable,"* which empowers people who are differently enabled, often referred to as *"People of Determination"* in the UAE.

During this week, DHL employees engage in activities that not only provide aid but also foster a culture of kindness and inclusivity within the organisation, reflecting DHL's ambition to play its role as a socially responsible leader.

The Jewel in the Crown

So what's the secret sauce that makes CSR more than just a buzzword? It's the real, transformative effect it has on employees. A study by Dr Shachi Yadav's shows that CSR can reshape the employee experience in three powerful ways:[104]

1. **Enhancing Interpersonal Skills:** CSR initiatives, whether community outreach or sustainability projects, actively improve interpersonal dynamics within the organisation. They help employees develop empathy, leadership, and problem-solving skills. These are the very qualities that improve teamwork and innovation.

Younger generations, in particular, thrive when their work connects to broader societal goals. In this sense, CSR becomes a non-traditional yet highly effective form of professional development.

2. **CSR as a Training Tool:** Surprisingly, CSR can be a more powerful training tool than formal courses. Instead of training rooms and seminars, CSR initiatives provide hands-on experience in real-world problem-solving. Employees are forced to think on their feet, develop leadership skills, and communicate effectively.

3. **CSR as a Driver of Organisational Performance:** Here's where CSR flexes its muscles—it drives organisational performance. Companies with strong CSR programmes retain more talent, boost creativity, and see improvements in problem-solving and productivity. Why? Because employees are more engaged when they feel part of something that matters. A socially responsible company inspires its people to go the extra mile—for the business AND for the greater good.

The Critical Link

An intriguing finding from Dr Yadav's study is the subtle yet notable gender differences in CSR participation. The data shows that women tend to engage more in CSR activities than men. This raises the question of how organisations can tailor initiatives to appeal across the board.

One thing is certain: communication is key. Employees can't engage with CSR if they don't know it exists! Organisations that communicate their CSR efforts clearly and transparently via different channels see much higher levels of participation. But it's more than broadcasting—it's creating a two-way conversation, giving employees a voice and allowing them to feel ownership over the initiatives. When people see the tangible impact of their work, their engagement skyrockets.

To make CSR more effective, it's essential to align initiatives with local causes that resonate with the employees' lives and involve them in decision-making. Finally, recognition for these efforts and clear communication about their impact also play a critical role in sustaining their participation and enthusiasm.

🖐 Case in Point

Fuelling Sustainability: Dubai Airports' Next Steps

When Sven Deckers, Director of Sustainability, Innovation & Partnerships at Dubai Airports, gets up in the morning, he feels incredibly fortunate. He's thankful for his loving family, his beautiful home, and the joyful energy of Emma, his ever-enthusiastic dog. And while his mornings often begin with Emma tugging at his feet, Sven's mind is already turning to the dynamic challenges of his role at Dubai Airports.

Over the past decade, Sven has been deeply involved in the corporate strategy of the largest international airport in the world. More recently, he started focusing on initiatives ranging from AI innovation to sustainability.

When he talks about the airport's forward-thinking projects—especially in CSR—there's a certain spark in his eye. His focus is more than working on strategic projects for airport. It's about contributing to a legacy that connects people and drives global progress.

At Dubai Airports, the challenges are as vast as its operations. With 1,800 direct employees, an additional 3,000 outsourced workers, and an ecosystem of roughly 100,000 people—ranging from suppliers to emergency services—the scale is massive. Ensuring consistent service quality across such a broad network is no easy feat. Sustainability, employee, and stakeholder engagement are deeply intertwined with these operational hurdles, making the task of balancing efficiency and responsibility a central focus.

To address one of the most pressing issues, service consistency, the international airport launched *"oneDXB."* Through oneDXB, the airport community ensures a unified service experience for passengers, no matter who is providing the service. Whether they're helped by a Dubai Airport employee or someone from any other airport partner, the aim is the same: consistent, high-quality service for all. In an airport as vast as Dubai's, where a significant portion of interactions come from outsourced staff, this initiative is a game changer.

Dubai Airports also face a unique challenge with their diverse passenger base, many of whom are first-time travellers. In fact, between 5% and 10% of all passengers are flying internationally for the first time, which means many are unfamiliar with processes and may even struggle with language barriers. As the middle class in Asia continues to grow, Dubai is increasingly becoming the first stop on many international journeys. The Dubai Airports team knows that for these passengers, a smooth, welcoming experience is key, and they work tirelessly to ensure that every traveller feels supported.

But the passengers aren't the only ones requiring attention. Employee engagement continues to be a key priority, especially with an impressive average employee tenure of more than 10 years. This kind of job stability points to high levels of satisfaction and work-life balance. Employees are proud of their association with Dubai Airports, and there are strategies in place to ensure that employees continue to remain actively engaged in shaping the airport's future. The Dubai Airports team encourages employees to permanently move from passive pride to active engagement, pushing them to take ownership of the airport's evolving mission.

Sustainability is another major focus for Sven and his colleagues. Similar to the service challenge, sustainability is an effort that can only be effectively addressed when approached as an ecosystem. To this end, they recently launched the **oneDXB Sustainability Alliance**—a community of key airport partners with the highest carbon footprint—committed to decarbonising DXB.

This is a next-level challenge since aviation, as an industry, is something of a paradox. It's vital for global connectivity and economic growth, yet it also leaves a significant environmental footprint. The challenge is to find the right balance: reducing the industry's environmental impact while amplifying its positive contributions to the world. DXB is leading the charge, exploring innovative ways to reduce aviation's environmental toll.

One of the most exciting developments on the horizon is the use of *Sustainable Aviation Fuel* (SAF). The UAE is perfectly positioned to advance this cutting-edge technology, thanks to its abundant solar energy and lower production costs. Power-to-liquid fuel, created by combining solar energy, desalinated water, and captured carbon, offers a sustainable alternative to traditional jet fuel.

While electric and hydrogen-powered planes are on the horizon, both options still face significant technological and infrastructure challenges. In the meantime, power-to-liquid fuels could present a viable solution in the future, offering significant emissions reductions with minimal changes to existing aircrafts. This pragmatic approach underpins Dubai Airports' sustainability initiatives—not only focusing on what can be done now through the on-the-ground decarbonisation project, but also by being very vocal about the need to drive technological breakthroughs.

The CSR team's commitment to sustainability extends beyond Dubai's borders. Acknowledging that collaboration with global airport communities and research institutions is crucial, even for the world's largest international airport, Dubai Airports proudly champion the World Economic Forum's Airports of Tomorrow initiative, along with other partnerships.

Instead of making sweeping declarations about long-term net-zero targets, the strategy of Dubai Airports is more grounded. They believe in setting realistic, achievable goals, while focusing on internal targets and strong partnerships with the regulators, treating them as allies in the pursuit of sustainability rather than mere enforcers.

The *Dubai Climate Change Initiative* is central to these efforts, encouraging regulatory collaboration and knowledge-sharing across the industry. By aligning with

211

airports in global cities like London, Amsterdam, and San Francisco, DXB is not only learning from the best but also contributing to international sustainability efforts. Dubai Airports prioritise transparency, avoiding the temptation to make grandiose claims and instead working diligently towards actionable, measurable progress.

For Sven, leadership is about sparking collective inspiration, locally and globally. Together with other departments, his team helps encourage to understand their role in decarbonising aviation and supporting the UAE's broader goals of growth and sustainability.

The road ahead is ambitious but grounded in practical solutions, and everyone—employees, partners, and stakeholders—is part of this shared vision.

When Sven finally heads home, greeted by Emma's wagging tail and the warmth of his family, he knows that his work is contributing to something far bigger than the day-to-day running of an airport. He's helping shape the future of aviation, and it's that sense of purpose that keeps him motivated—ready for the challenges and opportunities that lie ahead. His three young daughters Valentina, Emilia, and Isabela, will be among those who will judge his success in the coming decades.

12

Driver 12. DEIB

"Diversity is inviting new people to the party. Inclusion is asking them to dance."

—*V. Slavich*

When we look at the world's working population, the sheer wealth and depth of diverse talent are striking. Even though this sounds like a promising opportunity, this diversity also brings its own challenges. Diversity can boost engagement or, at times, undermine it.

I saved this one for last, not only because it's my favourite but because I view it as the turbo engine of employee engagement. It's the new kid on the block, which also means that, at the same time, it's the least mature one.

Doesn't this present a tremendous opportunity in today's global workspace? I often say that Diversity, Equity, Inclusion, Belonging (or DEIB) is currently where the other driver of engagement, CSR, was a decade ago. Sustainability has evolved into a strategic pillar in policy-making. And DEIB is heading very fast in the same direction.

"We don't hire Turks, Greeks, Poles, Indians, Ethiopians, Vietnamese, Chinese or Peruvians. Nor Swedes, South Koreans, or Norwegians. We hire individuals. We don't care what your surname is. Because ambition and determination have nothing to do with your nationality. McDonald's is one of the most integrated companies in Sweden, with as many as ninety-five nationalities working for us.
Join us at mcdonalds.se."

—*McDonald's Sweden's recruitment campaign*

From Diversity, Equity, and Inclusion to Belonging

While diversity, equity, inclusion, and belonging are often mentioned together, the distinction between them isn't always clear. Let's break down the differences.

Diversity refers to the many traits that differentiate people from each other. These characteristics aren't just gender or ethnicity, but also age, physical ability, race, religion, sexual orientation, socioeconomic status (income, education, and occupation), neurodiversity, personality types, etc. An organisational culture that nurtures diversity places importance on what makes each of its people unique. **Equity** (not to be confused with Equality)[105] is about ensuring fair access, treatment, opportunity, and advancement for all individuals. This involves identifying and eliminating barriers that have prevented the full participation of certain groups. **Inclusion** involves creating an environment where all individuals feel respected, heard, and empowered to contribute. It's cultivating a culture that encourages people to bring their

214

authentic selves to work. **Belonging** is the icing on the cake, fostering the emotional and psychological safety that helps people feel connected, valued, and genuinely part of the organisation. That last "B," belonging, is what completes DEI.

Challenging the Norm

People often perceive their experiences and perspectives as the norm. The *social identity theory*, developed by Henri Tajfel, explains that individuals categorise themselves into groups based on shared traits such as race or gender, which leads to an in-group bias.[106]

This bias makes people unconsciously favour their group and assume their behaviours, values, and experiences are the default. This can marginalise those outside the dominant group, reducing opportunities for inclusion and belonging.

As humans, we don't have the ability to recognise when we're biased—even if we see it in others. We believe ourselves to be fair and open-minded, but we're overestimating ourselves.

The *false consensus* effect is another cognitive bias where people overestimate the extent to which others share their beliefs and behaviours. In the workplace, this effect reinforces the notion that the majority's perspective is the standard, often sidelining underrepresented voices. People assume that their experiences are universally applicable, making it harder to recognise the need for more inclusive practices that address the diverse needs of all employees.

A study titled *The Weirdest People in the World* by Henrich et al. further explores this issue by examining how *Western, Educated, Industrialized, Rich, and Democratic (WEIRD)* populations often consider themselves representative of all human experiences.[107] The generalisation of *WEIRD* perspectives as universal parallels what can occur in corporate environments, where the dominant group's values may be regarded as the default, overlooking the experiences of marginalised groups. "*Cultural normativity*" in leadership is also quite common. It occurs when individuals from dominant groups perceive their leadership style, communication methods, or career paths as the standard or default.

These phenomena can hinder the understanding and appreciation of diverse perspectives, leading to unconscious bias. Recognising these unconscious biases is critical to creating environments where all employees feel valued and included.

DEIB initiatives are crucial to breaking these assumptions and fostering environments where diverse perspectives are recognised and valued equally.

✋Case in Point
Korn Ferry's INCLUDE Framework

I find the **INCLUDE** framework from Korn Ferry a practical guide to help organisations reduce unconscious bias and build an inclusive culture.

INCLUDE provides a language for what people can do at work to practice conscious inclusion:

Impact: Build awareness of how your biases drive your behaviour and can impact others, regardless of your intent.

Notice: Notice your reactions in moments that matter and ask yourself why you're thinking and feeling that way.

Communicate: Share your commitment in words and actions. Invite unconventional ideas and encourage others to do so.

Leverage: Demonstrate appreciation for different perspectives and look for ways to leverage them to achieve business results.

Uncover: Share more of who you are and encourage others to do the same, to build rapport and trust.

Disrupt: Pause before making decisions or taking actions that impact people, to disrupt ineffective biases.

Empathise: Understand and acknowledge the feelings and experiences of others, even if you don't agree with them.

The aspects Impact and Notice describe inward-focused aspects of driving inclusion. By practicing these skills, people will build more self-awareness. The other aspects of INCLUDE are outward-focused. They're the visible behaviours that we can demonstrate when we're acting inclusively.[108]

Making DEIB a Reality

DEIB and Organisational Performance: The Numbers

- *Corporations identified as more diverse and inclusive are 35% more likely to outperform their competitors (McKinsey).[109]*
- *Diverse companies are 70% more likely to capture new markets (Harvard Business Review).[110]*
- *Diverse teams are 87% better at making decisions (People Management).[111]*

- *Diverse management teams lead to 19% higher revenue (Boston Consulting Group).[112]*
- *Inclusive companies get 2.3 times more cash flow per employee and are 1.7 times more likely to be innovative (Josh Bersin).[113]*

As of 2023, approximately 12% of corporations have a dedicated DEIB team or leader, although many have incorporated DEIB functions into broader HR or operational roles. For instance, while 60% of organisations claim to have a DEIB strategy, fewer have fully operationalised these efforts with distinct teams.

The focus on DEIB clearly isn't a box on a to-do list to check! It's central to helping organisations achieve better business outcomes. The challenge lies in moving beyond DEIB as a corporate value to an organisational priority and strategy instead. That's when it can become a superpower.

Diversity and Employer Branding

- *Around 63% of employees across all generations say they prioritise DEIB programmes when it comes to choosing which company to work for, while 73% of Gen Z and 68% of Millennial respondents said the same (EY).[114]*
- *Two out of three job candidates seek companies that have diverse workforces (Glassdoor).[115]*
- *About 78% of employees who responded to a Harvard Business Review study said they work at organisations that lack diversity in leadership positions (Harvard Business Review).[116]*

While challenging, creating genuinely more inclusive organisations is something companies can actually do. Moreover, organisations that want everyone to feel included cannot rely on the combination of lofty aspirations, sincere intentions, and the right messaging. Real, sustainable change comes from doing. Making a more inclusive organisation is about both employees and leaders throughout the organisation adopting new mindsets, changing behaviours, and learning to operate in and adapt to new and different systems. Testing, learning, and practice are key to making this happen.

Diversity doesn't automatically lead to better performance. It depends on the right leadership, team dynamics, and a strategic approach. Research points out that heterogeneous teams only outperform homogeneous ones when they are led by managers who fully understand how to leverage the diversity within the team.[117] This underscores the critical importance of good leadership in unlocking the positive effects of diversity. A survey by Workday echoes this, noting that leadership and commitment from the top (38%) are cited as the prime need for moving to the next stage in relation to DEIB. Additionally, 83% of respondents believe that diverse leadership is vital for successfully implementing DEIB initiatives.[118]

We're seeing more and more evidence that the more diverse the organisation, the more chance that your people are engaged.

"The strength of our nation lies in the diversity of its people."

—*King Abdullah II (Jordan)*

✋ Case in Point

The Pillar of Respect in DHL's DEIB Strategy

As a vast and global organisation, DHL and its various divisions have long been committed to creating an inclusive workplace where everyone acts as one, regardless of geographic location. The logistics division of the group, DHL Global Forwarding, exemplifies this concept.

I had an inspiring conversation with the CEO of the MEA region, **Amadou Diallo**. He highlighted the company's *Respect* programme, which enforces a zero-tolerance policy on disrespect. A Senegalese native with extensive experience in Europe, Diallo has become an influential leader in the region and a living example of how diversity leads to success.

"Diversity is what makes us sparkle," he remarked, emphasising the strength that comes from such a varied workforce. In the MEA region, where the *war on talent* brings together people from all over the world, from Peru to India, DHL's Respect programme is proof of its commitment to fostering a respectful and inclusive work environment.

This principle is not just a guideline, but a fundamental law within DHL Global Forwarding, extending to the Supplier Code of Conduct and even customer interactions. *"The company may tolerate a miss on results or excellence, but any breach of respect is non-negotiable."* This unwavering stance has led to tough decisions, including the closure of operations in certain countries, even Diallo's home country, where this core principle wasn't upheld.

Whenever I feel the need to brainstorm on DEIB, I reach out to my friend Sama Sellami, a DEIB expert with a PhD in Social Economic Sciences who advises numerous organisations in Europe.

Ask the Expert ✍

Dr Sana Sellami—Inclusion Strategist

"While DEIB is increasingly recognised as essential, turning that recognition into sustained, meaningful progress requires a more integrated, strategic approach."

DEIB remains a top priority for organisations worldwide, even amid economic challenges.[119] The Workday study reveals that 78% of organisations have increased their focus on DEIB over the past year, with 85% allocating specific budgets to these initiatives. These numbers underscore that companies recognise DEIB as a critical component of their strategy for driving success.

The Challenge: Moving Beyond Good Intentions

However, the tangible impact on the workplace lags behind. This gap exists because many companies grapple with *action anxiety*—the hesitation or inability to integrate DEIB into their core activities in a strategic, meaningful way. This anxiety, often fuelled by a lack of knowledge, courage, and vision leads to "piecemeal actions." Fragmented efforts, though well-intentioned, often fail to drive lasting change. To turn global DEIB recognition into sustained, meaningful progress, we need a more integrated and strategic approach.

Diverse, inclusive teams have the potential to be more creative and innovative—if that diversity is properly harnessed. An academic review by Roberson et al. confirms that organisations that are truly diverse in terms of knowledge are more creative.[120] This is because diversity fosters different ways of thinking.[121]

A key theoretical framework relevant to DEIB is Allport's *contact theory*, stating that positive contact between people from different ethnic backgrounds can reduce prejudice.[122] These findings, supported by other academic research,[123] suggest that when companies actively promote diversity and facilitate positive interactions between different groups, it can lead to a more inclusive, less-biased work environment.

Patrick Lencioni's theory on team dynamics provides an important complement to the contact theory. Lencioni argues that a strong team is characterised by trust, constructive conflict, commitment, accountability, and a results-oriented mindset. In the context of DEIB, this means that diversity in a team only leads to higher engagement if there is a culture of trust and inclusion. Without trust, team members may not feel free to express their opinions, undermining their engagement and, ultimately, the team's performance. This underscores that DEIB should go beyond merely increasing diversity numbers; it should centre on creating an environment where trust and respect are the norms.

The Integration Challenge

The greatest hurdle to harnessing the power of DEIB is the failure to fully embed it within organisational operations. There's often a lack of strategic vision and leadership, leading to superficial initiatives. The Workforce report notes, "One of the current challenges is that over half of respondents say the makeup of their existing leadership teams is harming DEIB efforts." This lack of diversity in leadership can lead to bias and flawed decision-making, which impacts the effectiveness of DEIB initiatives and inhibits the creative potential that a diverse group could bring.

Where and How Do We Start?

To successfully integrate and leverage DEIB as a driver of employee engagement, organisations need to look beyond superficial initiatives and focus on strategic, long-term goals. Here are 4 tips to get started:

1. **Develop an Integrated DEIB Strategy:** DEIB should be seen as an integral part of the business strategy, not just a series of separate initiatives. When shaping an inclusive work culture, we start with the foundation: policy. This includes the written commitment to DEIB, forming the basis of the organisation's values and mission. This policy acts as the first point of contact for employees, setting the tone for what is expected and accepted within the organisation. It involves setting clear goals and implementing policies aimed at creating an inclusive culture.

2. **Focus on Inclusive Leadership and Strengthen Team Dynamics:** The call for leaders who not only recognise the value of this diversity but also embrace and utilise it, is growing louder than ever. The time has come to see inclusive leadership as the standard, not a goal. It involves leaders who are proactive, using their influence to promote inclusion, break biases, and cultivate an atmosphere of openness and respect. Effective leaders act as role models, provide space

for diverse voices, foster a culture of psychological safety, commit to continuous education, actively pursue equity, and work towards long-term changes. Teams under inclusive leadership excel in innovation, thanks to a wealth of perspectives and experiences. Therefore, invest in leadership that can fully harness the diversity within teams and use Lencioni's principles to build strong, cohesive teams where trust and inclusion are central.

3. **Prioritise DEIB Skills Development:** DEIB skills aren't innate; they're developed through conscious effort, training, and experience. It's essential that employees learn about the experiences, contributions, and challenges faced by diverse groups, as well as develop cultural competence. The ability to communicate and interact respectfully with people from various backgrounds is fundamental to building empathy and appreciation for differences. A purposeful DEIB training programme equips employees with knowledge and inspires action, fostering a deeper appreciation for all cultural nuances.

4. **Monitor and Evaluate Continuously:** A crucial yet often overlooked step. It is essential to regularly measure progress and adjust the DEI strategy as necessary. This means setting KPIs for DEI and regularly conducting surveys to measure engagement and inclusion.

Conclusion: DEIB offers enormous potential for increasing employee engagement, but this potential is only realised when DEIB is strategically and deeply rooted in the organisation. Research shows that diversity does not automatically lead to better performance. It depends on the right leadership, team dynamics, and a strategic approach. Companies must go beyond superficial initiatives and work towards creating a culture where trust, cohesion, and inclusion are the norm. Only then can they reap the benefits of a diverse and engaged workplace, ultimately leading to more success.

The Fabric of Inclusion

"We're not asking you to fit in; we're asking you to be you."

—*Tara Ataya, Chief People and Diversity Officer Hootsuite*

In a fascinating article, Bain & Company calls inclusion a fabric.[124] Because it is something woven of diverse strands that retain their individual integrity even while being part of a whole. It is also a fabric in the sense of an underlying structure, a framework in which people can do their best work when the structure is sound. It's about the design and workmanship that shape a texture where people can feel they belong and are supported—where they're respected, free to be themselves, able to contribute, and feel connected. I'm quite fond of this metaphor.

Bain & Company interviewed 10,000 individuals—across diverse industries and demographic backgrounds to learn what actually makes people feel the most included. Across all groups, a common thread is the desire to grow and succeed. People describe what being included looks and feels like in remarkably similar ways.

And that brings me back to the UAE, and more specifically Dubai, the land of "*Come One, Come All.*"

I genuinely believe that Dubai can lead from the front and show the world what it looks like to engage citizens. We've seen the numbers on the effects of diversity on both employee engagement and performance.

Dr Tommy Weir notes that when you ask successful business leaders in Dubai about the key to leadership success, the answer is almost always openness.[125] This perception of Dubai as an open city has deep roots.

As early as the 1960s, Sheikh Rashid stood out as an open leader, known for maintaining connections far beyond his immediate circle. In both his office and his *majlis*, he welcomed diverse ideas, recognising that these perspectives were crucial to shaping Dubai's development.

Sheikh Rashid's openness was reflected in his close engagement with the business community, foreign governments, and his observations of other cities. He forged lasting ties with the British and Indian merchants in Dubai, ensuring their inclusion in the city's growth.

Despite concerns that the influx of foreign cultures might threaten Emirati traditions, Sheikh Rashid embraced diversity. A notable example was in 1966, when he donated land in the heart of Dubai for the construction of St. Mary's Catholic Church, laying the foundation for a place of worship that would later expand to accommodate the city's growing Catholic community.

Naturally, these acts garnered a lot of controversy. Some native Dubaians were overjoyed, while others felt threatened. They were afraid that outside ideas would compromise their beliefs and their way of life. The Sheikh however made it clear that intolerance wouldn't fly in Dubai and would only cause friction.

When conflicts (an inevitable effect of a diverse population) bubbled up between the Indian and Pakistani communities, he shifted the focus to a shared identity. He reminded both groups, *"Dubai is home to both Pakistanis and Indians. I want each of you to consider yourselves as esteemed guests here. But I have to warn you categorically that we will not allow foreign politics to be played out in the streets of the city."*

And that's where he drew the line on openness. Yes, absolutely, leaders need to be open, but not to the extent that it creates division. Rather, use openness to pull together, like weaving diverse communities into the very fabric of Dubai's society.

Part IV RECAP—The 12 Drivers of Employee Engagement

✹ **Purpose**

- A strong sense of purpose drives employees to go the extra mile.
- While many companies focus on know-how, it's the know-why that inspires true commitment.

✹ **Organisational Values**

- Practical, guiding behaviours help employees identify with the company's tribe.
- Make them memorable and meaningful, so shape everyday actions.

✹ **Leadership**

- Bosses, managers, and leaders—each play a unique role.
- The Trust Equation is Credibility, Reliability, and Intimacy over Self-Orientation.

✹ **Teamwork**

- Strong teamwork relies on 3 psychological safety, vulnerability, and shared purpose.
- Mantra: WOW goal, Open Communication, and Cheer each other to victory.

✹ **L&D**

- The learning organisation is about curiosity, leadership support, shared, knowledge, continuous feedback, and flexible learning.
- Clear career development pathways boost engagement and prepare for growth.

- ✹ **Well-being**
  - Holistic well-being, encompasses mental, physical, social, financial, and nutritional balance.
  - Comprehensive well-being programmes leed to substantial returns.
- ✹ **Employee Journey**
  - The employee journey, from recruitment to boomerang, is filled with touchpoints.
  - Recognise Moments That Matter.
- ✹ **Compensation and Benefits**
  - The cornerstone of an organisation's EVP.
  - Effective compensation strategies ensure internal and external equity.
- ✹ **Working Environment**
  - Strategic tool for engagement, designed to foster productivity, collaboration, and focus.
  - ABW, a variety of settings tailored to different tasks.
- ✹ **Flexible Work**
  - The future of work is flexible, extending beyond remote work to embrace Smart Working practices.
  - We must learn from remote-first companies.
- ✹ **CSR**
  - CSR 2.0 embeds doing well by doing good into business strategy, creating a transformative effect on employee experience.
  - Effective CSR requires outcome-focused communication.

✱ DEIB

- The turbo engine of engagement, if unconscious bias is monitored
- Transforming awareness into sustained progress requires an integrated, strategic approach

PART FIVE

❧

THE PULSE OF ENGAGEMENT

> *"Everything that is measured and watched, improves."*
>
> —*Bob Parson, Founder GoDaddy*

To measure what drives employees, we take inspiration from the world of marketing and technology.

We'll explore how organisations use data-driven insights to measure engagement effectively. From pulse surveys and eNPS to more advanced people analytics, tracking engagement is no longer a guessing game.

But where do we stand today? Many organisations still struggle to translate engagement data into meaningful change. We'll examine case studies from businesses that have successfully measured and acted on employee feedback, proving that engagement isn't just about satisfaction—it's about performance, retention, and business impact.

Finally, we'll look ahead to the future, where AI revolutionises how we track, analyse, and enhance the employee experience. What does a world driven by real-time engagement data look like? And how can organisations prepare for it?

The answers lie in understanding the pulse of engagement—because what gets measured gets improved.

1

What Would Marketing Do?

"Marketing without data is like driving with your eyes closed."
—Dan Zarrella, Social Media Scientist

How can we truly grasp what's on our colleagues' minds? What worries them, what fuels their passion?

Let's step into the magical world of marketing for a moment to see how they go about it.

If a marketer needed to understand their audience, they would likely start with a survey of the current customers: *"What do our customers think of us? Where can we improve? What should we focus on more—or less? How do we make a difference in their lives?"*

Based on this feedback, they would adjust their strategies, implement solutions, and use the data to attract new customers— often by identifying *look-alikes*, customers with similar profiles and aspirations, or by targeting adjacent segments. A critical part of this process is understanding media consumption and mapping the customer journey.

Now, if we applied this approach to the employee journey, we'd ask ourselves similar questions: *"Where does talent discover us? On which platforms are we most visible? Do people find us mainly through word of mouth, or are they responding to our advertisements? Are we relying on external recruiters to scout talent, or does talent naturally seek us out, leaving us to focus on selection?"*

Once a potential employee has made initial contact, how does the next step unfold? *"Do we know if a candidate has visited our website multiple times? Can we track whether the person who sent an enquiry is the same one who downloaded our white paper on corporate social responsibility? How are our pre-boarding and onboarding processes shaping up? Are there insights we can leverage to enhance the experience for future hires? What does a candidate's journey look like before joining, and how does that crucial first day unfold? Is an onboarding coordinator or buddy assigned to ease their early days? And, most importantly, does their perception change once they're onboard?"*

The only way to uncover these insights is to ask. To measure is to know. An experienced marketing professional would suggest starting with a focus group of recently hired employees to map out their talent journey. *"What were the key moments of truth? At what point did they truly decide to join us? How did they discover us? What role did our website play in their decision? How significant was their conversation with the manager or the CEO?"*

Then you would extrapolate and validate them across the organisation. Ideally, this wouldn't be a one-off exercise but an ongoing process. It's relatively straightforward to set up a regular employee survey to keep your finger on the pulse. One useful metric is the *Employee Net Promoter Score* (eNPS).

And here's something that still gets overlooked—an interview with a future immediate colleague. Many potential misunderstandings can be avoided if candidates also have the chance to speak with the people they'll be working closely with. This helps ensure the candidate leaves with a clear and realistic impression of the organisation and the team.

A marketing-inspired approach applies to the entire employee journey. By mapping engagement, you gain a clearer understanding of how committed employees are to their work and the organisation's success, and how the company's purpose and values resonate. Once you grasp these elements, you have the foundation to enhance them. When employees trust you, they'll share feedback—sometimes uncomfortable, but always necessary—that can drive real improvement.

🖐 Case in Point
Insuring a Cultural Shift: How P&V Rewrote Its DNA

"The leader will change, or we will change the leader."
—Johan Dekens, Board Member P&V Group

When Johan Dekens joined the Executive Committee of the insurance group P&V, he was tasked with the monumental responsibility of leading a cultural overhaul. P&V had realised that, in order to meet their growth targets, they needed more than a business transformation alone—they needed a shift in their culture. Changing systems and operations would not be enough if the people behind them did not evolve as well. And with 1,500 employees, this was no small feat.

Despite his background in IT, Johan was the perfect fit for the role due to his unique combination of analytical thinking and emotional intelligence—a blend likely shaped by his upbringing as the son of two musicians and his engineering education. Transitioning from his role as IT director to leading this transformation was a significant leap.

But Johan's logical approach guided him to recruit top talent to help realign the organisation, especially after a series of acquisitions had left the company somewhat fragmented. After a year of intense negotiations with trade unions, a unified HR framework was finally in place.

Johan recognised that real change starts at the top, so he focused on reshaping the culture within the executive committee itself. P&V had traditionally operated with a hierarchical, top-down structure. This a common trait in the insurance sector, but one that has become increasingly outdated in this new world that prioritises agility, trust, and ownership.

The first step in the transformation process was a culture survey, which revealed a strong consensus among P&V leaders: change was necessary, and it was urgent! Employee feedback was gathered, and, after considerable refinement, a new cultural framework was developed and approved by the Board.

However, not everyone was on board. Some board members who couldn't align with the new direction chose to step aside, illustrating that successful cultural change demands unified leadership.

Cultural transformation isn't a quick fix—it's a journey that goes beyond people, requiring an overhaul of governance, processes, and systems. Even with the right mindset, real change is impossible without these foundational shifts.

But how do you measure success? The market provides the answer. Customers began to notice the positive changes at P&V, with satisfaction levels rising. This was reflected in a higher *Net Promoter Score* (NPS)—a clear indication that the cultural transformation was making an impact. Johan proudly marked a major milestone: their internal culture measurement revealed a substantial decrease in the entropy score (a measure of organisational frustration), dropping from 31 to 18—a 40% improvement in just two years.

In a business built on managing risk, it's safe to say that betting on culture paid off. Now, that's something worth insuring!

2

How Are You—Really?

> *"Approach people as true partners, involving them in continuous dialogues and processes about how to design and alter their roles, tasks and working relationships – which means that leaders need to make it safe enough for employees to speak openly of their experiences at work."*
>
> —William Kahn, Godfather of Employee Engagement

"**H**ow are you?"

It's one of those default phrases we toss around, often with little thought, and just as quickly, we get the typical responses: "*I'm fine,*" or "*All good.*" And that's it, conversation over. But throw in the word "***really,***" and suddenly, things shift. It makes us stop, and actually consider the answer for a moment.

And rightly so. While leaders may still get a decent sense of how their smaller teams are doing, scaling that insight across an entire organisation is a whole different ballgame. Especially in a hybrid setting. Let's not kid ourselves—many employees put on a brave face during video calls, but underneath, they might be battling feelings of isolation, anxiety, or dealing with personal problems. Earlier in the book, we touched on the declining well-being of employees, and this is where it happens.

Video calls may be convenient, but they come with real limitations when it comes to reading someone's emotional state. They still lack the emotional richness of in-person interactions. The absence of physical presence—critical for building rapport—further complicates communication in a hybrid or remote setting.

As Andy Holmes, a Korn Ferry Associate Client Partner, aptly puts it, *"Being on video calls all day is a struggle because our brains are saying: I can see you, I can hear you, but I can't feel you."* We are biologically conditioned to be empathetic and to feel each other, says Holmes, and doing so through a screen remains very difficult.[126] One major issue with video meetings is the restricted visual field—being *"boxed"* into a small window—where body language cues below the shoulders are missing. Without full-body signals, we're left relying solely on facial expressions, which leads to cognitive strain.

Additionally, the constant self-view on video calls, known as the *"mirror effect,"* forces us to self-monitor more than we would in person. This drains mental energy as we become hyper-aware of our appearance, adding to the mental toll. Research from the University of Arizona shows that this effect hits women and new employees particularly hard, as they often feel more pressure to prove their competence.[127]

Stanford University research has shown that **in-person communication** makes our brains happier.[128] Brain scans reveal that face-to-face interactions activate the brain's reward centres more than virtual meetings. This is because, in person, we experience a full range of sensory and emotional cues that help us connect and engage, like eye contact, subtle gestures, and body posture.

By contrast, virtual interactions can feel intense, as we see people's faces at unnatural sizes or distances, often much closer than we would in real life. Silences that might feel natural in face-to-face discussions often become tense and uncomfortable in digital meetings. Our brains may interpret these factors as threats, increasing stress levels. The difficulty of making direct eye contact in virtual meetings, coupled with audio lags and technical glitches, further hampers our ability to relate to others. Ironically, this phenomenon can be more pronounced on video calls than over the phone, where voice alone allows for greater focus on emotional tone.

Virtual interactions also make it easier for participants to zone out. People naturally pay more attention during face-to-face interactions, while screen-based meetings often invite distractions like other browser tabs or notifications. The need to work harder to fill in missing non-verbal cues, combined with the mental load of staring at a screen for extended periods, leads to cognitive exhaustion by the end of the day. This phenomenon, commonly known as *"Zoom fatigue,"* has become a familiar part of remote work.[129]

Given these challenges, leaders must find alternative ways to keep the pulse of their teams regularly and intentionally. Since casual conversations at the coffee machine are no longer a regular part of daily life, alternative methods—like sending regular pulse surveys—are essential for understanding how employees are truly feeling.

These pulses can provide a clear view of the overall health of your team and identify potential concerns early on. This approach shortens the learning curve and allows leaders to take corrective action swiftly, addressing concerns before they escalate. In the following section, we'll dive deeper into how to measure employee sentiment.

3

Measuring Engagement

"I feel listened to, but I don't feel heard."

—*Anonymous Employee*

When we launched the *BRAVOS! Employee Engagement Awards* in 2020, we had one clear mission: to give every organisation, regardless of size or profit motive, the chance to celebrate their exceptional culture.

But as with any great mission, reality likes to throw in a few surprises. At our first jury meeting, the debate quickly centred around how to measure employee satisfaction and engagement. Some jurors, having cut their teeth on prestigious marketing awards like the *Effies*, naturally expected the candidates to provide hard, numerical data for evaluation.

They weren't wrong. Data matters. But we were quickly caught off guard. It turned out that only medium to large companies had robust data to present. The world of engagement metrics still hadn't fully made its way into the SME landscape. If we had insisted on hard data across the board, we would have effectively shut out a lot of smaller companies from the competition—missing the very essence of what we were trying to achieve. Our solution? We applied stricter criteria for the large companies but kept the door wide open for others.

And here's where we realised, we had a unique opportunity to do more than hand out awards. We could raise awareness. By spreading the word on the importance of measuring engagement, we could encourage SMEs and non-profits to get on board with it too.

The good news? This doesn't have to be a daunting, bank-breaking affair. With the tools and tech now available, measuring engagement can be as simple or as sophisticated as you want it to be.

If you're ready to dip your toes into measuring employee engagement, you'll find plenty of tools available on the market. Some are a bit pricier than others, depending on how deep you want to go. If you're after something basic, you could knock together a DIY survey or buy a simple tool off the shelf.

But (and there's always a "*but*") the limitations soon rear their head. You'll find yourself needing to dig deeper, add custom questions, or perhaps, worst of all, trying to compare incompatible results across time. It's like trying to compare apples with oranges. Not to mention, you could find yourself juggling multiple tools, none of which play nicely with each other. Before you know it, you're knee-deep in spreadsheets, trying to manually piece it all together and spending far more time and energy than anticipated.

It's the Platform, Stupid

If you want to move beyond basic surveys and quickly translate insights into action, exploring a platform is your best bet. **The beauty of a platform lies in its flexibility.** You can collect data in two main ways: either automatically: by gathering data from calendars, behaviours, office movement sensors (and so much more), or by engaging your employees directly on the platform.

You get a much richer, integrated view of what's going on, and the ability to act on it fast. This platform should seamlessly integrate with your existing office tools. The smoother the integration, the quicker you can implement change without wasting time or resources on manual workarounds. After all, the goal is to make engagement easier to manage.

The 5 I's of a Powerful Engagement Platform

An engagement platform is most effective when it delivers on five core functionalities, which we refer to as **the 5 I's**:[130]

1. **Inform:** *Make sure employees have the information they need to understand what is expected of them.*
2. **Inspire:** *Connect employees to the organisation's purpose, vision, and values.*
3. **Instruct:** *Provide the necessary training to ensure employees can achieve their goals with the right skills and knowledge.*
4. **Involve:** *Allow people to actively participate in decisions that affect their work.*
5. **Incentivise:** *Implement systems to measure, reward, and reinforce desired behaviours that align with the organisation's goals.*

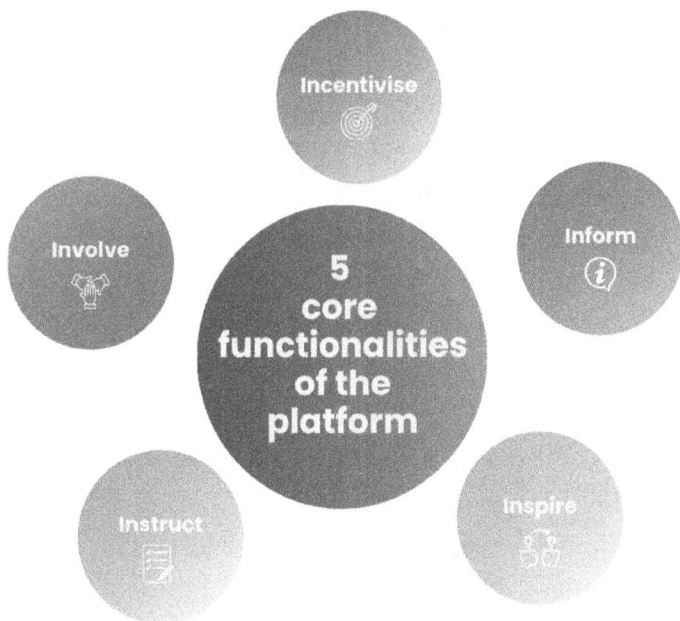

Figure 10. The I's of the Engagement Platform

Capturing the Employee Voice

This may not hold true for the future, but in today's workplace, surveys remain one of the most effective tools for gathering feedback. They offer a direct line to employees, capturing their thoughts and experiences in real time.

While there are many approaches to conducting internal surveys, I advocate for lighter, ongoing questionnaires that touch on a range of topics over time. The traditional annual satisfaction survey is simply too slow and becomes outdated too quickly. Human memory rarely stretches beyond three months, and if you rely on just one yearly measurement (or even every two years), you become overly dependent on the timing of the survey.

Some organisations avoid this by scheduling their satisfaction surveys at what they believe is a strategic moment. This approach risks reducing the survey to nothing more than a snapshot—a limited and potentially misleading view of employee sentiment at that moment.

The same issue arises with managers who urge their team members to give the organisation top scores simply to be rated the best place to work, rather than seeking honest, valuable input. Unfortunately, this is a phenomenon I've witnessed all too often, especially in the UAE. Let's avoid the trap of fooling ourselves into seeing only what we want to see, rather than what's really going on.

The key is to keep the conversation with employees ongoing. You can't make improvements if you don't listen. Surveys help uncover the barriers to engagement and are a powerful tool for democratising feedback, making sure everyone is heard. **Good or bad, feedback is a gift.** You would be surprised, but the best ideas come from your team itself. There is always more innovation in your own team than you think. And that's where we see many companies still missing the mark. *"Alright, team, we're serious about employee engagement now. Here's the plan: we'll host the annual marathon, scale Kilimanjaro with the CEO heroically leading the charge, hand out fitness trackers to everyone, and then—just to keep it balanced—we give everyone a fancy bottle of wine at year-end. Perfect, right?"* But who said your employees actually want this? It's all too common for management to misread feedback—or, even better, assume everyone shares their own taste and preferences.

Once you gather the results, put them into a clear dashboard and share them with the organisation. This gives you an objective starting point for action, creating greater understanding and goodwill around the changes to come. It shortens the organisation's learning curve and undoubtedly saves time and money.

But beware. This isn't a free pass to rush in without communication. First, explain why you're doing this and what you plan to do with the feedback. Asking for someone's opinion, whether it's on work or something as simple as dinner plans, implies that you value what they have to say. At the very least, it creates an expectation that their input will be acknowledged.

If you don't respond to employees' concerns, it can have disastrous effects on your organisational culture. It breeds apathy, or worse, resentment. If employees feel their voices make no difference, they'll start to disengage. And there you are, stuck with your well-intentioned survey, wondering why it backfired!

8 Tips for a Successful Survey

1. *Start with Why: Before you even think about sending out your survey, let your people know why you're doing it and what you plan to do with the results. And here's a golden rule: don't make promises you can't keep.*
2. *Mind Your Tone: The tone of voice is everything. Keep it conversational and familiar, in line with how you'd normally speak to your team internally. Don't suddenly switch to corporate-speak or management jargon.*

3. ***Speak Their Language—literally:*** *Wherever possible, ask your questions in your employees' native language or a language they are proficient in. If not, you risk losing important nuances. Plus, it's a simple way to show you've thought about them and want genuine feedback.*

4. ***Frame It Positively:*** *While it might be tempting to dive into what's going wrong, it's much more productive to focus on the factors that influence engagement. Frame your questions around what drives motivation and ask for feedback specifically on those areas.*

5. ***It's a Process. Remember:*** *Surveys aren't a one-and-done deal. Make it part of an ongoing process by following up with micro-surveys, whether weekly or monthly.*

6. ***Give Space for Open Comments:*** *Not mandatory, and I know some may disagree, but don't underestimate the power of a free-text box. Sometimes the best insights come from those unstructured comments. You'd be surprised at how much you can learn when people have space to share their thoughts. I'd suggest including just one open box at the end of the survey to keep things manageable—unless, of course, you're a fan of collecting people's finest grammar and spelling mishaps!*

7. ***Say Thank You, Quickly:*** *Always thank your employees immediately after they've completed the survey. It's a simple courtesy that shows you appreciate their time and input. A little gratitude goes a long way.*

> **8. Aim for High Participation:** *A successful survey means getting a solid cross-section of opinions. Aim for a participation rate of over 70%, and make sure to encourage every employee to take part (according to Culture Amp, a good participation rate depends on the size of the company).[131] You're looking for a true reflection of the organisation, after all.*

What about Survey Fatigue?

"We already ask our employees for feedback on so many things. Aren't we overdoing it? What about survey fatigue?"

This is a common concern, and a fair one at that. But let me ask you this one thing: is it **survey fatigue**, or rather **lack-of-action fatigue**? The key is to be thoughtful about what you ask and what you do with the feedback afterwards. You don't need to bombard employees with endless questions, but you do need to ask the right ones.

And don't treat it like a casual check-in. Institutionalise your surveys and make them a continuous feedback loop. When an employee provides thoughtful feedback, there's an implicit contract—they're sharing their views, and in return, you're expected to show how you're addressing them. The process involves listening, acting, and then listening again.

If the survey leads to changes and is communicated effectively, people are likely to be more open to participating in future surveys. Even if these changes weren't exactly what they had personally hoped for. Seeing that action has been taken based on survey results allows employees to view surveys as a tool for meaningful change. However, if nothing changes, they may participate reluctantly or ignore the survey altogether. After all, why should they invest their valuable time in answering questions that lead nowhere? Fail to act on feedback or communicate the results, and that's when you get *lack-of-action fatigue*.

Is there a magic frequency for how often you should survey your employees? I don't think so. It depends on several factors: the type of survey, the industry, the purpose behind it, and the actions taken since the last one. For a comprehensive engagement survey, once or twice a year may be appropriate. In between these larger surveys, it's useful to run smaller, pulse surveys—simple questions that provide quick insights into the organisation's current state.

Oh, by the way, even if you do listen and act, don't assume people will automatically connect the dots. One crucial task that your communication specialists will tell you, is reminding employees of what they told you and what you've done in response. People have short memories and often focus on different priorities than you might. That's why it's so useful to remind them of what they shared and explain the actions taken in response. Then, assess whether those changes have resolved the issue or if additional steps are still needed.

In the online ***The Question Master***, I've included a checklist of questions per engagement driver that you can tailor to fit the tone of your organisation. This gives you a solid starting point, so you don't have to reinvent the wheel every time.

Thanks to years of research from organisations like Gallup or Culture Amp, we now have a wealth of global data on engagement. This offers a fantastic benchmark to help you see where your company stands compared to others.

Another simple but powerful benchmark is the *eNPS*, or *Employee Net Promoter Score*. Ingenious in its simplicity, the *eNPS* is a highly effective parameter that can give you valuable insights into employee sentiment.

Power of eNPS

In the world of marketing, the *NPS (Net Promoter Score)* has long been a trusted metric for gauging customer satisfaction.[132] Created by Fred Reichheld, Partner at Bain & Company, back in 2003, the *NPS* was designed as a straightforward way to measure customer loyalty with one simple question: ***"How likely are you to recommend our company, product, or service to a friend or colleague?"*** The genius of NPS lies in its simplicity, which is why it quickly caught on with companies around the globe.

The calculation itself can be a bit of an eye-opener. Only the highest scores—9 and 10—and the lowest scores—those from 0 to 3—are factored into the final result, which can lead to some pretty confronting numbers. The final score, calculated across all customer responses, can range anywhere from -100 to +100. A score above zero is good, while anything over 50 is considered excellent.

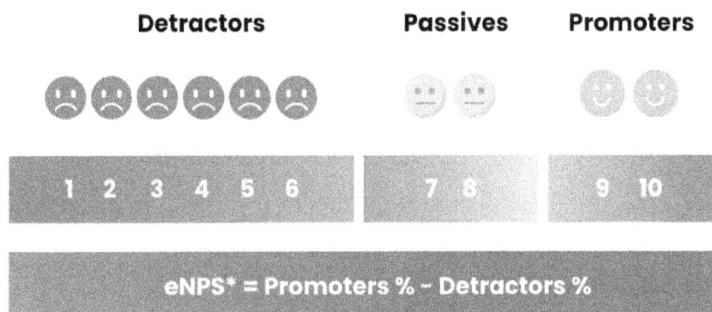

Figure 11. Employee Net Promoter Score

More recently, the same concept has been adapted to measure employee engagement and loyalty through the *eNPS* (Employee Net Promoter Score). Using the same calculation method, but now applied to employees, it asks: ***"How likely are you to recommend this organisation as a workplace to friends, family, network?"*** This score gives a quick snapshot of employee engagement. The *eNPS* also ranges between -100 and +100, with scores between 10 and 50 considered solid.

Now, if you ask a data expert, they'll tell you there's a whole lot more nuance involved in truly understanding engagement. And I would agree—no single metric can capture the whole picture. But in all its simplicity, the *eNPS* does a brilliant job of boiling things down to the essentials, and it serves as an excellent benchmarking tool.

What makes this method particularly interesting is the potential to link the *eNPS* with the traditional *NPS*, allowing companies to explore how employee satisfaction impacts customer delight. After all, happy employees often create happy customers, and the *eNPS* helps map that connection clearly.

✋Case in Point
The Evolution of NPS and eNPS at DHL

Together with Amadou Diallo, CEO of DHL Global Forwarding MEA, we explored the evolution of the *NPS* and *eNPS* within his Middle East and Africa region.

Initially, DHL found that measuring these metrics once a year wasn't sufficient to capture the dynamic nature of employee and customer satisfaction.

To address this, DHL Global Forwarding shifted to more continuous feedback mechanisms using *NPS* and *eNPS*, enabling real-time insights and quicker responses. When Amadou started, the *NPS* was 15. Now it's 55, and productivity has increased by 30%. This remarkable improvement is directly related to well-trained, motivated people, as the systems and products across the industry are quite similar.

The company's balanced scorecard approach assigns 50% weight to financial performance, 15% to customer satisfaction, and 15% to employee satisfaction. The five values of *passion, speed, can-do attitude, right-first-time,* and *customer service* have become true cornerstones, embedded in DHL's culture and driving the company's reputation as an attractive employer.

This strategic move has significantly contributed to DHL's standing as a top employer in the MEA region, particularly in the UAE, where they have garnered numerous accolades. DHL has been recognised as a *Top Employer* by the Top Employers Institute and has won the *Aon Best Employer* award, underscoring its reputation as a company that values its employees.

Seven Steps for Communicating Survey Results

Selecting the right questions and administering your employee engagement survey is only half the battle; the real work begins once the survey closes.

One of the biggest challenges is delivering results in a timely and insightful way, keeping the key stakeholders in mind: the executive team, department heads, and employees. You need buy-in from these groups to collect feedback, execute improvements, and foster trust.

Here are the 7 steps Culture Amp recommends for communicating your engagement survey results:[133]

1. **Thank Employees:** Acknowledge the time and effort employees took to provide feedback, preferably with a quick note from your CEO or the People team. Remind them of the survey's goals, share the participation rate, some preliminary findings, and a timeline of when you will share a more detailed breakdown of company-wide engagement scores.

2. **Share High-Level Results:** Offer a broad overview of the main findings, preferably one to two weeks after closing the survey. Keep it transparent and don't paint too rosy of a picture. Strike a balance by sharing both the strengths and areas for improvement that employees have highlighted in the survey. Communicate any actions already taken in response to the feedback, along with a clear action plan outlining future steps to address issues raised. This approach holds you accountable, while also demonstrating how the organisation is actively working to resolve known concerns.

3. **Share with Executives:** Your senior leadership team should be among the first to review the engagement survey results. Discuss key metrics and company-wide insights—both positive and negative—and compare them with previous surveys or benchmark

data for context, giving leaders a quick overview of the organisation's health. Next, highlight the key findings and propose two to four actionable recommendations. This is when you want to hear their feedback and earn their buy-in.

4. **Review with Department Heads:** The next step is to provide department heads with an overview of their team's overall health. Share insights on how their department's performance has evolved over time and how it compares to the wider organisation. Engage in an open discussion about the strengths and weaknesses identified in the survey, with particular attention to manager satisfaction scores.

5. **Engage People Leaders:** This review level is arguably the most important, as your managers have the most influence over day-to-day employee experiences. Follow the same approach as before: review key findings and scores and present your recommendations for improvement. This is also the perfect opportunity to coach managers on how to present survey results to their teams and facilitate open conversations. Some teams will be too small to conduct this level of analysis anonymously. If that's the case, share high-level findings, but don't drill down to that level of detail for these more intimate teams.

6. **Have People Leaders Review Results with Their Teams:** Encourage managers to go over team-specific data with employees, ensuring an open, productive discussion. Each team should leave with a clear understanding of the positive changes to be

implemented. For these discussions to be effective, managers must create a safe space where team members feel comfortable sharing their opinions. Starting with the positive survey results is a great way to warm up the team before moving into more constructive feedback. Remind managers to remain objective, future-focused, and results-oriented in order to understand employee pain points better.

7. **Follow Up on Progress:** As mentioned before, it's easy to move on after completing a survey. But it's essential not to report the scores once and then abandon the action plan. To show employees their feedback is a priority, you must continuously update them on the progress of initiatives. Regularly communicating ongoing efforts builds credibility and trust. When employees see that engagement surveys are taken seriously, they'll be more inclined to participate and share feedback on future surveys.

"If you believe people are good, you must be unafraid to share information with them."

—*Laszlo Bock, Former Senior Vice President People Operations, Google*

Engagement surveys require effort but are vital for strengthening company culture and improving employee engagement. It's crucial to clearly communicate why and when an employee engagement survey will be held. If there's one thing we've learnt from this book, businesses need to keep investing in ways to stay connected to their employees. Engagement surveys can help you do just that.

Transparency: A Bold Move?

Transparency is the key to building trust in any organisation. Stephen Covey said that *"Transparency is about being open, real, and authentic. It's about telling the truth in a way people can verify."*

If your company claims that people are the most important asset, then real transparency is essential to backing up that claim. Without openness, you risk being dishonest—not just with your employees, but with yourself.

Recent global shifts, such as the pandemic and rapid technological advances, have shown how quickly the world can change. By sharing results openly and almost instantly, organisations can quickly identify areas that need attention. It also brings clarity, helping to prioritise issues, and saving precious time in decision-making. Once that clarity is achieved, the next step is to involve employees in finding solutions.

True transparency shows that you trust your employees' judgement and value their contributions. It's sharing the full picture, even when it's not pretty. This means making survey results visible to everyone. This might seem daunting at first, but it's the most effective way to earn employees' trust and demonstrate that their voices matter. In the Herculean platform, for instance, a dashboard displays the key drivers of engagement, along with the organisation's performance on each. This approach includes the good, the bad, and, yes, the ugly. But as the saying goes, *"feedback is food for champions."*

For many managers, this level of openness is well outside their comfort zone. It's common for them to review the results privately, filtering what is communicated to their teams. Fear of negative feedback is understandable. However, a more transparent approach encourages respect and dialogue. Managers should start by preparing communications carefully and making it clear that transparency is a two-way street. This is a learning process for everyone.

Ray Dalio, founder of Bridgewater Associates, champions what he calls *radical transparency* in his organisation, a concept that pushes openness to the extreme. At Bridgewater, nearly all meetings are recorded and accessible to employees, and feedback—often referred to as *"tough love"*—is openly shared. Dalio's philosophy ensures that nothing is hidden, whether it's successes or mistakes, and that decisions are made based on merit rather than hierarchy.

While this approach has worked for Dalio's organisation, not every company may be ready for this intense level of openness. Radical transparency demands a significant cultural shift and isn't without its challenges. However, it serves as a powerful example of how far some organisations are willing to go to build trust from within. It's about creating a culture where feedback flows both ways, and trust is built through mutual understanding. This process requires patience and clear communication. After all, transparency is a learning curve for everyone involved. It's not something that happens overnight, but part of an ongoing journey—one where both employees and leaders grow together.

4

Where Are We Now?

"Be good with numbers. Be better with people."

—Unknown

Data is all the rage! However, data in its raw form holds limited intrinsic value, while digital tools generate vast streams of information. And that's where HR analytics steps in: transforming data into actionable insights to tackle both workforce and business challenges.

HR analytics is also referred to as talent analytics, workforce analytics, or more recently, people analytics. Though these terms are often used interchangeably, there's a subtle distinction. **HR Analytics** traditionally stems from data within Human Resources, focusing on enhancing HR functions specifically. **Workforce Analytics** is the use of data to understand, predict and optimise workforce data (e.g. forecasting workforce demands, skills, or trends). **People Analytics** reaches beyond HR to pull in data from various departments—marketing, finance, and customer insights—to tackle a broader spectrum of business questions.[134]

At its core, HR analytics is about gathering, analysing, and reporting HR data to drive meaningful business results. It enables organisations to understand their workforce better, make data-backed decisions, and track the impact of various HR metrics, ultimately enhancing business performance across the board. We generally distinguish four levels of HR Analytics: descriptive, diagnostic, predictive, and prescriptive.

The 4 Levels of HR Analytics

1. *Descriptive HR Analytics: analyses historical data to understand what has happened over a specific period and to identify patterns (e.g. what was the average salary for a specific job role, or how many employees left and their absenteeism rate).*

2. *Diagnostic HR Analytics: takes a deeper look at data to uncover the reasons behind certain outcomes (e.g. examining unplanned absence data to identify absenteeism drivers).*

3. *Predictive HR Analytics: explores current and historical data and uses statistical models and forecasts to predict future trends (e.g. exploring recruitment data to discover the key attributes of an ideal candidate).*

4. *Prescriptive HR Analytics: suggests potential future outcomes and scenarios and proposes recommendations for addressing them (e.g. develop an algorithm predicting what type of onboarding a new hire will need according to experience and skill level).*

The Rise of HR Analytics

The arrival of HR analytics is no surprise. As discussed in Part II, HR management has evolved dramatically over the past century, shifting from an operational role to a far more strategic one. This data-driven approach is perfectly aligned with that progression.

Some 10–15 years ago, marketing itself was far less data-driven than it is today. Previously, marketing was more *touchy-feely*, relying on intuition and creative ideas rather than on quantifiable metrics. Today, marketing relies on data of every kind, with organisations conducting customer segmentation, journey mapping, competitor analysis, and more. They measure and test nearly every interaction people have with their brand or product. Amazon, for instance, tests its homepage daily; the version of the homepage you see may differ entirely from what others experience. Using data, Amazon decides which content to display for each visitor to optimise engagement.

Given these changes in marketing, it was only a matter of time before the same shift came to HR. Back in 2016, Prasad Setty, Google's VP of People Analytics & Compensation, declared that all people-related decisions at Google would be based on data and analytics. HR departments worldwide are following suit, recruiting data scientists and analysts to harness the vast amount of employee data they already have.

The potential is thrilling: data-driven insights allow for informed, predictive decision-making, moving beyond instincts or opinions. Analytics can test the effectiveness of HR policies and interventions. Imagine the cost savings if your organisation could anticipate how long a candidate might stay or identify which departments will need specific skills soon. Consider the competitive advantage of spotting these trends early. Just think of all the time HR would save—time that could be redirected to the human touch.

Benefits of HR Analytics

The use of HR/People Analytics brings substantial strategic and operational benefits to HR. It helps identify talent, improve HR performance, analyse turnover and its causes, and, when applied effectively, strengthens HR's role as a strategic partner to the business.

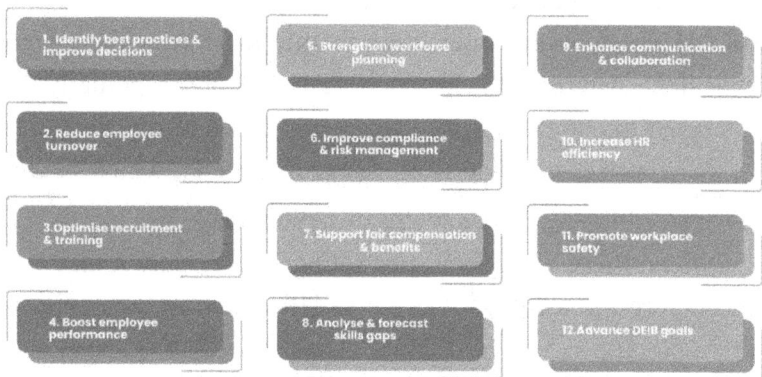

Figure 12. Top Benefits of HR Analytics

Key HR Metrics

HR metrics are essential data points for tracking human capital and assessing the impact of HR initiatives.[135]

HR Metric	Definition	How to Calculate
Revenue per employee	The revenue generated by the business for each employee, after accounting for expenses like salary and benefits.	Total revenue / total number of employees
Time to fill	The time taken to fill an open position, measured from job posting to offer acceptance. This metric reflects the hiring team's efficiency in sourcing and progressing suitable candidates through the recruitment process.	Number of days from posting the job to someone accepting an offer
Turnover rate (voluntary and involuntary)	The percentage of employees who leave the company. The voluntary turnover rate indicates how effectively the company retains employees, while the involuntary rate reflects its success in hiring the right talent and managing them effectively.	(Number of terminations during period / Number of employees at beginning of period) × 100
Absenteeism	The total number of days an employee is absent, excluding approved leave like holidays, over a given period. This metric is particularly useful for roles with high absence rates, such as in retail.	(Number of absent days / Total working days) × 100
Retention rate	How effectively the business retains its employees, measured either company-wide or at the manager level.	(Number of employees staying during a given period / Total number of employees over the same period) × 100

✋ Case in Point

Powering Up Attendance: E.On's Data Success Story

E.On, a Germany-based electric company with around 78,000 employees, faced rising absenteeism levels that exceeded the acceptable benchmark set by its HR department. This trend posed a significant financial risk, as absenteeism costs can range from 2,660 to 3,600 euros per employee per year—amounting to hundreds of millions for an organisation of E.On's scale.

In response, E.On turned to people analytics to identify the root causes of increased unscheduled time off. The people analytics team developed 55 hypotheses based on available data, tested 21, and ultimately validated 11. Their findings revealed that the duration and timing of employees' vacations had the greatest influence on unplanned absences for the rest of the year. Surprisingly, selling back vacation days—previously thought to affect absenteeism—showed no significant impact.

With these insights, E.On adjusted its time-off policies to encourage managers to be more flexible in allowing employees to schedule multiple breaks throughout the year, including at least one longer vacation. This policy change helped reduce absenteeism significantly and provided the HR team with a framework for future testing and insights into other potential factors affecting employee attendance.[136]

Essential Skills for HR Analytics

Realising the full potential of HR analytics requires more than just data. Robust analytics capabilities demand skilled leadership and a specific set of competencies within HR. In analytics, asking the right questions is paramount and that's not just true in HR Analytics.

This is where the insight of a seasoned HR professional becomes invaluable. An HR professional with a strong grasp of HR processes, organisational dynamics, and tools is a powerful asset. They ensure that the right organisational questions are posed, identify where analytics can deliver the greatest impact, and guide the data-driven analysis that ultimately supports strategic, evidence-based decisions.

Fragmented systems and gaps in analytics expertise remain significant challenges. Many organisations still rely on basic, *ad hoc* reports that don't deliver predictive insights. Bridging this gap requires HR leaders who combine traditional HR acumen with advanced analytical skills. Korn Ferry highlights that data-driven HR leaders need to be both adaptive and strategic, managing the technical aspects of analytics while building strong relationships across functions.[137] With the right mix of skills, these leaders can transform HR data into a strategic asset, enabling organisations to optimise workforce performance, enhance operational efficiency, and ultimately achieve long-term business success. It's the ultimate blend of art and science.

Companies with advanced people analytics are not only more likely to achieve efficiency gains and secure the right talent, but they are also 3.5 times more likely to place the right people in the right roles. To fully unlock the potential of people analytics, the extended HR team must develop key skills that bridge both data expertise and human insights:

1. **Data literacy:** Understanding data concepts and terminologies is foundational for any HR professional working with analytics. This skill ensures that HR teams can navigate data confidently, interpret data sources accurately, and draw insights that are both reliable and impactful.

2. **Statistical knowledge:** Proficiency in statistical analysis allows HR professionals to identify trends and correlations within data. By translating complex data sets into clear patterns, they can pinpoint issues such as engagement hotspots or turnover triggers, informing decisions that boost engagement and retention.

3. **Analytical and consulting skills:** HR analytics goes beyond simply managing numbers; it requires the ability to interpret data in a way that aligns with business goals. Strong analytical and consulting skills enable HR professionals to ask the right questions, identify critical workforce issues, and deliver insights that directly impact organisational strategy.

4. **Storytelling and data visualisation:** Communicating complex findings to stakeholders is crucial for driving change. Skills in storytelling and data visualisation make data insights accessible and actionable, allowing HR teams to share results that resonate across the organisation and inspire informed action.

How to Implement People Analytics

There's no single blueprint for implementing a people/HR analytics strategy. The key is finding a balance of metrics and tools that provide meaningful insights into the people side of your business without draining your budget. While a lack of data can seriously hinder your efforts, overspending on analytics that doesn't match your business size can be just as problematic.

HR data analysis unfolds in several phases, and understanding the process is essential for effective application. Erik van Vulpen, Founder of AIHR, outlines five straightforward steps to get started.[138]

5 Steps to Implement People Analytics

1. Ask a Relevant Business Question: Your aim with HR analytics should be to make a measurable impact on business outcomes, so start with the end goal in mind. Define the focus area and determine what you want the data to reveal, framing it as a question. For instance, if you're looking to improve succession planning, the question might be: "Which employees show the highest potential for progression and leadership?"

2. Data Selection: Next, identify the data required to answer your question and where to find it. Most of the needed information will reside in your HR tech stack/ employee engagement data lake or other internal sources. But external benchmarking may also be useful in some cases. This step is much smoother with a system that can organise and categorise data and ideally integrates with your reporting tools.

3. Data Cleaning: Once gathered, the data will likely contain duplicates, errors, or inconsistencies. Left uncorrected, these issues can lead to flawed analysis. Cleaning involves removing duplicates, fixing errors, and ensuring completeness. Also, watch out for any structural inconsistencies.

4. Data Analysis: At this stage, summarise and analyse the data to uncover trends, correlations, and patterns that address your original question. Analysis can be done with various tools like Excel, ChatGPT, Copilot, R, or Python. The goal here is to draw out insights that directly answer your question.

5. Actionable Insights: Now it's time to interpret what the data is telling you and turn that into courses of action. Based on the findings, you can evaluate the impact of HR processes and policies and make decisions or recommendations for improving them.

Predictive Power: Boon or Bane?

The most captivating aspect of People Analytics is undoubtedly its **predictive power**. Imagine being able to identify the ideal candidate for a role or determining the best approach to closing a skills gap: Is it by recruiting new talent or upskilling existing employees? People Analytics can even identify which employees may be most likely to leave in the near future, analysing parameters such as salary, productivity, employee sentiment, and work environment. Given the high cost of turnover for many organisations, this could truly be a game changer.

When I spoke with Peter Vermeulen, former CHRO at Amazon, it was no surprise that Amazon—now with over 1.53 million employees worldwide—has advanced considerably in this area. Several years ago, Amazon developed its own tool, *Nostradamus,* to reduce staff turnover. This AI-driven tool, customised by Peter's department and fine-tuned with various parameters, can accurately predict which employees may leave soon. Equipped with these insights, managers can take proactive steps, such as conducting *stay interviews* as a positive alternative to traditional exit interviews, to retain valued employees.

Does this all sound a bit unsettling, as though Big Brother is peering over our shoulder? There's no denying a potential dark side to it. Data could, after all, be used to make decisions that negatively impact employees—like calculating mass redundancies or manipulating behaviours. The notion that employees' every move, facial expression, or action is tracked can feel intrusive.

This is a delicate balance that organisations must navigate with great care. Given the vast amounts of sensitive and confidential data managed by HR, privacy and security will remain top priorities, and this topic will continue to spark intense debate in the years ahead!

5

Where Are We Going?

"We need to understand people, before we can develop technology to help them grow."

—*The Nedap Story*

The buzz around Artificial Intelligence, and more specifically Generative AI (GenAI), has reached a crescendo, capturing far more attention from the public than even the most enthusiastic AI advocates could have predicted. AI has swept into workplaces with monumental impact, swiftly becoming a transformative force that reshapes how organisations operate and connect with their people. It's boosting productivity, sparking fresh approaches to engagement, and adding some turbo-charged fuel to business success—so, yes, a little cheer is in order!

AI continues to evolve, and its potential to influence the next generation of workers—for better and for worse—only grows. **Over half of executives (54%) believe that their businesses won't survive beyond 2030 without adopting AI at scale.**[139] The adoption of AI raises important questions around ethics, privacy, and its long-term effects on employee engagement.

According to Bryan Offutt from Index Ventures, we have entered AI's "***Messy Middle***," another term borrowed from marketing. This is that challenging intermediary and even awkward stage, with a lot of tweaks, pivots, experimentation, and adjustments.

"People love to think about before and after. But most of the time, we are in the during phase, where we are learning, growing, making mistakes, and trying again. Embrace the messy middle."

—*Daily Jay (The Calm App)*

Benefits and Risks of AI

AI tools bring undeniable advantages, particularly by automating repetitive tasks and freeing employees to focus on high-value, creative work that taps into human ingenuity. From AI-powered project management software to virtual assistants and predictive analytics, these tools simplify routine tasks like scheduling and basic decision-making, enabling employees to shift towards strategic activities.

According to Gartner, over half (52%) of HR leaders plan to use AI to enhance the employee experience by automating low-value tasks, personalising interactions, and establishing real-time feedback loops that amplify the employee voice.[140] However, adopting AI also brings notable risks, underscoring the need for well-considered AI governance in HR:

1. **Unintended use and bias:** Gen AI can develop capabilities that surprise even its creators. While these emergent abilities can offer new advantages, their unpredictability presents governance challenges. The black box nature of AI can expose organisations to significant risks, particularly in sensitive areas

like credit assessments, medical diagnoses, and talent decisions. If you've worked with tools like ChatGPT, you've likely encountered answers that were downright delusional or embellished—and with no way to trace the sources of these fabrications. In some cases, this leads to confusion and wasted time as you search for reliable information to replace AI's misleading responses. With two in five organisations already using AI in HR, there is a risk of generating biased outputs that entrench inequalities. The lack of transparency in many AI models requires organisations to be prepared to defend AI-driven decisions against both legal and public scrutiny.

2. **Privacy and security:** Familiar risks—cyber attacks, data privacy breaches, misuse of technology, and copyright infringement—take on heightened relevance in the AI landscape. AI's dependency on vast data sets amplifies privacy concerns, and without rigorous oversight, it may inadvertently perpetuate biases. Organisations should implement robust data protection measures, a sentiment echoed by AI experts who stress the importance of responsible, transparent data use.

3. **Job security concerns:** Job-related anxiety is creeping in as AI disrupts the job market. While fears of AI-induced redundancy have dropped from 53% in 2022 to 10% today, over 21% of employees now worry that AI advancements will heighten performance expectations, increasing pressure to work faster or produce more.

The debate over AI-driven job loss is lively, to say the least, but here's some perspective. According to the World Economic Forum's *Future of Jobs Report 2020*, AI is projected to displace 85 million jobs worldwide by 2025.

Yet the same report also foresees the creation of 97 million new roles.[141] The catch? These new roles are markedly different from those AI may replace. As AI automates entry-level positions like data entry and processing, which were traditionally stepping stones for new graduates, the workforce itself is evolving, shifting towards roles that require adaptability and advanced skills.

While navigating economic uncertainty, executives are revealing their priorities: 43% plan to double down on AI investment, 40% on reskilling, and 39% on digital transformation. Only one in five executives expects to reduce workforce numbers. This trend signals a refreshing break from the high turnover *"churn and burn"* mentality. It suggests HR leaders are focusing on developing talent from within. **Notably, nearly 63% of executives believe it is jobs, not people, that should be made redundant.**[142]

Rather than employee redundancy, AI presents exciting potential for improving employee engagement by enabling people to focus on work that demands creativity, problem-solving, and innovation. Beyond freeing employees from tedious tasks, AI contributes positively to mental and physical well-being. Tools like AI-driven chatbots now provide round-the-clock mental health support, personalised wellness tips, and predictive insights to help prevent burnout. These resources not only increase productivity but create a workplace where employees feel valued and supported.

AI tackles critical workforce challenges, like talent shortages and rising labour costs, by identifying skill gaps and suggesting personalised development paths. Real-time feedback and sentiment analysis tools empower organisations to proactively respond to employee concerns, fine-tune policies, and adapt the workplace environment based on continuous insights.

Moreover, AI has the potential to enrich the human-machine interface and empower employees. By reducing the time leaders spend on routine decision-making, AI allows them to prioritise the human aspects of leadership. And that's obviously building rapport with their teams, fostering collaboration, and enhancing overall morale.

In reality, the future of work is more about **human–machine teaming**, where AI augments human capabilities and enhances the overall work experience. This collaboration is already reshaping roles to promote both personal and professional growth.

> *To fully seize what may be the most profound technological leap of our era, organisations must ensure that their strategies for both business and people foster genuine human progress.*

The Lean and Mean Human–Machine Team

Indeed, organisations are racing to harness the advantages of this augmented intelligence. In fact, according to Mercer's *Global Talents Trends 2024*, 56% of executives consider AI as a job creator within their companies, though one in four say it will transform their business model, meaning change will ripple across nearly every role.[143]

Executives view human–machine teaming as a productivity game changer, economists say it'll reshape markets. And employees? They're already reaping the benefits firsthand—or at least the most agile ones. You don't need to be a futurist; just watch what's happening in your organisation and how some savvy employees are already harnessing AI. We're increasingly noticing that AI's real value lies in amplifying human intelligence to elevate the quality of work. Human–machine teaming could help address some of today's most pressing talent challenges—limited talent pools, rising labour costs, clunky talent mobility, low workforce energy levels, and more.

As technology progresses from written prompts to multimodal models and domain-specific knowledge applications, AI's power to amplify human intelligence will shape hiring and mid-career transitions alike. Combined with richer talent insights, diverse voices, and an emphasis on sustainable work habits, AI is poised to become a true productivity catalyst that benefits everyone.

You may be wondering: if these new technologies are designed to skyrocket efficiency, why are productivity gains still so hard to come by across the organisation? One reason is that, in too many cases, tech deployments aren't translating into new ways of working, and there's often not enough time and effort invested in supporting people through the change. In my opinion, the best response is to **prioritise reskilling and upskilling**, and **cultivating the Growth Mindset** in the organisation.

The initial productivity gains from AI and quantum computing are certainly enticing (often thanks to quick cost savings). But it's human-centric design—not just tech installs—that will unlock lasting productivity and spark innovation. To make this real, work needs to be reimagined to fit how people want to work, with skills nurtured and evolved alongside tech advances.

Managing the Superhuman

Skills Amplified: Enter the AI Genius

The BCG Project: Could HR leaders soon be writing code? Building predictive models? Traditionally, the answer might be no, but new research points to a future where generative AI makes this a reality.[144]

A recent project by Boston Consulting Group (BCG) tested if generative AI could enable users—including HR leaders—to tackle tasks previously beyond their skill set.[145] In this experiment, 480 BCG consultants took on complex tasks typical of data scientists, such as writing Python code and building predictive models, with the help of an AI tool. Their results were then compared with 44 data scientists performing the same tasks without AI assistance.

The study revealed that AI-augmented workers could successfully perform beyond their traditional skill boundaries, suggesting it may be time for HR leaders to rethink skill development strategies. Those using generative AI scored 86% of the data scientists' benchmark, a 49-point improvement over non-AI-assisted users. They also completed tasks roughly 10% faster than the data scientists.

AI's ability to automate routine tasks is reshaping work, and it's not just affecting those in frontline or "*automatable*" roles. It's transforming roles across the board. McKinsey estimates that by 2030, up to 30% of business activities could be automated.[146] Picture a workforce harnessing generative AI to produce outputs beyond an employee or department's skillset.

So here we are. Welcome to the era of **Superhumans**! The superhumans can be found everywhere. They're individuals able to accomplish feats once thought impossible. HR leaders, as the guardians of people and processes, need to understand this trend and embrace it wholeheartedly to remain relevant.

The question we need to ask is: *"How do we lead these superhumans? And what does it mean to show up as leaders in this AI-enhanced era?"* As digital transformation expert Charlene Li points out, *"Leadership is, at its core, a relationship: when you give up the need to be in control because you realise you were never in control in the first place."*[147]

For us—and for HR—to fully leverage AI's potential, we must understand both its capabilities and its limitations. Without this understanding, we won't be able to harness it for positive impact, despite knowing it can serve many other purposes. HR, in particular, needs a disruptive mindset—viewing AI as a strategic partner in decision-making and leveraging its advanced reasoning capabilities to support more data-driven, informed choices.

It's encouraging to see today's most innovative HR leaders setting new standards by using AI to streamline operations like recruitment, onboarding, and payroll. This shift allows them to concentrate on high-value tasks such as talent development and shaping organisational culture.

This shift means that HR professionals shouldn't just view AI as an efficiency tool but as an assistant. A right hand capable of handling tasks more effectively than ever before. At the core of this is the concept of ***chain-of-thought reasoning***—a technique used by advanced models like ChatGPT-4, which enables AI to break down complex issues into sequential, logical steps, simulating human reasoning for intricate challenges. When addressing multifaceted HR issues, for instance, an AI-equipped with this capability can examine each element, evaluate options, weigh pros and cons, and suggest a range of thoughtful solutions.

As it happens, this very book took shape through the reasoning chain of thought process thanks to my collaboration with GenAI. My GPT-4 co-writer, whom I affectionately call CloClo, became my virtual buddy, sparking countless conversations (and the occasional friendly quarrel) along the way (I miss you already, CloClo!).

The best HR leaders are standing at the forefront, ensuring employees' careers, livelihoods, and organisational connections are nurtured. They understand that HR professionals are not passive observers in this AI journey, but active architects, assimilating AI into the fabric of their organisation.

The Future of Employee Engagement

"On its own, AI is just tech.
True transformation is the people part."
—Charlene Li, Digital Transformation Expert

The future of employee engagement belongs to organisations that embrace a balanced, human-centred approach to AI.

How? By prioritising **transparency**, **privacy**, and **inclusivity**, they will use AI as an invaluable asset to elevate employee engagement, creating a workplace where technology and human creativity flourish side by side.

When applied responsibly, AI becomes more than a technological upgrade; it has the potential to shape a culture that's both highly efficient and deeply empathetic. According to the *McKinsey's* report, *Human-centred AI: The Power of Putting People First*, human-centred design is key to using AI in ways that genuinely benefit the workforce. AI systems should act as co-pilots, enhancing employees' skills while preserving their autonomy, dignity, and well-being.[148]

Future work experts advocate for AI principles that are rooted in transparency, ethical use, supportive design, and privacy to foster organisational trust. This framework underscores AI as a support system—not an overbearing authority—transforming AI into a catalyst for a resilient workforce.

It will be crucial to have AI managed by cross-functional teams that align its applications with strategic goals, towards a balanced, people-first approach. On a personal level, this can leave employees feeling more valued, supported, and energised. It's also the perfect opportunity for leaders to really step into their roles as mentors and coaches, using their soft skills and emotional intelligence to strengthen their teams.

So, after this initial era of excitement, what's next? I'm honestly unsure about the long-term benefits—it's starting to go beyond what I can currently grasp. What I do believe is that this ultimately depends on us. It's called machine learning for a reason. It won't just learn from the knowledge we feed it; it will also continue to learn by observing and recording our behaviour.

In the short term, we should prioritise **ethical AI**, ongoing upskilling, and a commitment to lifelong learning. My wish is that these steps will gradually improve our odds of using AI to foster a more inclusive, diverse, and flourishing workplace in the long run.

Based on what I've learned so far, here's my advice: Don't limit yourself to exploring what AI—or any technology—can do for you as a leader, marketer, or HR expert. Instead, reflect on what YOU can do to address the human questions that AI raises. And show the world what **human-to-human behaviour** looks like.

Part V RECAP—Measure Engagement

✹ **Measuring Engagement:** Surveys provide a clear, real-time understanding of organisational health.

✹ *eNPS* is a powerful tool offering a quick benchmark, especially when linked to the NPS.

✹ **The 5 I's of Platforms** should Inform, Inspire, Instruct, Involve, and Incentivise.

✹ **Transparency and Trust:** Transparent communication fosters trust, showing employees their voices matter.

✹ **Benefits of HR Analytics:** They support decision-making by converting raw data into insights on talent, retention, workforce planning, and performance, enabling HR to act as a strategic partner.

✹ **AI supports engagement** by automating repetitive tasks, personalising employee interactions, and offering real-time feedback. However, this requires careful attention to ethics, privacy, and AI's impact on roles.

✹ **Human–machine teaming** is reshaping roles, allowing AI to augment human abilities. While still in the *messy middle,* HR must prepare to manage a workforce of S*uperhumans* who leverage AI to achieve beyond traditional limits.

THE ART & CRAFT OF EMPLOYEE ENGAGEMENT

"You never really understand a person until you consider things from his point of view... Until you climb inside of his skin and walk around in it."

—Harper Lee (To Kill a Mockingbird)

We've journeyed through the essentials of why engaged employees and a strong organisational culture are non-negotiables for success. We've unpacked the twelve drivers of engagement, explored how to measure them, and underscored the need for HR to step up as a strategic business partner and the architects of culture, talent, and employee experience. This evolution includes mastering digital tools and building a solid HR tech infrastructure to power the organisation forward. Let's not forget, engagement isn't solely HR's responsibility; it's a shared commitment that comes to life on the frontline, where team leaders drive it and everyone else fuels it.

In any organisation, you'll find varying levels of engagement, both among individuals and across teams. And the importance of leadership in shaping and guiding this engagement cannot be overstated. By *"leader,"* I'm not just talking about the CEO—this term encompasses project managers, team leaders, HR managers, and anyone who works closely with people and feels a sense of responsibility.

While the pandemic has often been described as a period that exposed leadership flaws, it also brought to light some unexpected positives. During this challenging time, new leaders emerged; people who discovered leadership qualities within themselves that they might not have even realised they possessed.

According to Gallup, overall, managers are more engaged than employees. While only 30% of managers and 23% of employees overall are engaged globally, some organisations reach much higher levels of employee engagement and well-being. Best-practice organisations across industries and geographies have three-fourths of their managers engaged and seven in 10 non-managers. This is the equivalent of 14 engaged employees for every one actively disengaged employee, a ratio 11 times the global average.

It is the moral duty of the leader to identify the different levels of engagement and to grasp them. In this final chapter, I will give you some practical tools for communication, marketing, and coaching in order to help you successfully expand your role, regardless of your position. This empowers you to help others elevate themselves and craft a legacy that stands the test of time.

1

The Shift from Disengaged to Engaged

"You don't have to see the whole staircase, just take the first step."

—*Martin Luther King, Jr.*

Convince, Encourage, and Inspire

In today's workplace, employees frequently juggle roles across various teams and countries—a reality that organisational charts rarely reflect. Consequently, the reporting lines can look as tangled as a bowl of spaghetti to anyone not involved in the daily grind. In today's hybrid work environment, team-level collaboration has become central. An employee might feel like a rockstar in one team yet like a fish out of water in another.

Here are 3 key steps to help you mentor your team members and give their engagement levels a well-deserved boost:[149]

1. Persuade. *Take the Safe First Step*

Imagine someone stuck in the gears of a change process, feeling uncomfortable in the new situation. The magic trick here is to gently nudge them to take just one safe step. By doing this, you create a safe space and an emotional cushion. You're not asking them to dive headfirst into the deep end; you're merely suggesting they dip their toes in the water. One effective way to do this is by offering some educational opportunities or training sessions—essentially, their safety floaties.

2. Encourage. *The Feel-Good Factor*

The secret sauce to encouragement? Making people feel good about themselves. Rather than taking the easy route of criticism, invest time in recognising their strengths. Acknowledge what they've already accomplished and express your unwavering belief in their ability to tackle future challenges. A heartfelt conversation can be a real game-changer. Give it a try and see the impact!

3. Inspire. *Storytime Magic*

To inspire wield the mighty power of storytelling. Every great leader knows that a good story can move mountains. Stephen Covey, author of *The Seven Habits of Highly Effective People*, swears by the mantra: "*Start with the end in mind.*" Paint a vivid picture of a positive future work experience and trace the steps backward from there. Engage your colleague in this vision, sketch it out, and make it feel real. Because it has already happened, so to speak, there will be less trepidation in the conversation. Guiding people to visualise a compelling future can be a powerful way to lift them out of disengagement.

✋Case in Point

The Happy or Not Initiative: A Small Tool, Big Impact at DHL

I have mentioned the charismatic CEO of DHL MEA, Amadou Diallo, a few times throughout this book. Amadou shared an innovative yet straightforward approach that he championed at DHL Global Forwarding UAE.

Diallo, a dynamic leader known for his close connection with employees, always ensures he is deeply involved with frontline operations. DHL has been working with Lean Six Sigma methodologies for years. Diallo exemplifies this by regularly going to the *Gemba*—a Japanese term meaning "*the real place*" or "*the place where it happens.*" Gemba walks include observing processes in action, engaging with employees, and identifying opportunities for improvement. Although Diallo is a big Gemba fan, he still believed something extra was needed. There was no KPI to measure the sparkles in the employees' eyes.

That's how he came up with the "*Happy or Not*" parameter. This daily tool measures employee mood throughout the day, providing executives with a real-time snapshot of workplace sentiment.

Each morning, executives receive a report in their inbox, allowing them to address any issues promptly and make adjustments as needed. Although it may not be the most scientific method, it offers direct, actionable feedback that is highly effective in driving continuous improvement and maintaining high levels of employee engagement.

Dealing with the Actively Disengaged

"It is a misconception that you can do little with employees who show low engagement. Give them the chance to give their own content to their job."

—*Ronald Everaert,*
Former CEO of Mercator and Telindus

Actively disengaged employees are like a ticking time bomb, posing a danger to both the company and themselves. Not only do they drag their feet in terms of productivity, but they also have the potential to sabotage operations in a big way. Their negative energy can spread faster than a rumour at the coffee machine, affecting other employees. And, as you may recall, about 17% of employees are actively uninvolved.[150]

The *Employee Engagement Report* by BlessingWhite categorises employees into various engagement levels, including those who are disengaged, with labels such as *Spinning*, *Settling*, and *Splitting*.[151] Each term represents a distinct way in which disengagement is expressed.

3 Levels of Disengagement

*1. **Spinning:** Refers to employees who are busy and active but lack a clear direction or purpose. They are often involved in various tasks and activities, but their efforts do not necessarily contribute to meaningful progress or the organisation's goals. Characteristics:*

- *Highly active but not necessarily productive.*
- *They may appear engaged because of their activity level, but their work lacks focus and alignment with the organisation's objectives.*

- *They often feel overwhelmed or stressed due to their lack of direction.*
- *They may engage in busywork that gives the appearance of productivity but has little impact.*

2. Settling: *Describes employees who have become complacent and are no longer striving for growth or improvement. They have settled into their roles, often doing the bare minimum to meet expectations without seeking additional responsibilities or opportunities for development. Characteristics:*

- *Content with the status quo and resistant to change.*
- *Lack motivation to pursue new challenges or career advancement.*
- *Often disengaged due to a perceived lack of opportunities, recognition, or meaningful work.*
- *Their behaviour typically reflects coasting—doing just enough to meet expectations without going above and beyond.*

3. Splitting: *Refers to employees who are mentally or emotionally disengaged, leading to a division between their personal interests and their work responsibilities. These employees may physically be at work, but their mind and focus are elsewhere, resulting in minimal contribution to the organisation. Characteristics:*

- *Physically present but emotionally detached.*
- *May be actively looking for other opportunities or just going through the motions.*
- *Their disengagement can lead to decreased productivity and potential errors in their work.*
- *They might display a negative attitude, be indifferent to organisational goals, or have conflicting priorities that pull their focus away from work.*

Do you have spinners, settlers, or splitters in your team? I can assure you: **Nothing ruins a positive work environment quicker than seeing a negative team member being tolerated.** As a leader, it's your duty to make it crystal clear: those who choose to be actively disengaged need to either step up their game or step out.

Spotting the Disengaged

How do you spot the party poopers? Here's a simple litmus test: ask yourself if you or your team would feel a sense of relief if certain individuals decided to leave. If the answer is a resounding yes, it's time to dig deeper. Identify the root cause of their disengagement. Is it due to specific circumstances, or is it a matter of a sour attitude? Are others in the organisation showing similar behaviour?

Here's the truth: Even your most dedicated employees can hit rough patches. Imagine facing a tough merger, dealing with an overbearing boss, or years without a promotion or pay raise. When there's a real reason behind their disengagement, recognise it and take action. If these employees are valuable to the organisation, pull out all the stops to turn things around.

When Attitude Is the Culprit

If you find that their disengagement stems from a generally negative attitude rather than specific circumstances, swift action is necessary. Let them know, without sugar-coating it, that their behaviour is unacceptable and won't be tolerated in your organisation. Have a candid, personal conversation, clarifying that while you're addressing the circumstances, they must take responsibility for their attitude.

5 Coaching Steps for a Candid Conversation

1. ***Personal Interaction:*** *Keep the conversation personal and engaging.*

2. ***Specificity:*** *Be clear and precise about the issues.*

3. ***Behaviour Focused:*** *Address their behaviour, not their personality.*

4. ***Actionable Advice:*** *Provide realistic steps they can take to improve.*

5. ***Documentation:*** *Record everything.*

Actively disengaged employees pose a serious threat to the organisation. Give them a fair opportunity to re-engage, but if they can't—or won't—demonstrate commitment, it's essential to take responsibility and make the tough calls.

Facing the Brutal Facts

As humans, we often hire quickly and fire slowly. We shy away from confrontation, hoping (in vain) that these situations will magically improve on their own. But they rarely do. If this resonates, let it be your wake-up call to take decisive, bold action. Anyone who has read *Good to Great*[152] by Jim Collins knows the importance of facing brutal facts, no matter how optimistic you are about the outcome. Toxic team members are one such brutal fact. Ignoring red flags because you want to see the good in everyone will often lead to more harm than good.

Experience shows that letting people go due to their attitudes is often a long, dragged-out process. When the decision is finally made, it's usually met with relief from colleagues. Here, the key lesson from the Netflix Culture Code is: *"No brilliant jerks allowed.*" Your responsibility is to the organisation, and often, colleagues have sensed the problem long before any action is taken. As the French say, "*Quand les dégoûtés s'en vont, il n'y a que les dégoûtants qui restent,*" when the disgusted leave, only the disgusting remain. Make sure it never gets to that point.

2

Employer Branding and Communication

"A brand is the promise of an experience."

—Alexander Isley, Graphic Designer & Educator

A true leader is a maestro in communication. Masterful leaders excel at conveying messages with clarity and adapting their tone and attitude to suit their audience Even if you're not a marketing wizard, it's crucial for you to keep an eye on your organisation's employer branding campaigns to attract the best team members. Keeping tabs on your organisation's employer branding efforts is key to attracting top talent. With GenAI elevating your Superhuman marketing skills, you might be amazed at what you can accomplish.

Purpose and Principles

We've touched on this before. Your company's purpose and values form the bedrock of any effective employer branding campaign. With a dual focus on attracting talent and validating employees' choices, employer branding creates value both externally and internally.

Attracting the right employees becomes a breeze once you've defined a **powerful purpose** that people are eager to champion. A real purpose means you can skip the cliché ads. You know the ones, featuring an overly polished team with just the right blend of ethnicities beaming from a rafting boat under the tagline: *"Are you the team player we've been searching for?"* Instead, let your values and mission do the talking. They will naturally draw in candidates who are genuinely passionate about what your company represents.

A robust employer branding campaign is rooted in strong values and paints an aspirational picture for job candidates. Think about it. Who wouldn't want to join a company committed to *"democratising design"* (Ikea), *"being in business to save our home planet"* (Patagonia), *"encouraging people to exercise"* (Nike), or *"realising childhood dreams"* (Disney)?

One good measure of your attractiveness in the job market is the number of spontaneous applications you receive. Take Emirates Airlines in the UAE, for example. The ones from *"Hello Tomorrow."* Known for being a highly attractive employer, they received a staggering 3.2 million applications in one year, with the highest number in a single week hitting 110,000 applications. If I were in my twenties, I'd know where to start my career! This phenomenal volume underscores their strong employer brand and wide appeal.

Now let's add a key qualifier: **relevance**. How many of these spontaneous applications are from top performers you'd love on your team? Is your company a magnet for talent, or do you have to shell out big bucks to attract top candidates? The strength of your employer brand is what makes the difference.

Obviously, no strong employer branding can exist without a strong employer brand. It seems obvious, yet one cannot exist without the other. Every marketer knows that the fastest way to kill a bad product is a good campaign. You might get people to try your product with a snazzy campaign, but if the product itself falls short, sales will plummet, and social media backlash will be swift and merciless.

Marketers know to focus on perfecting the product before pushing it through campaigns. Similarly, a strong employer brand isn't built through employer branding campaigns alone. The foundations—a solid organisational culture—must be in place first. Only then can you effectively market your company as a top employer.

✋ Case in Point

From Tobacco over Smoke-Free to… Health? The Smoke-Free Journey of Philip Morris International

It might feel jarring to see a tobacco giant featured in a book on well-being and engagement. You're probably wondering: what place could Philip Morris International (PMI) possibly have here? But before you slam this book shut and toss it away, hear me out.

PMI is on an extraordinary journey—one that defies assumptions and sets them apart from every other player in their industry, drawing some of the world's top talent to their mission.

PMI has arguably built the world's most successful cigarette company, with the world's most iconic brands and famous marketing campaigns that are still studied at university. Then, just over a decade ago, they made a monumental choice: to launch the first smoke-free product in the industry. PMI is building its future on smoke-free products that—while not risk-free, let's be very clear about that—are far less harmful than cigarettes. PMI's goal is that these products will one day replace cigarettes; a vision as ambitious as it is controversial and driven by a clear commercial strategy as well.

I'm fully aware of the debate surrounding both tobacco and these new alternatives. And, as a health advocate myself, my intention isn't to promote these products. What intrigues me is PMI's willingness to confront its own past and completely reinvent itself—an unprecedented move in this industry. Few organisations of this scale have the courage to own their legacy, transform their business model, and build a compelling culture that pulls in top talent from Big Tech, pharmaceutical, and luxury consumer brands. I remember the first time I heard PMI's slogan about a smoke-free future; it stopped me in my tracks. I had to wonder: could they actually make such a bold vision work?

To delve deeper, I spoke with Tom Verbeke, VP of People and Culture in Japan.

PMI's origins began in 1847 when Philip Morris opened a tobacco shop on London's Bond Street, and by the 1970s, brands like Marlboro had become cultural icons, thanks in part to unforgettable Formula One campaigns. But, beginning as far back as the early 2000s, a visionary group led by PMI's current chairman, André Calantzopoulos, decided it was time for change. And not just incremental change—radical transformation from the inside out. The goal was bold: reduce harmful substances in their products by leveraging technology and science. The research lab in

Neuchâtel, Switzerland was built with the aim to remove the most dangerous compounds from smoke. Their premise was simple but groundbreaking: if people don't quit smoking, could they instead choose something less harmful? After nearly a decade of R&D, PMI claimed they had removed the overall majority of the carcinogenic substances from their new product line.

The result was IQOS, a series of devices that heat specially designed tobacco units called heatsticks to a lower temperature as an effort to provide smoke-free alternatives for adult smokers who would otherwise continue smoking. IQOS took off, generating over $10 billion in revenue and scaling faster than some of the world's biggest tech disruptors. But this success demanded an organisational overhaul: PMI is now a consumer electronics company with a vastly different business model. They needed new capabilities in everything from tech development to customer care.

It is something that has never been done before. PMI needed to reshape its workforce and culture, attracting people who, a decade ago, wouldn't have dreamed of joining a tobacco company. PMI is focused on helping legal-age smokers switch to better alternatives. They use stringent marketing strategies and do not target youth, non-users or non-smokers. With this commitment, they are redefining ethics in the industry, a factor that's increasingly critical to their employees.

Tom shared that PMI's culture has become more purpose-driven than ever before. *"We're at an all-time high,"* he said. *"Our organisational culture doesn't have to be pushed, as our purpose leads the way."* With clear reports to the stock market and street on the growing user base exceeding 30 million users now, the transformation is clear and direct.

Most of it is trial and error, but it all starts by attracting the right people and developing internal talent. And the right people means something different than what it meant 20 years ago. The renewed purpose has attracted waves of new talent, especially within the executive team. In the past five years, in Japan, 300 out of 450 members of PMI's are new, drawn in by this mission of reinvention. Within the global 80,000+ headcount workforce, it's a melting pot of legacy and new: scientists, technologists, marketers, data analysts, manufacturing talent, and so much more.

PMI's HR team is now re-evaluating core capabilities across the organisation. *"Transformation is never structured,"* Tom told me. *"Sometimes you have to take a step back in order to avoid losing people through rapid transformation. It's always keeping that fine balance to make sure that you're on the right track, rather than rushing to the next goal. Making sure people never lose our purpose, the why, the end game out of sight, makes all the difference."*

And the change continues. PMI is now venturing into wellness, exploring applications for inhalation technology that extend far beyond tobacco. In collaboration with scientists, PMI has begun to test and use applications in medication, relaxation, and sleep aids. Imagine, for example, the difference if an inhaled aspirin took effect in two minutes rather than thirty. This wellness expansion is set to shape PMI's future, transforming their product portfolio well beyond smoke-free alternatives.

So, could PMI actually become a wellness and health company in the next few decades? There's a long way to go, and the idea is still met with scepticism. But it is a very powerful illustration of a transformational change with tremendous impact that will touch many lives and attract new and unexpected talent. Whatever the future holds, PMI's journey reveals the incredible power of purpose to drive organisational change and rewrite legacies. And that's a story worth reading.

Right Media

Communication Checklist

When communicating with your (future) workforce, ask yourself these questions to ensure you're using the right media channels:

- *Which channels are we using?*
- *What message are we delivering in which channel?*
- *How is your funnel management coming along?*
- *What messages do candidates see before they are hired and are they consistent after the onboarding phase?*
- *What communication channels do we use to communicate with our employees on an ongoing basis?*

These are just a few of the questions a typical marketer considers when figuring out how to attract new customers and keep existing ones satisfied. As a leader, are you thinking along these lines, or are you still relying on the occasional *ad hoc* job posting to attract talent?

Social media is a powerful magnet for attracting candidates to your website. But let's not forget: you don't own the data collected there. The Zuckerbergs of the world do. Moreover, you need to be wary of putting all your eggs in one social media basket because trends can change faster than you can say *MySpace.*

Your website should be the central hub in your social media ecosystem. Picture this: your website is the window display, and social media platforms like LinkedIn, Facebook, Instagram, and possibly TikTok are the spokes. Use these spokes to build reach and create awareness, but the magic happens on your website—where you capture data and build lasting relationships.

Imagine your website the way a meticulous shopkeeper thinks about their window display. A candidate will probably visit your website more than once, so keep it fresh and engaging. Offer different content each time and initiate a dialogue with candidates using sales automation tools. It's like having a friendly chat with a regular customer, making them feel valued and special.

It's incredibly powerful when your own employees spontaneously share content about your company. The spontaneous creation and sharing of content by employees on external channels is the holy grail of engagement. That's the essence of *"HR is the new marketing."* Unfortunately, not all employees—even the engaged ones—are eager to blur the lines between their professional and personal social media. Typically, only about 10–15% are willing to do so. They might claim they want to keep work and personal life separate, but platforms like LinkedIn, which are inherently professional, make that excuse fall flat.

It always helps if you can explain to them the personal benefits of sharing professional content: They build more professional connections, establish themselves as thought leaders in their field of expertise, learn from other specialists, and enhance their personal branding.

If creating content isn't their forte, provide them with ready-made motivational content. Several excellent tools on the market can generate post-ready content and appropriate hashtags with just a few clicks. These tools can measure content distribution, track which types of content achieve the greatest reach, and identify optimal posting times. While they may not be the magic solution for massive social media sharing, they're valuable enough for your marketing/communications team to keep promoting them. Experimenting with these tools is worthwhile to find what works best for your organisation.

Hygiene—Hub—Hero

In the world of marketing, the *Hygiene, Hub, and Hero* model is a trusty framework. It's all about deciding in advance which channels to use for your communication efforts and allocating your resources wisely.

1. **Hygiene:** Think of hygiene as the daily brushing and flossing of your communication strategy. It's the constant stream of relevant information that's *always on.* Your website is the shining beacon here, chock-full of valuable content aimed at interesting target groups. To keep it polished, use a sophisticated *SEO (Search Engine Optimisation)* and *SEA (Search Engine Advertising)* approach. You want to be the first result when someone googles: "*awesome places to work,*" or "*best organisational culture.*"

2. **Hub** means that you will select a number of important periods where you put in extra effort. Maybe it's during

a business expansion or to cover a holiday period. During these times, you ramp up your visibility as an employer. Hub activities are like those seasonal deep cleans—It's not just a quick wipe-down.

3. **Hero** are those moments where big *all-hands-on-deck* efforts go to attract top talent. An example of this is opening up your site to visitors from the local area and using that to make the company known to a wider audience. These are grand events where you pull out all the stops to draw in the right candidates. Make sure to register visitors, agree on follow-ups, and, if the chance arises, have those one-on-one chats to tell them you're on the lookout for talent like theirs.

A sophisticated communication plan is your secret weapon in the war for talent.

Keeping Communication Alive

Once the recruitment dust settles, the role of communication becomes even more crucial. As a marketer, you use communication to reaffirm customers in their choice and continue to build brand attitude. This involves various touchpoints, preferably *phygital* (both physical and digital).

For your employees, the approach is quite similar. When new hires come on board, they often experience cognitive dissonance, questioning if they made the right choice. "*Did I do the right thing?*" becomes a nagging thought. This is the phase where most questions arise, and communication is key to easing these doubts.

But the need for communication doesn't stop there. Consistent updates about the company's goals, achievements, and internal happenings are essential. How can employees know what they are contributing to if they're not kept in the loop? In many companies, employees can't even name the top three priorities for the year. Not because they don't care or because they lack intelligence, but because the information wasn't communicated clearly or frequently enough.

What about you: Do you know them by heart? Are you confident your employees and management do? Thought so.

In a hybrid setting, people often complain that the feeling of proximity is lacking. Companies have launched numerous initiatives to maintain connection and promote well-being. But these efforts often only talk to the brain and not to the heart. Some managers hesitate to communicate personally, fearing they need all the answers. But your employees know you don't have a crystal ball. They've been through the pandemic, remember? You only fail if you don't communicate. Authentic leadership is about acknowledging you don't have all the answers while conveying a message of solidarity and hope tied to the company's mission.

Storytelling remains one of the most powerful and effective ways to engage your audience. Given the diversity of your workforce, use all available channels—videos, memes, speeches, blog articles, competitions, online events, surprise boxes, awards, and more. Finding the right mix to suit your internal audience is key. And if you worry about over-communicating, just keep in mind that it's better to over-communicate than under-communicate. Repetition is allowed. Repetition is allowed.

Conversations: Stepping Away from the Transactional

Executive coach Joe Sejean believes that conversations are a powerful tool for fostering employee engagement. These rare one-on-one chats can create a significant impact throughout the year. Joe shares three tips to make your conversations count.

1. Relationship focus: Go beyond tasks and metrics. Connect with employees on an emotional level, seeing them as human beings, not just *human doings.* Build genuine relationships by understanding their feelings, motivations, and challenges. Practical questions to use:

- *How are you feeling today?*
- *What's your biggest challenge right now?*
- *How can I support you?*

2. Paying attention: Show that you truly notice your employees' efforts and dedication. Recognise not just their achievements but also the process and hard work involved. Examples of questions/feedback:

- *I noticed you handled that project really well. Can you walk me through your process?*
- *What challenges did you face during this task, and how did you overcome them?*
- *I saw a quality improvement in your deliverables [be specific] and the impact is positive. Well done.*
- *I sense this project is challenging [give an example]. What's the situation and how can I help?*

3. Curiosity about achievements: If direct observation isn't possible, engage in conversations to explore how achievements were made. Show that you value their input and development.

Questions to ask:

- *How did you manage to achieve this outcome?*
- *What were some key decisions you made along the way?*
- *Were there any unexpected challenges, and how did you handle them?*
- *What support or resources were most helpful to you during this process?*

By incorporating these elements into your conversations, you can nurture a more engaged, motivated, and productive team.

🖐 Case in Point

From Ohio to Abu Dhabi: Cleveland Clinic's Cure for Engagement

In 2022, Cleveland Clinic launched a comprehensive listening effort as part of its four-part engagement strategy to create a more connected, engaged, and motivated workforce. This initiative was designed to address the critical need for real-time dialogue and deeper connections between leaders and staff, moving beyond the limits of traditional engagement surveys.

One of the key components of this strategy is leader listening sessions, available to all leaders across Cleveland Clinic's global footprint, from Ohio to Canada to Abu Dhabi. These sessions provide a structured yet open forum for leaders to share their experiences, challenges, and needs, offering a more meaningful alternative to the typical one-way communication of surveys.

As Executive Vice President and Chief Caregiver Officer Kelly Hancock explains, *"Listening to what employees tell you they need goes a long way. When workers feel like their feedback isn't being heard, they can become disengaged."*[153]

This listening initiative is just one aspect of the Clinic's broader engagement strategy, which is built around four pillars: listening, connecting, developing, and taking action. Through Leader Conversations, executives, including Hancock and the CEO, engage directly with system leaders to ensure that feedback from listening sessions leads to action. This transparent follow-up helps build trust and solidifies the connection between employees and the organisation's leadership.

Another critical element is development. Cleveland Clinic recognises that growth opportunities are essential for engagement, particularly in a demanding healthcare environment. They've enhanced leadership development programmes to equip leaders with the skills they need to manage teams effectively and empathically.

Finally, the engagement strategy hinges on accountability and action. Insights from listening sessions are promptly analysed and turned into actionable steps, allowing employees to feel heard and observe tangible results, based on their input. This commitment to follow-through builds trust and keeps the engagement strategy dynamic and responsive.

By launching this listening initiative and embedding it into its overall strategy, Cleveland Clinic has created a robust model for employee engagement, one that goes beyond the superficial layer of surveys and fosters deeper, ongoing connections across the organisation.

3

It Begins and Ends With...

"You are what you believe yourself to be."

—*Paulo Coelho, Author*

YOU! That's right, you're the starting point—and the finish line—of employee engagement.

When you've found that sweet spot in your work—doing something you're passionate about and skilled at, something that energises and challenges you, offers new opportunities, and allows you to collaborate with great colleagues in a place where you feel at home—well, that's when you know you're in the right place. You're not just engaged; you're radiating that positivity to everyone around you, including your family and friends.

The goal of this book was to help you elevate your own commitment, giving you more energy and a greater sense of fulfilment. I also aimed to provide you with tools, tips, and tricks to better understand and amplify engagement within your organisation, especially during these disruptive times that are redefining work.

I hope that, by now, it's clear that employee engagement is a never-ending process. Even if you mapped out the perfect strategy for the year ahead, it won't be long before it needs tweaking—especially in today's fast-paced environment. Hence the tagline we came up with when creating Herculean Alliance: "*Crafting powerful workforces.*" Engagement isn't a one-time task; it's an ongoing shaping and refining.

No matter what GenAI or the future of work brings, one thing is certain: employee engagement is a marathon, not a sprint. Take the time to focus on it now. Bring your people along for the ride, involve them in the process, and empower them. Use your purpose, company culture, and values—those very things that drew you to your organisation in the first place—as your guiding compass and make it fun! You know the drill by now: it's now or never.

Let's wrap up with a bit of wisdom from Simon Sinek: "*True love exists in business. It's when employee and employer are amazingly grateful to have each other. We should all have true love at work.*"

My sincere wish for you is that you find that true love at work. You deserve it.

Inge

Part VI RECAP—The Art and Craft of Employee Engagement

- **Shift from Disengaged to Engaged:** Gradual shift from convincing to encouraging to inspiring.
- **Spinning, Settling, Splitting:** 3 levels of disengagement.
- **5 Coaching Steps:**
  1. Personal interaction
  2. Specificity
  3. Behaviour focus
  4. Actionable advice
  5. Documentation
- **Facing the Brutal Facts:** Confront disengagement head-on, making tough decisions when employees fail to re-engage.
- **Employer Branding and Communication:** Purpose & Principles form the foundation of employer branding.
- **Right media** and the ***Hygiene—Hub—Hero* model.**
- **Keeping Communication Alive:** Storytelling, varied channels, and consistent communication maintain engagement.
- **3 Steps for Meaningful Conversations:**
  1. Relationship focus
  2. Paying attention
  3. Curiosity about achievements

Bringing It All Together

In a rapidly evolving world where change is constant and some challenges seem insurmountable, leaders face an unprecedented test: how to keep people engaged and motivated amidst uncertainty? Inge's second book is a guiding light for any leader who believes we are experiencing a rapid global transformation, impacting people's lives.

When I finished my MBA in the 90s, the job of managers was straightforward: "*Use resources to increase revenue and decrease costs to drive profit.*" Decentralisation through Web 3.0, climate pressure, geopolitics, and artificial intelligence are just a few of the transformational phenomena. Balancing all these challenges while trying to run a business with engaged employees who drive customer happiness is a challenge for every leader.

Incomplete, contradictory, or changing requirements characterise a wicked problem. Inge described how poor the numbers are. Balancing twelve major drivers in employee engagement in this fast-changing world is a Herculean challenge. While the mathematician in me fantasises about developing an algorithm to solve this, the reality is that no formula can fully address the intricacies of human dynamics. Solutions to wicked problems are neither true nor false; they can only be good or bad.

Unlike so-called *"tame"* problems, which have clear solutions, wicked business problems cannot be solved with a simple formula or process. In fact, applying old orthodoxies often makes them worse. They will not be solved by the same tools and processes that are complicit in creating them, but require ongoing experimentation, learning, and adaptation.

We can only solve wicked problems by creating a diverse community of people who are curious, and who share, listen, connect, and innovate. That's why we founded the Herculean Alliance, an ecosystem of experts and formats. Through formats like *Hercules Trophy, Pink Ladies Games, and Bravos! Employee Engagement Awards*, we are nurturing a global community that thrives on connection, curiosity, and collaboration.

I firmly believe in the power of diverse communities or networked organisations to create a culture of performance and customer delight. With the right people doing the right things right at the right time, sharing a **Big Hairy Audacious Goal (BHAG)** that they can't conquer on their own. Focusing on each other's strengths while having truthful conversations. A culture in which everybody is committed to becoming their best version. An environment where people cheer each other to victory, especially when things get rough.

The pandemic, another one of these wicked problems, was a unique social experiment we had to endure. It proved once again that the individual is lost without meaningful connections and strong leadership. Anger, anxiety, loneliness, and other low-frequency emotions kicked in for too many people. When the individual is lost, organisations are lost.

We are as strong as the sum of the strength of our connections and trust is the currency. Surround yourself with a diverse tribe of good people. People who lift you—people who don't judge and will patiently cheer you to victory. People who don't push you deeper by pointing out your weaknesses from their moral high ground. But successful people with whom you can maintain truthful conversations to hold you accountable for becoming the best version of yourself.

As Stanley McChrystal writes in his book *Team of Teams: New Rules of Engagement for a Complex World*, we have to allow leaders to grow themselves, evolving from chess players to gardeners. Just as gardeners nurture the conditions for nature to thrive, leaders must create the environment for their people to flourish. This shift in perspective, from controlling to cultivating, is at the heart of building resilient, self-sustaining communities. You can't ask a tree to grow faster, but you can influence the circumstances for it to flourish. Practice patience and believe that amicable conversations with plants help them grow. Leaders should become brokers of trust, building and interconnecting communities in a decentralised world. Transforming from "*a team of greats to a team of great teams*"— like a flock of starlings—becoming a liquid organisation with mass relationships.

I'm absolutely delighted to see Inge spotlight the UAE as a shining example of engagement—a country I deeply admire. Relocating here with the family at the onset of the pandemic wasn't just daring; it embodied the resilience and adaptability she mentions. The leadership and people of the UAE have shown us that through true engagement, even the most complex challenges can be turned into opportunities for growth. Moving here has reshaped nearly every part of our lives, and not a day goes by that I don't feel grateful for weathering this journey together. I hope this book inspires others to draw on the lessons of adaptability from this remarkable region.

As a final note, this book marks both the end of an era and the beginning of a new chapter for Herculean Alliance. Just one week after completing her book, Inge embarked on her next journey as Senior Client Partner with Korn Ferry Middle East. Mabrook! After spending half her career in corporate and half as an entrepreneur, an exciting new opportunity opened up—just the right next step for growth. It's true: the Universe has a way of providing exactly what we need to evolve.

I couldn't be prouder. Inge embodies impact, customer delight, professionalism, and so much more. Taking on a role in the Middle East with the global market leader is the perfect challenge to match her values and vision. I have no doubt this next step will allow her to realise her full potential. They're truly fortunate to have her.

What a journey it's been, Inge—thank you. I can't wait to see what the future holds.

Yves Vekemans, Founder Herculean Alliance

Bibliography

[1] Ben Horowitz, the well-known venture capitalist and co-founder of Andreessen Horowitz, often advises against treating employees like family. He believes that businesses and families operate on different principles. In a family, relationships are unconditional, and support is given regardless of performance. In contrast, a business focuses on performance, results, and alignment with company goals.

[2] William A. Kahn, *"Psychological Conditions of Personal Engagement and Disengagement at Work,"* https://cygnetinstitute.org/wp-content/uploads/2021/02/William-Kahn-Employee-Engagement.pdf, Academy of Management Journal; Dec 1990; 33, 4; ProQuest.

[3] Institute for Employment Studies. Dilys Robinson, Ies Opinion. Employee Engagement. https://www.employment-studies.co.uk/system/files/resources/files/op11.pdf

[4] Jacob Morgan. *The Employee Experience Advantage: How to Win the War for Talent by Giving Employees the Workspaces they Want, the Tools they Need, and a Culture They Can Celebrate,* John Wiley & Sons Inc., 2017.

[5] Don Phin, *Employee Engagement.* Course on LinkedIn Learning.

[6] Gallup, State of the Global Workplace: 2024 Report, https://www.gallup.com/workplace/349484/state-of-the-global-workplace.aspx

[7] If you're curious about how your country stacks up in terms of engagement and well-being, head over to Gallup website for the full scoop.

[8] Daniel H. Pink, *Drive. The Surprising Truth About What Motivates Us,* Canongate Books Ltd., 2018.

[9] Van den Broeck, A., Ferris, D. L., Chang, C. H., & Rosen, C. C. (2016). *Review of Self-Determination Theory's Basic Psychological Needs at Work.* Journal of Management, 42(5), 1195-1229. http://doi.org/10.1177/0149206316632058. Also retrieved from Supporting Work.

[10] Harvard Business Review, Robert E. Quinn and Anjan V. Thankor. *"Creating a Purpose-Driven Organisation,"* 2018.

[11] Ray Baumruk. *"The missing link: The role of employee engagement in business success."*

[12] James K. Harter, Frank L. Schmidt, and Theodore L. Hayes, *"Business-unit-Level Relationship Between Employee Satisfaction, Employee Engagement, and Business Outcomes: A Meta-Analysis."*

[13] Harter, J.K., Schmidt, F.L., & Hayes, T.L., Psychology, 2002 Vol. 87, No. 2.

[14] Towers Watson, 2009.

[15] Towers Watson, 2010.

[16] The Conference Board, 2006.

[17] Towers Perrin, 2008.

[18] The Conference Board, 2006.

[19] The Conference Board, 2006.

[20] Center for Creative Leadership, 2009.

[21] Gallup Germany, 2011.

[22] Towers Perrin *"European Talent Survey: Reconnecting with Employees: Attracting, Retaining, and Engaging"*, Towers Perrin, 2004

[23] *"The Impact of Employee Engagement,"* Kenexa.

[24] Reid Hoffman and Chris Yeh, *Creating an Alliance with Employees.* LinkedIn Learning.

[25] Gartner, *Customer Experience Survey 2018.*

[26] Blake Morgan, *"The Customer of the Future: 10 Guiding Principles for Winning Tomorrow's Business,"* Harper Collins, 2019.

[27] Alex R. Zablah, Brad D. Carlson, D. Todd Donavan, James G. Maxham, III, and Tom J. Brown. *A Cross-Lagged Test of the Association Between Customer Satisfaction and Employee Job Satisfaction in a Relational Context,* Online First Publication, Journal of Applied Psychology, 18 January 2016.

[28] Press Release Worldbank, *"Demand for Online Gig Work Rapidly Rising in Developing Countries"* https://www.worldbank.org/en/news/press-release/2023/09/07/demand-for-online-gig-work-rapidly-rising-in-developing-countries, 7 September 2023.

[29] Boston Consulting Group, Judith Wallenstein, Alice de Chalendar, Martin Reeves, and Allison Bailey, *"The New Freelancers: Tapping Talent in the Gig Economy,"* https://www.bcg.com/publications/2019/new-freelancers-tapping-talent-gig-economy, 17 January 2019.

[30] McKinsey & Company, *"Freelance, side hustles, and gigs: Many more Americans have become independent workers,"* https://www.mckinsey.com/featured-insights/sustainable-inclusive-growth/future-of-america/freelance-side-hustles-and-gigs-many-more-americans-have-become-independent-workers, 23 August 2022.

[31] Deloitte, Sue Cantrell, Karen Weisz, Michael Griffiths, Kraig Eaton, co-authored by Lauren Kirby, *"Unlocking the workforce ecosystem,"* https://www2.deloitte.com/us/en/insights/focus/human-capital-trends/2023/contingent-talent-management.html, 9 January 2023.

[32] Dr Tommy Weir. *Leadership, Dubai style. The habits to achieve remarkable success*, EMLC Press, 2013.

[33] A Majlis is an Arabic term meaning *"sitting room"* or *"assembly."* It refers to a space where people gather for various purposes, such as socializing, discussing community issues, or holding formal meetings. The concept of a majlis is deeply rooted in the cultural and social traditions of many Middle Eastern and North African countries.

[34] Korn Ferry, George Bongiorno, Joseph McCabe, *"Measuring up: HR's new need for leaders in data analytics,"* https://www.kornferry.com/insights/this-week-in-leadership/measuring-up-hrs-new-need-for-leaders-in-data-analytics.

[35] As stated by Don Phin in his LinkedIn Learning course *"Engagement = Success."*

[36] Source: https://www.brandlearning.com/views-ideas/latest-views-ideas/hr/what-can-hr-learn-from-marketing/.

[37] *The New HR Imperative 2020*, Report by Brand Learning (Accenture).

[38] HR.com's *Future of the HR Function 2024*.

[39] World Economic Forum, *Future of Jobs Report*.

[40] World Economic Forum, *Future of Jobs Report*, https://www3.weforum.org/docs/WEF_Future_of_Jobs_2023.pdf, Insight Report, May 2023.

[41] *The New HR Imperative 2020*, Report by Brand Learning (Accenture).

[42] Harvard Business Review, Hubert Joly, *"Does Your Company's Culture Reinforce Its Strategy and Purpose?"* https://hbr.org/2022/06/does-your-companys-culture-reinforce-its-strategy-and-purpose, 10 June 2022.

[43] More info on the Culture Factor: https://www.hofstede-insights.com/the-culture-factor.

[44] Erin Meyer. *The Culture Map. Breaking Through the Invisible Boundaries of Global Business*, PublicAffairs, 2016.

[45] The Culture Factor, https://news.theculturefactor.com/news/noorbank.

[46] *Jumeirah Jane*: Expat housewife, typically living in the Jumeirah neighbourhood. *Chammak*: A very colloquial way to describe teens that hang around malls at night and try hard to be part of the cool group. *Khalli walli*: A very Dubai-specific way of saying forget about it. *Shway shway*: little by little.

[47] Mohammed bin Rashid Al Maktoum. *My Story*, Explorer Publishing & Distribution. February 2019.

[48] Rutger Bregman, *Humankind. A Hopeful History*, Bloomsbury Publishing, 13 May 2021.

[49] Goudsmet's current model contains four levels instead of five. It was also further enriched and cast in a data model. This gives companies the opportunity to have their maturity model captured through the platform with objectively measurable criteria.

[50] The Herculean Index is publicly available at https://employeeengagement.io/.

[51] Hubspot *Company Values Glossary*, offers.hubspot.com/hubfs/HubSpot-Company-Values-Glossary.pdf

[52] Lattice Company Values: https://lattice.com/blog/lattices-company-values.

[53] Shawn Pope and Arild Wæraas, "*How to Create Company Values That Actually Resonate,*" How to Create Company Values That Actually Resonate (hbr.org).

[54] Stephen M .R. Covey. *The SPEED of Trust: The One Thing That Changes Everything.* Free Press, 2008.

[55] "*The Trust Equation: A Simple Summary,*" https://worldofwork.io/2019/07/the-trust-equation/

[56] Paul J. Zak. "*The Neuroscience of Trust. Management behaviors that foster employee engagement,*" https://hbr.org/2017/01/the-neuroscience-of-trust.

[57] Joe Sejean: Joe Sejean – Executive Coach and Founder.

[58] Inspired by Derek Gaunt. "*Five Reasons Fear-Based Leadership Is Ineffective.*" Black Swan Group. 5 Reasons Fear-Based Leadership Is Ineffective (blackswanltd.com).

[59] Amy C. Edmondson. *The Fearless Organization: Creating Psychological Safety in the Workplace for Learning, Innovation, and Growth.* John Wiley & Sons Inc, 2018.

[60] Patrick Lencioni, *The Five Dysfunctions of a Team: A Leadership Fable,* John Wiley & Sons Inc, 2002.

[61] Jocko Willink and Leif Babin, *Extreme Ownership: How U.S. Navy SEALs Lead and Win,* St Martin's Press. 2017.

[62] Daniel Coyle, *The Culture Code. The Secrets of Highly Successful Groups,* Bantam Books. 2018.

[63] General Stanley McChrystal, Tantum Collins, David Silverman, Chris Fussell, *Team of Teams: New Rules of Engagement for a Complex World,* Portfolio. 2015.

[64] Adrian Gostick and Chester Elton, *The Orange Revolution. How One Great Team Can Transform an Entire Organisation,* Simon & Schuster. 2010.

[65] Satya Nadella, *Hit Refresh. The transformation of Microsoft and the search for a better future for us all,* AW Bruna. 2017.

[66] Jacob Morgan, *The Future of Work. Attract New Talent, Build Better Leaders, and Create a Competitive Organisation,* John Wiley & Sons Inc. 2014.

[67] Common classification of the generations: The Builders (Born <1946), Baby Boomers (Born 1946-1964), Generation X (Born 1965-1979), Generation Y (Born 1980-1994), Generation Z (Born 1995-2009), Generation Alpha (Born 2010-2024) and Generation Beta (Born 2025-2039).

[68] The term *"Zoomers"* is a playful nickname for Generation Z (those born approximately between 1997 and 2012). It's a clever spin on the nickname *"Boomers,"* used for the Baby Boomer generation. Since Gen Z loves to poke fun at us in Generation X by calling us Boomers, I consider calling them Zoomers a delightful bit of sweet revenge. After all, if they're going to lump us with our parents, we might as well return the favour!

[69] These beliefs are: *"We Grow Talent, Talent Grows Us," "Every Moment Matters, Act Now!" "Think Yes! We're Better Together, Yes I Can!"* And: *"Be True."*

[70] Randstad, *"Randstad Survey Reveals More Employees Leave Jobs for Career Growth Than Money."* 2016. https://www.randstadusa.com/about/news/randtad-survey-reveals-more-employees-leave-jobs-for-career-growth-than-money/

[71] Gena Smith, *"How LVMH navigates the dynamic workforce through strategic upskilling,"* https://www.hrdive.com/news/LVMH-learning-development/703821/

[72] Gallup *State of the Global Workplace 2024 Report*, https://www.gallup.com/workplace/349484/state-of-the-global-workplace.aspx

[73] Kate Pritchard, *"What is 'wellbeing washing,' and is your org guilty of it?,"* Wellbeing washing: What is it, and what's HR's role in tackling it? (hrexecutive.com), 6 December 2023.

[74] Fortune, Orianna Rosa Royle, *"Gen Z and young Millennial employees are missing the equivalent of one day's work every week due to mental health concerns, research shows,"* https://fortune.com/europe/article/what-is-mental-health-doing-to-gen-z-workplace-anxiety-stress-burnout/, 31 October 2024.

[75] Tim Barker, Forbes Business Council, *"Gen-Z in the Modern Workplace: Mental Health and Well-Being Matters,"* Gen-Z In The Modern Workplace: Mental Health And Well-Being Matters (forbes.com)

[76] Hanju Lee, *"Gen Z in the Workplace: How Should Companies Adapt?,"* https://imagine.jhu.edu/blog/2023/04/18/gen-z-in-the-workplace-how-should-companies-adapt/ John Hopkins University, 18 April 2023.

[77] Korn Ferry, Ron Seifert, Ronald Porter, Mark Royal, *"Mental-Health Help: Why Unused?,"* https://www.kornferry.com/insights/this-week-in-leadership/mental-health-help-why-unused

[78] Emilie Shumway, *"One-quarter of HR professionals feel uncomfortable using mental health benefits, SHRM researcher says,"* https://www.hrdive.com/news/HR-professional-burnout/719938/, 26 June 2024.

[79] Report Winckworth Sherwood: https://wslaw.co.uk/wp-content/uploads/2024/06/Wellbeing-Strategies-Effective-in-Managing-Sickness-Absence-Insights-and-Recommendations-for-Employers.pdf.

[80] Jim Clifton and Jim Harter. *It's the Manager: Moving From Boss to Coach*, Gallup Press, 2019.

[81] Melanie Katzman, *"To Promote Mental Health at Work, Focus on Good Management,"* To Promote Mental Health at Work, Focus on Good Management | Psychology Today, 3 March 2022.

[82] Ignace Van Doorselaere. *The Road to Infinity. How to build a business for eternity.* Published at 4F. 2019.

[83] Jacob Morgan. *The Employee Experience Advantage: How to Win the War for Talent by Giving Employees the Workspaces they Want, the Tools They Need, and a Culture They Can Celebrate.* John Wiley & Sons Inc. 2017.

[84] People Element, *"Exit Interviews: Ultimate Guide to Capturing Feedback,"* Exit Interviews: The Guide to Exit Feedback | People Element

[85] Helen Tupper and Sarah Ellis, *"It's Time to Reimagine Employee Retention,"* https://hbr.org/2022/07/its-time-to-reimagine-employee-retention, Harvard Business Review, July 2022.

[86] Society for Human Resources Management, *"2016 Employee Job Satisfaction and Engagement: Revitalizing a Changing Workforce,"* April 2016. https://www.shrm.org/hr-today/trends-and-forecasting/research-and-surveys/Documents/2016-Employee-Job-Satisfaction-and-Engagement-Report.pdf

[87] Workforce 2024, Korn Ferry's *Global Insights Report,* https://www.kornferry.com/insights/featured-topics/workforce-management/workforce-planning-insights

[88] Indeed Hiring Lab. *"The Indeed Job Happiness Index 2016: Ranking the World for Employee Satisfaction,"* 2016. http://blog.indeed.com/hiring-lab/indeed-job-happiness-index-2016

[89] Herzberg published the Two Factor Theory of Motivation-Hygiene theory in 1959, about people's motivation at work. According to this theory, people are influenced in two ways: Namely by motivation factors and hygiene factors. Motivational factors can cause an employee to be satisfied with their work and hygiene factors can cause an employee to be dissatisfied with their work. However, it is not the case that if a supervisor will reduce the hygiene factors, an employee will immediately be satisfied with his work. Conversely, this means that if little or no attention is paid to the motivational factors, an employee will not be immediately unhappy in his work.

[90] Reed Hastings and Erin Meyer. *No Rules. Netflix and the Culture of Reinvention,* Ebury Publishing. 2020.

[91] Columbia University, Zuckerman Institute, *"New study sheds light on how the brain learns to seek reward,"* https://zuckermaninstitute.columbia.edu/new-study-sheds-light-how-brain-learns-seek-reward, 13 December 2023.

[92] Steelcase *Global Report*, Steelcase Global Report | Employee Engagement and the Global Workplace.

[93] CBRE, *"The Complete Guide to Activity Based Working,"* https://www.cbre.com/insights/articles/the-complete-guide-to-activity-based-working

[94] The *"Love That Design"* website shows you some pictures of what it looks like: Fine Hygienic Holding, Dubai - Manufacturing Interior Design on Love That Design

[95] J. Heerwagen, Leah Zagreus, *"The human factors of sustainable building design: post occupancy evaluation of the Philip Merrill Environmental Center,"* https://escholarship.org/uc/item/67j1418w, https://pubmed.ncbi.nlm.nih.gov/6143402/, UC Berkeley, CBE, Center for the Built Environment, 2005.

[96] Dr Nigel Oseland, *Beyond the Workplace Zoo: Humanising the Office*, Routledge, 2021.

[97] More info on the Habitarmonia approach: habitarmonia.com.

[98] Quixy, *"50+ Hybrid Workplace Statistics that you should know in 2024,"* 50+ Essential Hybrid Workplace Statistics to know in 2024 (quixy.com)

[99] Andy Lake, *Beyond Hybrid Working: A Smarter & Transformational Approach to Flexible Working*, Routledge, 22 December 2023.

[100] Human Resource Executive. Interview with Ty Breland. *"How Marriott boosted engagement by focusing on flexibility over remote work,"* Marriott International reimagined flexibility amid remote work push (hrexecutive.com)

[101] Veldhoen + Company. Mid-Year Update: Part 2 - How to Hybrid Work (veldhoencompany.com)

[102] Jim Clifton and Jim Harter, *It's the Manager: Moving From Boss to Coach*, Gallup Press, 2019.

[103] McKinsey & Company. Alex Camp, Phil Kirschner, Laura Pineault, Patrick Simon, *"Hybrid can be healthy for your organization—when done right,"* https://www.mckinsey.com/capabilities/people-and-organizational-performance/our-insights/the-organization-blog/hybrid-can-be-healthy-for-your-organization-when-done-right

[104] McKinsey & Company. Alex Camp, Phil Kirschner, Laura Pineault, Patrick Simon, "Hybrid can be healthy for your organization—when done right," https://www.mckinsey.com/capabilities/people-and-organizational-performance/our-insights/the-organization-blog/hybrid-can-be-healthy-for-your-organization-when-done-right

[105] Equity differs from Equality, which would give all individuals the same access to resources without consideration of their diverse needs.

[106] Henri Tajfel, *"Differentiation between Social Groups: Studies in the Social Psychology of Intergroup Relations,"* 1978.

[107] Joseph Henrich, Steven J. Heine, Ara Norenzayan, *"The weirdest people in the world?"* https://www2.psych.ubc.ca/~heine/docs/weirdpeople.pdf. Behavioral and Brain Sciences (2010).

[108] Korn Ferry, *"Building a more diverse and inclusive culture,"* https://www.kornferry.com/insights/featured-topics/diversity-equity-inclusion/building-a-more-diverse-and-inclusive-culture

[109] McKinsey, Dame Vivian Hunt, Dennis Layton, and Sara Prince *"Why diversity matters,"* https://www.mckinsey.com/capabilities/people-and-organizational-performance/our-insights/why-diversity-matters, 1 January 2015.

[110] Harvard Business Review, Sylvia Ann Hewlett, Melinda Marshall and Laura Sherbin, *"How Diversity Can Drive Innovation,"* https://hbr.org/2013/12/how-diversity-can-drive-innovation, December 2013.

[111] People Management, *"Diversity drives better decisions,"* https://www.peoplemanagement.co.uk/article/1742040/diversity-drives-better-decisions.

[112] BCG, Rocío Lorenzo, Nicole Voigt, Miki Tsusaka, Matt Krentz, and Katie Abouzahr, *"How Diverse Leadership Teams Boost Innovation,"* https://www.bcg.com/publications/2018/how-diverse-leadership-teams-boost-innovation, 23 January 2018.

[113] Josh Bersin, *"Why Diversity and Inclusion Has Become a Business Priority,"* https://joshbersin.com/2015/12/why-diversity-and-inclusion-will-be-a-top-priority-for-2016/, 16 March 2019.

[114] EY Press release, *"EY survey finds global workers feel sense of belonging at their workplaces, yet most are uncomfortable sharing all aspects,"* https://www.ey.com/en_gl/newsroom/2023/09/ey-survey-finds-global-workers-feel-sense-of-belonging-at-their-workplaces-yet-most-are-uncomfortable-sharing-all-aspects-of-their-identities, 6 September 2023.

[115] Glassdoor Team, *"What Job Seekers Really Think About Your Diversity and Inclusion Stats,"* https://www.glassdoor.com/blog/diversity/, 12 July 2021.

[116] Harvard Business Review, Sylvia Ann Hewlett, Melinda Marshall and Laura Sherbin, *"How Diversity Can Drive Innovation,"* https://hbr.org/2013/12/how-diversity-can-drive-innovation, December 2013.

[117] DiStefano & Maznevski (2001).

[118] Workday, *"Global blueprint for belonging and diversity - Focusing on strategic maturity and positive impact for the business,"* https://forms.workday.com/content/dam/web/be/documents/reports/de-i-study-and-report-v1-en-BE.pdf

[119] Workday & Sapio Research (2024), Global Blueprint for Belonging and Diversity. https://forms.workday.com/en-us/reports/global-blueprint-for-belonging-and-diversity-2023/form.html?step=step2_hr

[120] Review by Roberson, Holmes, and Perry's (2017).

[121] Research from Quintana-García and Benavides-Velasco (2008), but also and Van de Ven and De Dreu (2010). Van de Ven, C., & de Dreu, C. (2010), *"Myths about diversity: Science and practice do not learn sufficiently from each other,"* Personnel Management Guide, 89(11), 34.

[122] Gordon W. Allport *"The nature of prejudice."* New York, NY: Basic Books, 1954.

[123] Pettigrew et al.'s (2011) meta-analysis, Pettigrew's meta-analysis, which analysed 515 studies, supports this by showing that in 94% of cases, prejudice was reduced through contact with people from another ethnic group.

[124] Bain & Company, Julie Coffman, Bianca Bax, Alex Noether, and Brenen Blair, *"The Fabric of Belonging: How to Weave an Inclusive Culture,"* https://www.bain.com/insights/the-fabric-of-belonging-how-to-weave-an-inclusive-culture/

[125] Dr Tommy Weir. *"Leadership, Dubai style. The habits to achieve remarkable success."* EMLC Press, 2013.

[126] Korn Ferry. *"Crafting the Workplace Culture of Tomorrow,"* https://www.kornferry.com/insights/featured-topics/future-of-work/crafting-the-workplace-culture-of-tomorrow

[127] Sofia Sanchez, Eller College of Management. *"Turning Cameras Off During Virtual Meetings Can Reduce Fatigue, UArizona Research Finds,"* https://news.arizona.edu/news/turning-cameras-during-virtual-meetings-can-reduce-fatigue-uarizona-research-finds

[128] Jeremy N. Bailenson. *"Nonverbal Overload: A Theoretical Argument for the Causes of Zoom Fatigue."* Volume 2, Issue 1. DOI: 10.1037/tmb0000030. https://tmb.apaopen.org/pub/nonverbal-overload/release/2

[129] Korn Ferry, *"The Real Culprit Behind Zoom Fatigue,"* https://www.kornferry.com/insights/this-week-in-leadership/the-real-culprit-behind-zoom-fatigue

[130] Temkin Group. 2018.

[131] In small companies (less than 50), we should be aiming a little higher than the 65–85% range. As we move to larger companies, we can scale our expectations down—with 500 employees, we will probably get a good sense of where the company is with a 70% rate of participation, so 70–80% is a good benchmark. Companies of 1000+ can probably aim for a participation rate of around 65% as their lower bound—even though higher rates allow

a stronger sense of involvement psychologically. https://www.cultureamp.com/blog/what-is-a-good-survey-response-rate

[132] Fred Reichheld, Darci Darnell, and Maureen Burns "*Winning on Purpose: The Unbeatable Strategy of Loving Customers*". It focuses on the Net Promoter System (NPS) and emphasises the importance of enriching customers' lives as a core business strategy,

[133] Culture Amp, "*How to communicate engagement survey results to your team,*" https://www.cultureamp.com/blog/employee-engagement-results-communication

[134] CHRMP - Certified Human Resource Management Professional, "*Top 15 Key Benefits of HR Analytics,*" https://www.chrmp.com/benefits-of-hr-analytics/#The_Difference_Between_HR_Analytics_People_Analytics_and_Workforce_Analytics

[135] Forbes, Jeff White, "*HR Analytics: Definition, Best Practices & Examples,*" https://www.forbes.com/advisor/business/hr-analytics/, 28 May 2024.

[136] Effectory. Maaike Ankum, "*People Analytics: 5 Real Case Studies,*" https://www.effectory.com/knowledge/people-analytics-5-real-case-studies/, 4 March 2023.

[137] George Bongiorno and Joseph McCabe, "*Measuring up: HR's new need for leaders in data analytics,*" https://www.kornferry.com/insights/this-week-in-leadership/measuring-up-hrs-new-need-for-leaders-in-data-analytics

[138] Erik van Vulpen, AIHR, https://www.aihr.com/blog/what-is-hr-analytics/, 23 February 2023.

[139] Mercer, *Workforce 2.0. Unlocking human potential in a machine-augmented world. Global Talent Trends, 2024.*

[140] Gartner, "*AI in HR: The Ultimate Guide to Implementing AI in Your HR Organization,*" https://www.gartner.com/en/human-resources/topics/artificial-intelligence-in-hr

[141] World Economic Forum, *"The Future of Jobs Report 2020,"* https://www.weforum.org/publications/the-future-of-jobs-report-2020/digest/, 20 October 2020.

[142] Mercer, *Workforce 2.0. Unlocking human potential in a machine-augmented world. Global Talent Trends 2024.*

[143] Mercer, *Workforce 2.0. Unlocking human potential in a machine-augmented world. Global Talent Trends 2024.*

[144] HR Executive, Jill Barth, *"How are HR leaders like data scientists? Ask gen AI, says a new study,"* https://hrexecutive.com/how-are-hr-leaders-like-data-scientists-ask-gen-ai-says-a-new-study/, 9 September 2024.

[145] BCG, Daniel Sack, Lisa Krayer, Emma Wiles, Mohamed Abbadi, Urvi Awasthi, Ryan Kennedy, Cristián Arnolds, and François Candelon, *"GenAI Doesn't Just Increase Productivity. It Expands Capabilities,"* https://www.bcg.com/publications/2024/gen-ai-increases-productivity-and-expands-capabilities, 5 September 2024.

[146] McKinsey & Company, Aaron De Smet, Sandra Durth, Bryan Hancock, Marino Mugayar-Baldocchi, Angelika Reich, *"The human side of generative AI: Creating a path to productivity,"* https://www.mckinsey.com/capabilities/people-and-organizational-performance/our-insights/the-human-side-of-generative-ai-creating-a-path-to-productivity, 18 March 2024.

[147] Charlene Li, *"Winning with Generative AI, the 90-day blueprint for success,"* https://charleneli.com/winning-with-generative-ai/

[148] McKinsey & Company, Aaron De Smet, Sandra Durth, Bryan Hancock, Marino Mugayar-Baldocchi, Angelika Reich, *"The human side of generative AI: Creating a path to productivity,"* https://www.mckinsey.com/capabilities/people-and-organizational-performance/our-insights/the-human-side-of-generative-ai-creating-a-path-to-productivity, 18 March 2024.

[149] The outlines are loosely inspired by coach Don Phin's leadership course - Employee Engagement. Course on LinkedIn Learning.

[150] Gallup Q12® Meta-Analysis 2020.

[151] BlessingWhite, *"Employee Engagement Research Update,"* https://blessingwhite.com/wp-content/uploads/2018/11/Employee-Engagement-Research-Report-2013.pdf, January 2013.

[152] Never read this classic? Then this is the perfect time. Jim Collins. *Good to Great*, Vintage Publishing. 2004.

[153] K. Kelly Hancock, *"Successful Engagement Begins with Listening."* https://consultqd.clevelandclinic.org/successful-engagement-begins-with-listening, June 30, 2022.

Acknowledgements
(Shoukran)

First up, a massive high-five to the extraordinary people who made this book a reality. The list is long and deserves a red-carpet rollout, each of you shining in your own spotlight: Ahmed Soliman, Amadou Diallo, Andreas Creten, Andrew Stotter-Brooks, Awatif Alsuwaidi, Boris Fugger, Conny Vandendriessche, Eva Mattheeussen, Frank Van Massenhove, Hadi Kamouh, Harpreet Sing Chhatwal, Ignace Van Doorselaere, James Lafferty, Joe Sejean, Johan Dekens, Julie Barbier-Leblan, Karim Boutaour, Karin Van Roy, Maarten Van Cauwenberghe, Nuria Muñoz Arce, Peter Van den Broeck, Peter Vermeulen, Sabine Schellens, Sana Sellami, Shameem Farouk, Tatiana Parshina, Sven Deckers, Tom Verbeke, Wassim Karkabi, Wayne Visser, Yves Van Vaerenbergh, and Yves Vekemans. A special thought goes to the coauthor of my first book, Klaus Lommatzsch.

To my publisher, Susmita Dutta, and the powerhouse team at Global Book Publishing—you are nothing short of legends. Thank you for your skill, dedication, and commitment to making this book truly shine.

To my customers—thank you for keeping me on my toes and constantly feeding me with insights. Some of you have turned into more than customers; you've become dear friends. Your support and challenges have meant the world to me.

To my colleagues and mentors who've pushed, and sometimes dragged me forward: Ronald Everaert, Kris Talboom, Jan De Schepper, Marc Bresseel, Patrick Dejager, Frank Wouters, Danny Leinders, and so many more. Consider yourselves fully responsible for any wild success this book might achieve!

Then there's my gang of special people—the fierce, funny, and fabulous friends who remind me that I'm never alone on this journey: Jessica, Jill, Jirka, Lieve, Lynn, Nathalie, Yoke, and Yulia. You are my anchors, my cheerleaders, and my sanity savers.

To my family: my parents, who taught me kindness, respect, and *savoir-vivre*; my parents-in-law, the steady pillars we can always count on; my children, young adults becoming their best selves and making me incredibly hopeful for the future; and my husband, who deserves a lifetime supply of medals for his unwavering support, patience, and love. Thank you for being my constants through it all.

And finally, to you, the reader: whether you picked up this book for inspiration, insight, or a fresh perspective, I hope it serves you well. Now, go out there, make it happen —and remember another piece of Captain Jack Sparrow's wisdom: *"The problem is not the problem; the problem is your attitude about the problem."*

About the Author

Inge van Belle is a Senior Client Partner at *Korn Ferry* and co-founder of *Herculean Alliance*, the employee engagement company. Known for her passion and expertise in people-centric work, Inge's focus spans leadership, employee engagement, executive search, and organisational culture. She founded the *Bravos! Employee Engagement Awards* and has led intercultural projects across ten countries. A Board member in multiple organisations, Inge is also a committed advocate for women's empowerment. In 2024, she was named one of the *50under50* for the Middle East and Africa by UN Women. She currently lives and works in the United Arab Emirates.

Contact with author at:

- @ingevanbelle
- inge.vanbelle@kornferry.com
- https://www.linkedin.com/in/ingevanbelle

More Praise from Readers

"'Work is love made visible.' This powerful quote encapsulates the essence of employee engagement: a true symbiosis between individuals and the organisations they contribute to. I had the pleasure of reading this book with great interest and anticipation, as Inge Van Belle explores all key concepts of employee engagement through the unique prism of the UAE's multicultural corporate environment, where organisational cultures intersect with diverse national identities. This perspective is crucial in understanding how engagement strategies must adapt to varied cultural expectations and workplace dynamics.

At a time when AI and GenAI are transforming work environments, the human–machine relationship has never been more relevant. Inge masterfully highlights the importance of maintaining employee engagement in an era where technology is reshaping roles, interactions, and expectations. More than just a reflection on engagement, this book serves as a playbook for organisations, offering case studies and concrete application frameworks to reshape engagement strategies in a rapidly evolving workplace.

A must-read for anyone interested in the future of work, cross-cultural leadership, and employee engagement in the age of AI. Highly recommended!"

—Valerie Hawley,
Executive Director SCAI—
Sorbonne Centre for Artificial Intelligence

"This is not just another book about employee engagement. It's an invitation to reconsider how you live, breathe, speak, think, and connect with others. It urges you to be fully present, here and now, at work and beyond. It encourages you to embark on a transformative journey that impacts all aspects of your life.

It is a practi-sophical guide to be engaged and engage people you care about, well beyond employees. And above all, every word carries vibrance, heart, guts, and soul. Because Inge is not only talking the talk—she walks the walk. As she reminds us, the stakes are high: we're talking about happiness, fulfilment, and true love—even in business. And we are the ones who can make a difference. Yalla!"

—Johanne Dessard,
Senior Vice President
Enterprise Risk Mubadala

"In her book *Employee Engagement. What Else?"* Inge van Belle offers senior executive leaders' actionable insights to elevate employee engagement as a strategic driver of success. Drawing from her extensive experience in the UAE, particularly in Dubai, she underscores the transformation of engagement into a collective responsibility beyond just an HR function. Van Belle challenges leaders with a thought-provoking question: 'What can you do for your organisation?' This call to action has significantly influenced my leadership approach, fostering a culture of increased ownership and accountability among teams, ultimately enhancing motivation and performance.

The book also highlights the significance of cultural nuances in international management, using Dubai's resilience and diversity as prime illustrations. Inge's discussion on how

Dubai's leadership promotes inclusivity and adaptability mirrors my own experiences in fostering teamwork within diverse environments. Cultural awareness has played a pivotal role in improving engagement and collaboration within my teams across 19 countries.

Furthermore, the integration of marketing and technology in engagement strategies, as advocated by Inge, deeply resonates with me. Implementing real-time feedback systems to gauge and address employee sentiment has been a recurring practice, reinforcing the importance of adapting to evolving technological landscapes.

For senior leaders in people-centric industries, this book serves as a valuable guide to embed engagement as a core element of organisational triumph. It provides practical insights and strategies to drive success through prioritising and enhancing employee engagement."

—Dirk Goovaerts,
CEO Swissair Continental Europe,
Middle East, Africa, India & Global Cargo Chair

"Employee engagement—two words that have been thrown around boardrooms for years, yet few truly crack the code. In *Employee Engagement, What Else?* Inge Van Belle doesn't just talk about engagement; she unpacks it, challenges it, and injects it with the high-energy, forward-thinking mindset of Dubai—a city that has mastered the art of attracting, retaining, and inspiring people from all walks of life.

At its core, this book isn't just about policies and strategies; it's about people. Engagement isn't a metric—it's a connection, a relationship, an ecosystem where employees feel a deep sense of belonging, feel valued, seen, and part of something bigger than themselves. Inge blends sharp insights with compelling storytelling, diving into purpose-driven leadership, AI's rising role in engagement, and how culture can be the ultimate game-changer. And the Dubai influence? It's not just a backdrop; it's a case study of ambition, innovation, and belonging.

If you think you've read everything there is to know about engagement, think again. This book will challenge your perspective, spark new ideas, and leave you asking, What else? And that's exactly the kind of thinking the future of work demands."

—Dr. Heba Makram,
AI & Future of Work Futurist